LUTHER'S WORKS

American Edition

VOLUME 38

Published by Concordia Publishing House

and Fortress Press in 55 volumes.

General Editors are Jaroslav Pelikan (for vols. 1–30)

and Helmut T. Lehmann (for vols. 31–55)

LUTHER'S WORKS

VOLUME 38

Word and Sacrament

IV

EDITED BY

MARTIN E. LEHMANN

GENERAL EDITOR

HELMUT T. LEHMANN

FORTRESS PRESS / PHILADELPHIA

Library of Congress Catalog Card Number 55-9893

ISBN 0-8006-0338-9

Printed in the United States of America *1–338*

GENERAL EDITORS' PREFACE

The first editions of Luther's collected works appeared in the sixteenth century, and so did the first efforts to make him "speak English." In America serious attempts in these directions were made for the first time in the nineteenth century. The Saint Louis edition of Luther was the first endeavor on American soil to publish a collected edition of his works, and the Henkel Press in Newmarket, Virginia, was the first to publish some of Luther's writings in an English translation. During the first decade of the twentieth century, J. N. Lenker produced translations of Luther's sermons and commentaries in thirteen volumes. A few years later the first of the six volumes in the Philadelphia (or Holman) edition of the *Works of Martin Luther* appeared. But a growing recognition of the need for more of Luther's works in English has resulted in this American edition of Luther's works.

The edition is intended primarily for the reader whose knowledge of late medieval Latin and sixteenth-century German is too small to permit him to work with Luther in the original languages. Those who can will continue to read Luther in his original words as these have been assembled in the monumental Weimar edition (*D. Martin Luthers Werke.* Kritische Gesamtausgabe, Weimar, 1883-). Its texts and helps have formed a basis for this edition, though in certain places we have felt constrained to depart from its readings and findings. We have tried throughout to translate Luther as he thought translating should be done. That is, we have striven for faithfulness on the basis of the best lexicographical materials available. But where literal accuracy and clarity have conflicted, it is clarity that we have preferred, so that sometimes paraphrase seemed more faithful than literal fidelity. We have proceeded in a similar way in the matter of Bible versions, translating Luther's translation. Where this could be done by the use of an existing

English version—King James, Douay, or Revised Standard—we have done so. Where it could not, we have supplied our own. To indicate this in each specific instance would have been pedantic; to adopt a uniform procedure would have been artificial—especially in view of Luther's own inconsistency in this regard. In each volume the translator will be responsible primarily for matters of text and language, while the responsibility of the editor will extend principally to the historical and theological matters reflected in the introductions and notes.

Although the edition as planned will include fifty-five volumes, Luther's writings are not being translated in their entirety. Nor should they be. As he was the first to insist, much of what he wrote and said was not that important. Thus the edition is a selection of works that have proved their importance for the faith, life, and history of the Christian church. The first thirty volumes contain Luther's expositions of various biblical books, while the remaining volumes include what are usually called his "Reformation writings" and other occasional pieces. The final volume of the set will be an index volume; in addition to an index of quotations, proper names, and topics, and a list of corrections and changes, it will contain a glossary of many of the technical terms that recur in Luther's works and that cannot be defined each time they appear. Obviously Luther cannot be forced into any neat set of rubrics. He can provide his reader with bits of autobiography or with political observations as he expounds a psalm, and he can speak tenderly about the meaning of the faith in the midst of polemics against his opponents. It is the hope of publishers, editors, and translators that through this edition the message of Luther's faith will speak more clearly to the modern church.

J.P.
H.T.L.

CONTENTS

ABBREVIATIONS

CL — *Luthers Werke in Auswahl*, edited by Otto Clemen, *et al.* (Bonn, 1912-1933; Berlin, 1955-1956).

C. R. — *Corpus Reformatorum*, edited by C. G. Bretschneider and H. E. Bindseil (Halle, 1834-1860).

EA — *D. Martin Luthers sämmtliche Werke* (Frankfurt and Erlangen, 1826-1857).

LW — American edition of *Luther's Works* (Philadelphia and St. Louis, 1955-).

MA[3] — *Martin Luther*. Ausgewählte Werke, edited by H. H. Borcherdt and Georg Merz (3rd edition; München, 1948-).

MPL — *Patrologia, Series Latina*, 221 vols. in 222, edited by J. P. Migne (Paris, 1844-1904).

PE — *Works of Martin Luther* (Philadelphia, 1915-1943).

St. L. — *D. Martin Luthers sämmtliche Schriften*, edited by Johann Georg Walch. Edited and published in modern German, 23 vols. in 25 (St. Louis, 1880-1910).

S-J — *Luther's Correspondence*, 2 vols., edited by Preserved Smith and Charles M. Jacobs (Philadelphia, 1913-1918).

WA — *D. Martin Luthers Werke*. Kritische Gesamtausgabe (Weimar, 1883-).

WA, Br — *D. Martin Luthers Werke*. Briefwechsel (Weimar, 1930-1948).

WA, TR — *D. Martin Luthers Werke*. Tischreden (Weimar, 1912-1921).

INTRODUCTION TO VOLUME 38

Luther's love for the church was deep and genuine. "The church shall be my fortress, my castle, and my chamber," he exclaimed in the midst of his *Lectures on Genesis*.[1] The church was in his view the community of believers where man's search for faith had to take place because this community had been entrusted with the gospel of Jesus Christ. Indeed, for Luther the gospel of the sinner's justification before God through trust in Christ alone was the vital, vibrant center of the church's message in the world. He adhered to this basic belief throughout his career as reformer.

"Nothing in the church," he stated in his *Explanations of the Ninety-five Theses* of 1518, "must be treated with greater care than the holy gospel since the church has nothing which is more precious and salutary. Therefore it is the only single work which Christ enjoined upon his disciples at so many different times. . . . It is better to omit the sacrament than not to proclaim the gospel. Therefore God has placed greater importance on the gospel than on the mass, for without the gospel man does not live in the Spirit, but he does without the mass."[2]

The word of God was, as he expressed it in 1533, "the greatest, most necessary, and most sublime part in Christendom."[3] Elaborating on this point of view, he explained that the sacraments could not exist without the word, but that the word by itself would continue to be God's saving power even without the sacraments. He asserted that if a person should die before receiving the desired baptism, he could still be saved without the sacrament by simply believing the gospel. Still later in life—in 1539—Luther reiterated this essential position in his theology by calling the word of God "the principal item, and the holiest of holy possessions by reason of which the Christian people are called holy," summing it all up

[1] *LW* 8, 183. Cf. *WA* 44, 713.
[2] *LW* 31, 210.
[3] *WA* 38, 231.

in this terse sentence: "God's word cannot be without God's people, and conversely, God's people cannot be without God's word."[4]

Despite this high estimate of God's word, Luther never lost sight of the paramount significance of the sacraments of baptism and the Lord's Supper because of their inseparable connection with the word of God and because they enshrined, as it were, the message of the gospel. In the words of Heinrich Bornkamm: "The Sacraments are external signs of one and the same thing: the message of the Gospel. In the close compass of Luther's definition there is no room for the injection of a physical, magical, or subconscious element but only for that which fits into the area of promise—faith, the area about which Luther's whole theology revolves. To be sure, the Sacraments are outward signs, but they are signs of a spiritual act. Symbolically they proclaim a clear message and demand a clear and sure faith. 'For a Sacrament is an affair of faith in which nothing but the Word of God shall happen and be done through His Word.' "[5]

In baptism and the Lord's Supper the gospel and faith are therefore primary and central for Luther. God takes the initiative in word and sacrament, bestowing through them what he promises. So the believer accepts by faith the gift of forgiveness and new life through baptism, through the preached word, and through the Eucharist within the Christian church. God's saving action through these means of grace invests them with this fundamental and far-reaching importance. Thus the message of God's victory over sin, death, and the devil and the offer of restoration to sonship through Jesus Christ, the incarnate Son of God, who died on the cross for the world's sin and rose from the dead, are brought to mankind through the word and the sacraments.

It was no narrow literalism which caused Luther to uphold with unwavering conviction the real presence of Jesus Christ in the Holy Communion. Rather, it was his fidelity to the gospel as God's reliable word of promise which determined his doctrine of the Lord's Supper. In the spirit of Pauline theology he excluded the

---

[4] *LW* 41, 149-150. Cf. *WA* 50, 629.

[5] Heinrich Bornkamm, *Luther's World of Thought,* trans. by Martin H. Bertram (St. Louis: Concordia Publishing House, 1958), pp. 101-102.

rational, philosophical scruples of the Greek mind that sought the wisdom of human comprehension. In the same spirit of faith the cross of Christ did not become for him a stumbling-block, as it did for many Jews who were looking for visible signs of divine power and glory and who therefore rejected the crucified Messiah. Luther's theology of the cross was predicated on the gospel of the Suffering Servant, Jesus Christ, the Son of God, who conquered sin and death in weakness and shame on a cross, who rose again in power, and who shares his humanity, his body and blood, with the members of the redeemed community under the forms of bread and wine in the Holy Supper as a seal and earnest of their redemption.

The Marburg Colloquy and *The Marburg Articles*, offered in translation in this volume, testify to Luther's steadfast adherence to his teaching of Christ's real presence in the sacrament and to the failure of reaching a doctrinal consensus on this basic tenet of the faith with Zwingli and Oecolampadius, the leaders of the Swiss Reformation. According to these two Swiss theologians only a spiritual eating by faith took place in the Eucharist. Bread and wine in the Lord's Supper merely signified Christ's body and blood because his humanity was in their view spatially confined to a certain place in heaven and could not be communicated to believers with the bread and the wine.

The fruitless attempt at Marburg to break the deadlock between Luther and Zwingli over the right understanding of the Lord's Supper occasioned a continuing separation between the Lutheran Church and the Reformed Church in the centuries to come. This separate existence of the two churches persisted even though Calvin some years later modified Zwingli's eucharistic doctrine, teaching that by the action of the Holy Spirit the soul of the believer is lifted into heaven in the Holy Communion and is thus spiritually nourished by Christ's body and blood there.

In the context of twentieth-century ecumenism, the doctrinal difference with respect to the Lord's Supper between Lutheran church bodies and churches belonging to the Reformed tradition has been reexamined. Here in the United States a discussion of the desirability of a theological dialogue between representatives of certain Lutheran church bodies and representatives of Presbyterian and Reformed churches led to the approval of holding such conversations in the spring of 1961. After a preliminary meeting in New York City between spokesmen of the two separate traditions, subsequent consultations culminated in a meeting at Princeton, New Jersey, in 1966, at which the results of this ongoing dialogue were evaluated and summarized.

In the Summary Statement that was drawn up, broad areas of agreement on the doctrine of the Lord's Supper were acknowledged. "We are agreed that the presence of Christ in the sacrament is not effected by faith but acknowledged by faith. The worthy participant is the one who receives in faith and repentance the Christ who offers himself in the sacrament. The unworthy participant is the one who fails to acknowledge the Lordship of Christ, his presence in the sacrament, and the fellowship of the brethren in the common Lord. Such unworthy participation brings judgment."[6] While it is jointly agreed upon in the Summary Statement that the total Christ as the divine-human person is present in the sacrament, there is no specific explication of the more precise meaning of this presence. Consequently, no mention is made of the presence of the body and blood of Christ along with the bread and the wine and their oral reception by communicants. The concluding sentence in the statement makes it clear that the barriers to complete agreement between the denominations involved in the discussions have not been entirely removed. "Our churches are not in full agreement on the practice of inter-communion because they hold different views of the relation of doctrine to the unity of the church."[7] Nevertheless, the two confessional bodies that participated in the dialogue were encouraged to engage in further discussions with one another for the purpose of "looking forward to inter-communion and the fuller recognition of one another's ministries."[8]

---

[6] Paul C. Empie and James I. McCord (eds.), *Marburg Revisited: A Reexamination of Lutheran and Reformed Traditions* (Minneapolis: Augsburg Publishing House, 1966), p. 104.
[7] Empie and McCord, *op. cit.*, p. 104.
[8] *Ibid.*, p. 191. For a full discussion of the various attempts that have been made between Lutherans and other Protestant church bodies to reach some kind of consensus with regard to the doctrine of the Eucharist in our century, see Eugene M. Skibbe, *Protestant Agreement on the Lord's Supper* (Minneapolis: Augsburg Publishing House, 1968).

The conversations between representatives of the Lutheran Church in South India and leaders of the Church of South India—the latter body being a union of Reformed, Presbyterian, Methodist, Congregationalist, and Anglican churches—led to a final Agreed Statement in 1955 and to the approval of intercommunion between Lutherans in South India and the members of the Church of South India. Dr. Skibbe, in detailing this development in his book *Protestant Agreement on the Lord's Supper,* points out that in this particular case the doctrine of the real presence of the body and blood of Christ under the bread and the wine and the oral manducation of them by the communicants is taught in the Agreed Statement.[9]

In Holland discussions between the Lutheran and the Dutch Reformed churches about the Lord's Supper resulted in the Consensus on the Holy Communion in 1956. This Consensus openly acknowledges disagreement about the doctrine of the Lord's Supper and yet sanctions intercommunion between the two confessional church bodies. Thus, while adhering to and acknowledging the historical difference in the teaching on the Eucharist, the Lutheran Church in Holland and the Dutch Reformed Church have mutually agreed to allow their members to partake of the sacrament in each other's churches.[10]

In Germany doctrinal agreement on the Lord's Supper was reached by Lutheran and Reformed theologians after careful study of the problem in the light of the New Testament witness. Reports by various study groups preceded the final formulations by a commission. These formulations became known as the Arnoldshain Theses to which both Lutheran and Reformed theologians subscribed in 1957 as a basis of agreement on the teaching of the Lord's Supper. The Fourth Thesis, which Dr. Skibbe designates as "the heart of the Arnoldshain Theses," expresses the doctrine of the real presence of Christ in the sacrament in these words: "The words which our Lord Jesus Christ speaks when he offers the bread and the cup tell us what he himself gives to all who come to this Supper: he, the crucified and risen Lord, permits himself to be taken

[9] Skibbe, *op. cit.*, pp. 27-44. See especially the Agreed Statement on the Lord's Supper on pp. 31-32.
[10] *Ibid.*, pp. 45-68.

in his body and blood given and shed for all, through his word of promise, with the bread and the wine, and grants us participation, by virtue of the Holy Spirit, in the victory of his lordship, so that we, believing in his promise, may receive forgiveness of sins, life, and salvation."[11]

Although both Lutheran and Reformed theologians exhibit the tendency to interpret the theses in the light of their own traditional beliefs and although one prominent Lutheran member of the commission, Ernst Sommerlath, did not give his approval to them, the agreement nonetheless represents a significant attempt to overcome the confessional difference on the doctrine of the Lord's Supper that reaches back to the time of the Reformation in the sixteenth century. Albrecht Peters, in connection with a thorough study of Luther's teaching on the real presence of Christ's body and blood in the sacrament, notes that the agreement between the Reformed and Lutheran theologians brought about in the Arnoldshain Theses, must be regarded as a genuine rapprochement between the Lutheran and Reformed churches in Germany. "The Arnoldshain Theses," he writes, "have succeeded in overcoming the dilemma of the controversy in the sixteenth century."[12] Pointing out that several theses in the agreement are worded in a way that obfuscates doctrinal clarity with regard to the teaching of the real presence of Christ in the sacrament, he nevertheless believes that exegetical studies made possible the formulation of a doctrinal statement on the meaning of the Lord's Supper that proved to be acceptable to both Lutheran and Reformed theologians. At the same time he is at pains to make it clear that the theses are in reality " 'a study document' which points to the first steps for a correct understanding of the biblical expressions."[13] One can therefore say that, although the Arnoldshain Theses cannot be looked upon as a normative confession which has been officially adopted by the respective church bodies represented in the discussions, they might well form the provisional basis of a historic consensus on the teaching of the

---

[11] *Ibid.*, p. 91.
[12] Albrecht Peters, *Realpräsenz: Luthers Zeugnis von Christi Gegenwart im Abendmahl* (Berlin, 1960), p. 197.
[13] Peters, *op. cit.*, p. 202.

Lord's Supper between the Reformed and the Lutheran churches of Germany.

In 1530, approximately a year after the Marburg Colloquy, Luther wrote *Admonition Concerning the Sacrament of the Body and Blood of Our Lord.* It is a devotional writing of real significance, reflecting in an attractive literary form the Reformer's deep understanding and reverent appreciation of the sacrament in the light of the dominical words of institution: "Do this in remembrance of me." Though interspersed with a vigorous polemic against the abuse of the sacrament by the Church of Rome which had made it a sacrifice for the living and the dead and a source of financial gain, it clearly sets forth what Luther believes the proper use and benefit of the sacrament to be for Christians who are members of the church through baptism.

Three years later Luther directed a forceful attack against the then prevalent Roman Catholic practice of having the priest by himself celebrate the mass for the benefit of the living and the dead. In the same work he also scored the related practice of consecrating persons to the priesthood solely for the purpose of having them celebrate such private masses. This polemical piece is entitled *The Private Mass and the Consecration of Priests.* To Luther, who had recovered the New Testament emphasis on the community of believers and the communal character of the eucharistic service, these practices constituted a gross abuse of the real intention and meaning of the sacrament. He categorically rejected the teaching that the private mass was a sacrifice and good work carried out for the benefit of others. According to him the sacrament was God's gift to repentant believers, assuring them of forgiveness through the bestowal of Christ's body and blood. Sinful man, he held, could not offer anything to God to propitiate for his sins; he could only receive the forgiveness offered and respond in a grateful spirit of praise and thanksgiving to God for his grace in the sacrament. Thus he would allow the sacrifice of the heart and the lips to God as being the only valid sacrificial response that could be made by believers who participated in the Lord's Supper.

In Luther's theology the New Testament teaching of the priesthood of all believers precluded the concept of a special priesthood within the church. Therefore, priestly consecration for the purpose of setting a person apart to say private masses was, he contended, neither right nor necessary. According to his evangelical view of the office of the ministry and of preaching, ordination to the ministry did not invest a person with a special capacity or character but merely set him apart for the office of preaching the word and administering the sacraments in the service of God's people. Hence, believing that priestly consecration which enabled a person to celebrate private masses lacked scriptural warrant, the Reformer denied the validity of the practice in and for the church.

Because the private mass involved no participation by believers so that there could be no real communion of persons, in his book *The Private Mass and the Consecration of Priests* Luther expressed doubt as to whether the gift of the body and blood of Christ was present in the secret mass. This questioning of the genuine sacramental character of the secret mass in this writing of 1533 caused the charge of Zwinglianism to be leveled against him. For that reason *A Letter of Dr. Martin Luther Concerning His Book on the Private Mass* was written in 1534. Emphatically denying that he taught a merely symbolical view of the sacrament in this brief treatise, he underscored anew his belief in the real presence of Christ's body and blood in the Supper.

Present-day ecumenism within Christendom has provided the climate which has made it possible for Roman Catholics and Lutherans, on the basis of their common Christian heritage, to engage in dialogue about doctrinal differences that go back to Luther's day. Here in North America an initial discussion between Catholics and Lutherans, revolving around the meaning of the Nicene Creed, took place in 1965. A second gathering of Roman Catholic and Lutheran theologians in February, 1966, concerned itself with conversations about the teaching on baptism. Finally, at a third meeting in September, 1966, theologians from these two confessional bodies presented papers on the theme *The Eucharist as Sacrifice*. The discussions centered around two principal facets of the doctrine of the Lord's Supper, the Eucharist as sacrifice and the presence of Christ in the sacrament. Since Luther had retained the teaching of offering the sacrifice of our hearts and lips to God in the Eucharist out of gratitude to him, agreement in a joint report on this point was worded thus: "The confessional documents of both traditions agree that the celebration of the eucharist is the church's sacrifice of praise and self-offering or oblation."[14] However, with respect to the teaching of offering Christ in the Eucharist as a propitiatory sacrifice "for the living and the dead," there was neither extensive discussion nor expression of agreement.[15] It is nevertheless of special significance that the report states explicitly that "the Second Vatican Council in its Constitution on the Sacred Liturgy has declared that the nature of the mass is such that the communal way of celebrating is to be preferred to individual and quasi-private celebrations."[16]

As to the presence of the body and blood of Christ in the bread and the wine in the Eucharist, both Lutherans and Catholics subscribe to the reality of that presence, although agreement about the nature of the presence is acknowledged as not being complete. This much can be said: Contemporary doctrinal emphases and the resulting practices in the Roman Catholic Church with regard to the sacrament represent a different posture from the one with which Luther was confronted and which he attacked with such vigor and force. Still, between the two church bodies distinct differences in the total understanding of the meaning of the sacrament remain.

Luther was above all else an expositor and teacher of God's word. However, because he was compelled time and again by force of circumstance to clarify and defend his Christian teachings in debate, he developed a notable disputation style in his writings. Luther's *Disputation Against Scholastic Theology* and his *Ninety-five Theses or Disputation on the Power and Efficacy of Indulgences,*[17] both written in 1517, were drawn up in order to serve

---

[14] Paul Empie and T. Austin Murphy (eds.), *Lutherans and Catholics in Dialogue III: The Eucharist as Sacrifice* (published jointly in New York by Representatives of the U.S.A. National Committee of the Lutheran World Federation and in Washington, D.C., by the Bishops' Committee for Ecumenical and Interreligious Affairs, 1967), p. 188.

[15] Empie and Murphy, *op. cit.*, pp. 188-191.

[16] *Ibid.*, p. 191.

[17] *LW* 31, 9-16 and 25-33.

as a basis for disputations. The same observation can be made about the theses he prepared for the Heidelberg Disputation[18] of 1518 at which he presided. The Leipzig Debate of 1519, for which he published thirteen theses, likewise tested his mettle as a skilled debater.[19] It was Heinrich Boehmer who called attention to the debating style which Luther developed and employed in many of his writings: "As far as the external form of his books is concerned, he was satisfied at this time, at least when he wrote in German, briefly to formulate in the fashion of academic theses the thoughts which seemed important, and then simply to set them down in a numbered series, one after another."[20] For this reason it is not at all surprising that Luther, in the face of certain historical events, came to regard academic disputations as an important tool for teaching students how to develop precise theological expressions in setting forth the doctrines of the Christian faith.

It was in part the humanists' criticism of Scholasticism that resulted in the sharp decline of disputations at various universities in Germany in the sixteenth century. Wittenberg University was also affected by this trend. Melanchthon, however, though a leading humanist, did not share in humanism's disapprobation of disputations because he recognized their educational value. It was also in part the hostility to advanced learning by the radical Reformers that accounted for the waning of disputations at the universities. So, for example, Karlstadt, who was in charge of bestowing degrees upon two Augustinian monks at a disputation in Wittenberg, denounced this practice and resolved not to participate in such an event again. Luther, who as early as 1521 opposed the oath associated with the bestowal of degrees at disputations, was induced to side with Melanchthon's favorable estimate of them when he was confronted by the opposition of the radical Reformers to learning. Finally, it was in part the ecclesiastical struggle in which Luther and his colleagues were involved which was responsible for the

---

[18] *LW* 31, 35-69.

[19] *LW* 31, 317-318.

[20] Heinrich Boehmer, *Road to Reformation*, trans. from the German by John W. Doberstein and Theodore G. Tappert (Philadelphia: Fortess Press, 1946), p. 299.

decline of the disputations from 1522 to 1533.[21] There is only one reference to a disputation conducted by Luther between 1525 and 1533. John Mathesius, a friend and boarder at Luther's home from 1540 to 1542, and later pastor at Joachimsthal, in a series of sermons on Luther's life, states that the Reformer held a public disputation on the Lord's Supper in September of 1529 at Wittenberg University in preparation for the Marburg Colloquy.[22]

However, despite the energetic spirit with which both Melanchthon and Luther labored from 1533 onward to make the holding of disputations a regular part of the academic life at Wittenberg, the practice experienced only a temporary revival. The spirit of the times had changed. The golden age of disputations was past. In 1588 the statutes of the university provided for a total of only four theological disputations during the year. The complete demise of this once prevalent practice was thus foreshadowed.[23]

The public quarterly disputation presented in translation in this volume is entitled *The Disputation Concerning the Passage: "The Word Was Made Flesh" (John 1:14)*; it was held in 1539. Luther's deep concern about the doctrine of the incarnation of the eternal Word in this disputation is closely related to his teaching on the real presence of the body and blood of Christ in the sacrament. In fact he sees in the overarching mystery of the incarnation the valid basis for his faithful adherence to the literal sense of Christ's words in the Eucharist. The biblical doctrine that the infinite God became incarnate in finite man was for him the prior and pre-eminent miracle of God's grace. Thus his belief in Christ's promised presence of body and blood in the sacrament was authentically anchored in the incarnation.

This disputation points up the fact that Luther, in harmony with the classical Christology of the ancient church and of the early church fathers, championed what Holsten Fagerberg in his study of the Lutheran Confessions characterizes as "an assumption

---

[21] Paul Drews, *Die Disputationen Dr. Martin Luthers* (Göttingen, 1895), pp. x-xii.

[22] Johann Mathesius, *D. Martin Luthers Leben in siebzehn Predigten* (Leipzig, 1887), pp. 153 ff.

[23] Drews, *op. cit.*, p. xxv. Cf. *LW* 34, xiii-xv.

Christology."[24] That is to say, God assumed human nature; man was not raised to the level of the Godhead. The initiative and action in the incarnation therefore emanated entirely from God.

Upholding the biblical witness to the incarnation, Luther believed it to be a theological truth that was neither accessible to nor comprehensible by philosophy. Indeed, he contended that the language used in theology at times had a different meaning from that given to the same words in philosophy. For that reason he held that theology was bound by the very nature of its task to express the reality of God's revelation in Christ independently, utilizing philosophy and logic solely as subservient tools.

In his *Brief Confession Concerning the Holy Supper* of 1544, the Wittenberg Reformer bore witness for the last time to his unalterable adherence to the doctrine of the real presence of the body and blood of Jesus Christ in the Supper. The writing is a vigorous refutation of the views espoused by Karlstadt, Zwingli, Oecolampadius, Schwenckfeld, and others, all of whom he regarded as "fanatics" (*Schwärmer*). He intended this work to be a closing testimony to his eucharistic teaching and his serious, lifelong concern for doctrinal integrity. Though this product of his pen does not compare with the thoroughness and well-ordered progression of thought evident in his *Confession Concerning Christ's Supper* of 1528, it is nevertheless an important writing by the "old Luther." It bears witness to the fact that Luther's theology of the cross, whether taken from the early period or the later years of his life, is a consistent whole. Thus one is not justified in pitting the theological views of the "young Luther" against those of the "old Luther." To be sure, during his career the battle lines shifted, causing him to make different emphases at different times and in different ways; but throughout the vicissitudes of his reform work, even though he became more conservative socially and politically, he developed a theology that did not contradict itself but was consistently oriented around the gospel of God's grace in Christ.[25] The revealed Word, in

[24] Holsten Fagerberg, *Die Theologie der lutherischen Bekenntnisschriften von 1529 bis 1537* (Göttingen, 1963), p. 122.

[25] Hanns Lilje, *Luther and the Reformation* (Philadelphia: Fortress Press, 1967), pp. 220-222. Cf. Heinrich Bornkamm, *op. cit.*, pp. 32-35.

the context of a critical appraisal of church history with its great theological teachers and leaders, was and remained the firm foundation for his teachings. This particular volume of *Luther's Works* bears out the thesis that Luther's interpretation of the sacrament in reality grew naturally out of his conscientious and lifelong faith in and obedience to the word of God and its unrivaled importance in the life and destiny of the church on earth.

In the preparation of this volume valuable insights in the translation of the Marburg Colloquy were gained from Hermann Sasse's reconstruction of it in his book, *This Is My Body* (Minneapolis: Augsburg Publishing House, 1959), and from Walther Koehler's parallel effort in German under the title, *Das Marburger Religionsgespräch: Versuch einer Rekonstruktion* (Leipzig, 1929). I should like to express my deep appreciation and gratitude to Dr. Edmund Smits and Dr. Lowell C. Satre of the faculty of Luther Theological Seminary, St. Paul, Minnesota, who have helped me in many ways with their suggestions. My colleague in historical theology at Northwestern Lutheran Seminary, Dr. Dorris A. Flesner, assisted me with his counsel with regard to this introductory material. Lastly, I want to mention the important supportive role my wife has played in carrying out this assignment, not the least of which was her expert preparing of the bulk of the typescript.

M.E.L.

LUTHER'S WORKS

VOLUME 38

THE MARBURG COLLOQUY
AND
THE MARBURG ARTICLES

1529

Translated by

Martin E. Lehmann

INTRODUCTION

Luther's *Confession Concerning Christ's Supper* of 1528 was designed to be the Reformer's final defense of his teaching on the Lord's Supper. This work, dealing with the many objections brought forward against his interpretation of the sacrament by his opponents Zwingli, Oecolampadius, Bucer, and others, proved to be a masterful, detailed, and clear presentation of his interpretation of the doctrine of the Eucharist in particular and of his basic Christian beliefs in general.[1] Thus he held that he had confessed his faith with unmistakable clarity before the world so that henceforth there would be no doubt in the minds of his contemporaries and of posterity as to what he believed on the basis of God's word.

Actually Luther had not initiated the controversy over the Lord's Supper with Zwingli and his party, but had deliberately refrained from attacking the Zurich Reformer personally.[2] Gradually, however, he had been drawn into the conflict and so had felt obliged to defend his teaching on this sacrament. It turned out to be an acrimonious dispute with Zwingli, eliciting from Luther's pen the writing of 1527, entitled *That These Words of Christ, "This Is My Body," Still Stand Firm Against the Fanatics* and in 1528 the work which was mentioned above.

Since Luther believed that he had made a definitive statement about his teaching on the sacrament in his *Confession Concerning Christ's Supper,* he saw no further need of discussing this doctrinal issue with Zwingli. In fact he did not again deal with the same theme at length until 1544, at which time Schwenckfeld's heretical notions about the Eucharist compelled Luther to reiterate his own belief in his *Brief Confession Concerning the Holy Sacrament,*[3] a work that appears in this volume.

---

[1] See Introduction to *Confession Concerning Christ's Supper. LW* 37, 156-158. Robert H. Fischer, editor and translator.

[2] Walther Koehler, *Zwingli und Luther* (2 vols.; Leipzig, 1924, Gütersloh, 1953), I, 73. Cf. Hermann Sasse, *This Is My Body* (Minneapolis: Augsburg Publishing House, 1959), pp. 139 ff., and *LW* 37, 5 ff.

[3] *WA* 54, 141 ff.

Why then did the Marburg Colloquy take place? What was its purpose, and who were the persons chiefly responsible for planning and carrying it out?

Before the Marburg Colloquy in particular was proposed, the idea of a religious disputation had cropped up repeatedly. The Leipzig Disputation of 1519 had no doubt been responsible for popularizing this method of dealing with religious differences. Indeed, Zurich itself had formally declared its adherence to Zwingli's reform program only after a public disputation between the contending parties had taken place under the auspices of the city council in January of 1523.[4]

John Oecolampadius of Basel first broached the idea of arranging a disputation which would concern itself specifically with the then current dispute over the Lord's Supper in a letter to the humanist Willibald Pirckheimer of Nürnberg, in April, 1525. Subsequently, Zwingli, Capito, and Bucer proposed religious colloquies for the purpose of dealing with this controversy.[5] In 1526 Bucer, in a letter to Justus Jonas in Wittenberg, suggested that a personal meeting between the Zwinglians and the Lutherans take place in order that they might discuss their differences concerning the Eucharist.[6]

In 1526 Wolfgang Capito of Strassburg attended the First Diet of Speyer where he came into contact with the gifted and politically astute young Landgrave Philip of Hesse. Capito was able to initiate a correspondence between the landgrave and Zwingli, both of whom favored a political federation of all Protestants (excluding Anabaptists) to counterbalance the Roman Catholic territories.[7] In 1527 Philip of Hesse, in the interest of his political plan, proposed a colloquy with Zwingli to Luther. However, Luther decidedly rejected the proposal because he believed that both sides had written sufficiently about their views and that there were no new arguments that could be presented at such a colloquy.[8]

---

[4] John T. McNeill, *The History and Character of Calvinism* (New York: Oxford University Press, 1967), pp. 56 ff.

[5] Koehler, *Zwingli und Luther*, II, 1-3.

[6] Sasse, *op. cit.*, p. 192.

[7] Koehler, *Zwingli und Luther*, II, 12 ff.

[8] *WA* 30^{III}, 110. See *The Marburg Colloquy* below. Cf. Koehler, *Zwingli und Luther*, II, 24.

Despite this initial rebuff, Philip persisted in pursuing his political plan of bringing about some kind of agreement between the two reform movements. In his ardent desire to stage a colloquy the landgrave was able to count on both Zwingli's and Bucer's support. Zwingli held that the doctrinal difference between Zurich and Wittenberg with regard to the Lord's Supper in no way obstructed genuine fellowship between the two Protestant parties. "Luther and I possess one faith in him (Christ) . . . ," declared Zwingli. "There is no discord among believers because of the faith, for they possess one spirit."[9] Bucer concurred with such a view. At the beginning of the Public Disputation in Bern (1528), the latter stated that the doctrinal divergence about the sacrament between the Swiss and the Strassburgers, on the one hand, and the Lutherans, on the other, was not important because it did not concern "the essence of the faith."[10] It is understandable then why both Zwingli and Bucer welcomed a religious colloquy. Zwingli shared the landgrave's desire for a political union of the evangelicals in order to safeguard and strengthen the reform movement in Switzerland and Germany, while Bucer believed that a doctrinal compromise could be achieved without endangering the fundamentals of the faith.

At the Second Diet of Speyer in 1529, in the face of stringent measures designed to halt the spread of the Reformation, a solemn protest was made by the evangelical estates. Philip of Hesse, together with five other princes and fourteen cities, formally signed the protest and appeal. This action resulted in calling those who were at variance with the Roman Catholic Church "Protestants." The landgrave believed that the time was now ripe for making a broader political alliance with the Swiss. He therefore worked energetically toward the goal of holding a religious colloquy by telling Melanchthon, who was present at the diet, about a possible colloquy between Luther and Oecolampadius. At the same time he wrote to Zwingli, suggesting that the Zurich Reformer should be prepared to meet somewhere with Luther and Melanchthon for the purpose of discussing their religious differences.[11]

[9] Koehler, *Zwingli und Luther*, II, 4.
[10] *Ibid.*, II, 8.
[11] *Ibid.*, II, 25-27.

After Melanchthon had returned to Wittenberg, he set forth his opinion about a planned colloquy in guarded terms.[12] Luther, who was informed about the new evangelical alliance contemplated by Philip of Hesse, wrote a letter to his ruler, the elector John, and cautioned him against the proposal. However, the landgrave was able to win the Saxon elector's support for his plan of a meeting between Luther and Zwingli and therefore sent a letter to Luther, inviting him to attend a religious colloquy at Marburg. Although Luther was doubtful about the value of a personal meeting with Zwingli and a discussion of their differences, he accepted the invitation. At the same time he did not hesitate to point out to the landgrave in a letter that the projected colloquy might make matters worse between the two parties than the deadlock that existed.

"Therefore, if your Grace is willing to do it, I should be glad if your Grace . . . would inquire of the other side whether they are inclined to yield their opinion, so that the trouble may not become worse than ever. For your Grace can readily understand that all conferences are wasted and all meetings are in vain if both parties come to them with no intention of yielding anything. It has been my past experience that they will insist on their own ideas after our arguments have been fairly presented; that I cannot yield after their arguments have been presented, I know as certainly as I know they are in error."[13]

It is noteworthy that Luther, during the summer of 1529, prior to his going to Marburg, together with his Wittenberg colleagues drew up a theological confession which became known as the Schwabach Articles. This confession faithfully reflected Lutheran teaching, especially with respect to the doctrine on the Lord's Supper. With this confession as a kind of platform for unity among the evangelicals, Luther went to Marburg with a good conscience.[14]

The Swiss delegation consisted of Zwingli, Rudolph Collin, Ulrich Funk, and the printer Froschauer from Zurich, Oecolampadius and Rudolph Frey from Basel, and Hedio, Bucer, and Jacob

---

[12] S-*J* 2, 477-478. Cf. *C. R.* 1, 1066.

[13] S-*J* 2, 484. Cf. *WA*, Br 5, 101-102.

[14] Sasse, *op. cit.*, pp. 208 ff. Cf. Koehler, *Zwingli und Luther*, II, 41 ff.

Sturm from Strassburg. In addition to these, five servants, attending to their needs on the journey, accompanied them. On September 26 the party arrived at Marburg where they were hospitably received by the landgrave himself as guests in his castle.

The Wittenberg delegation was made up of Luther, Melanchthon, Justus Jonas, Caspar Cruciger, George Rörer, and perhaps Veit Dietrich. Arriving at their destination in Marburg on September 30, they, too, were given a most cordial welcome by Philip of Hesse and also remained in his castle as his guests. On Saturday afternoon, October 2, the Lutherans from South Germany arrived: Osiander from Nürnberg, Brenz from Schwäbisch-Hall, and Stephan Agricola from Augsburg. As a result of their late arrival these South German theologians missed the entire first session of the colloquy that had taken place on that morning.[15] According to Zwingli's estimate no more than twenty-four persons were assembled in a large living room of the castle to witness the debate. Brenz, by contrast, calculated that fifty to sixty persons were in attendance at the colloquy. In addition to the representatives of both parties mentioned, several men of noble rank besides Philip of Hesse, some laymen of prominence and a number of theological professors and pastors from various parts of Germany witnessed the proceedings.[16]

At the landgrave's request preliminary discussions were held in private between Luther and Oecolampadius and simultaneously between Melanchthon and Zwingli on Friday, October 1, in order that areas of possible agreement might be explored. While little is known about the content of the discussion between Luther and Oecolampadius, the gist of the conversation between Melanchthon and Zwingli has been preserved in the notes which Zwingli made and which Melanchthon confirmed as a reliable summary of their dialogue.

In dealing with the subject of word and Spirit and in touching upon the doctrine of original sin, Zwingli and Melanchthon had no difficulty in reaching agreement. When, however, the matter of Christ's bodily presence in the Eucharist came up for discussion,

[15] Koehler, *Zwingli und Luther,* II, 63 ff. Cf. Sasse, *op. cit.*, pp. 215 ff.
[16] Koehler, *Zwingli und Luther,* II, 65-66.

they discovered that they held to quite different interpretations of Christ's words of institution. The same points of disagreement again cropped up during the debate later.[17]

The colloquy proper, beginning on Saturday morning, October 2, at six o'clock, ended Sunday evening, October 3. Luther, Melanchthon, Zwingli, and Oecolampadius were seated at a special table before the landgrave and other dignitaries who were present. When Osiander, Brenz, and Agricola arrived on Saturday afternoon, they, too, were seated beside Luther and Melanchthon at the table.

Zwingli had earlier expressed the wish that the debate might be open to any who wished to attend. In opposition to this desire, Luther had stated that it would not be advisable to give the colloquy such wide publicity. Philip of Hesse agreed with Luther in this matter. Zwingli likewise would have preferred to use Latin for the debate because he believed that the Swiss dialect of the German language that he spoke might not be readily understood by those who were present. However, since the landgrave, who followed the entire debate with great interest, and others of the laity would not have been able to understand Latin, the German language was used. Finally, it was also Zwingli's desire that official minutes of the colloquy might be recorded, while Luther was not in favor of the proposal. In this instance, too, Luther's wish was granted. In fact, taking notes on the part of any of the auditors was expressly prohibited.[18] A reconstruction of the colloquy on the basis of the reports which were afterward made, either from notes taken during the sessions or entirely from memory, must consequently remain fragmentary.[19]

The seven separate reports on the colloquy, offered here in translation, are taken from *WA* 30^{III}, 92-159. They were made by various persons who attended the event, and so furnish information about the colloquy. On the whole, the colloquy was conducted

---

[17] Sasse, *op. cit.*, pp. 225-229. Cf. Koehler, *Zwingli und Luther,* II, 78-83.
[18] Sasse, *op. cit.*, p. 220. Cf. Oskar Farner, *Huldrych Zwingli* (4 vols.; Zurich, 1943, 1946, 1954, 1960), IV, 364-365.
[19] Two recent and notable reconstructions of the debate are: Walther Koehler, *Das Marburger Religionsgespräch: Versuch einer Rekonstruktion* (Leipzig, 1929), and Sasse, *op. cit.*, pp. 215-268. The latter volume also lists previous attempts at reconstructing the debate.

with courtesy and in an amicable spirit. Only on several occasions did Luther and Zwingli exhibit a spirit of animosity as they exchanged their views. A brief evaluation of the various individual reports follows here.

1. The report by Caspar Hedio of Strassburg in Latin, doubtlessly based on notes taken during the colloquy, is the most important source concerning the debate as a whole. His notes were seemingly not elaborated upon or changed afterward.

2. The report of Anonymous, also in Latin, is similar in nature to the one by Hedio. It appeared in print in 1574 and 1575 as an eyewitness account. There is evidence that the report was subjected to revision and formulated in clear and theologically precise language. The author of it remains unknown; but it is generally believed that he belonged to the circle of Luther's close friends. It has been surmised that either George Rörer, Luther's secretary, or Frederick Myconius, a pastor at Gotha, wrote the account.

3. Rudolph Collin, Zwingli's colleague and travel companion from Zurich, furnished an account of the debate in Latin that agrees in many respects with Hedio's. He may have made use of Hedio's notes in the composition of it, although some scholars are of the opinion that his was also an independent report.[20]

4. Osiander's report, in the form of a letter, was made to the city council of Nürnberg. Since he did not arrive at the start of the colloquy, he may have had recourse to some notes to supplement that part of the debate which he missed. The account is in German and furnishes some important information about the negotiations that followed the colloquy.

5. Brenz's letter, addressed to Schradin and the people at Reutlingen, is an account that does not make the claim of reproducing the original words of the debate. Brenz makes special mention of the fact that his report should not be published because he had not been requested to report on the proceedings at Marburg. The account is mainly in Latin with a short portion of it in German.

6. *Rhapsodies on the Marburg Colloquy*, like the report made

[20] Koehler, *Das Marburger Religionsgespräch*, p. 3.

by Anonymous, emanates from an unknown source. Veit Dietrich, Luther's secretary, made a copy of the *Rhapsodies*. The assumption that Luther himself may have been its author is not tenable. The concluding couplet with the signature of Martin Luther beneath it could be an indication that it was a summary account made by one of the Reformer's friends which Luther then sent to Spalatin. It contains important statements not found in the other reports and was written in Latin.

7. The *Summary Report Concerning the Marburg Colloquy* was made by Heinrich Utinger in the German tongue. Walther Koehler does not believe that the report is based upon notes made by Zwingli,[21] as is assumed in a discussion of it by the editor in *WA* 30^{III}, 101. The manuscript of this *Summary* was first discovered in the nineteenth century.[22]

After the colloquy had come to a close without resulting in an agreement on the doctrine of the Lord's Supper, Philip of Hesse nonetheless continued to seek ways and means by which to effect some political federation between the Lutherans and the Zwinglians. For this reason smaller groups from both sides engaged in dialogue on Monday morning, October 4, for the purpose of ascertaining whether fellowship between the two parties could be established in spite of the existing doctrinal difference. The Lutherans concluded that fellowship was not possible "for important Christian reasons."[23] At this juncture the landgrave requested Luther to draft articles of faith which would express those beliefs held in common by the two opposing parties. Using the Schwabach Articles as a basis for this assignment, Luther formulated the Marburg Articles. After completing the task, the Reformer did not expect Zwingli and his party to sign the articles he had drawn up; but much to his surprise they did so.

Agreement was reached by both parties on the first fourteen articles in the document. The fifteenth article, in the formulation of which Philip of Hesse appears to have had a part, stated that there was an agreement on five of the six points that dealt with the doc-

[21] *Ibid.*, p. 4.
[22] Sasse, *op. cit.*, p. 221.
[23] See Osiander's report below.

trine of the Lord's Supper.[24] To be sure, the sixth point was the sensitive and critically important one that had to do with the bodily presence of Christ in the sacrament. Zwingli and those who sided with him agreed to sign their names to the Marburg Articles, not because they were fully in accord with the details of the doctrinal formulations they contained, but because they, like the landgrave, believed in the need of achieving political solidarity with the Wittenbergers. The notes, which Zwingli later appended to the Marburg Articles as a kind of commentary and correction of the doctrines stated in them, reveal that his views differed from those of Luther.[25]

The Marburg Articles were dated October 3 by Luther in order to make the time of their composition coincide with the final day of the colloquy. Thus they were to be regarded as a tangible result of the meeting at Marburg. Actually the date of their composition was October 4.

It is worth noting, too, that the final negotiations had to be conducted with considerable haste because an epidemic of serious proportions, known as the "English sweat," had broken out in Marburg. Anxiety about the rapid spread of the disease caused Philip of Hesse to speed up the proceedings, although he had originally planned that the colloquy was to extend over a period of "not less than eight days."[26] Consequently, the landgrave himself left Marburg early on October 5. Luther and his party departed on the same day in the afternoon. It is probable that the Zwinglians and the Strassburgers began their homeward journey on the same date, since all had been urged to leave as soon as possible.

The Marburg Articles are presented in the Weimar Edition on the basis of three different available German texts. The oldest version is based on the Kassel manuscript, reflecting most faithfully the original wording of the articles. A facsimile and a printing of the text were made in Kassel in 1847 and in 1854.[27] Next in importance to the Kassel manuscript is the Zurich manuscript,

---

[24] Koehler, *Zwingli und Luther,* II, 127.
[25] *WA* 30^{III}, 160-171.
[26] Koehler, *Zwingli und Luther,* II, 131.
[27] For a discussion of the various manuscripts and texts see *WA* 30^{III}, 96-109.

which contains certain additions to the seventh, thirteenth, and fifteenth articles. The original Zurich manuscript with its ten signatures is in Zurich. Finally, a printed version, based on the Zurich manuscript, appears along with the two aforementioned texts, *WA* 30^{III}, 160-171. Our translation is based on the Kassel manuscript. The additions found in the Zurich manuscript are, however, included and are especially noted within the body of the translation. In the Wittenberg Edition of Luther's works the fourteenth article on infant baptism was inadvertently omitted and the fifteenth article became the fourteenth. The Erlangen Edition of Luther's works copied the error, as did the Walch Edition. The latter edition, however, later corrected the mistake.[28]

---

[28] See the details given by Sasse, *op. cit.*, p. 268, n. 112.

THE MARBURG COLLOQUY

The Report of Hedio

[October 2, 6 A.M.][1]

Luther, when requested to speak after the close of the chancellor's address, said: Most noble prince, gracious lord! I do not doubt that the colloquy has been planned and arranged with good intentions. Two years ago I rejected it because I knew that enough had been written on both sides and that no further arguments could be presented by either party. Besides, I had made up my mind that I would abide by my opinion until the end of my life. Nor was it my intention to write anything more on the subject. However, when at the Diet of Speyer, my lord, Landgrave Philip, proposed such a colloquy I gave my approval to it;[2] not that I wished to change my conviction of which I am completely sure, but that I might demonstrate the reason for my faith and show where others are in error. But before we can actually begin I want to know about certain opinions that are being put forward by the churches of Zurich, Basel, and Strassburg and which, if actually held, would be in error. They concern the Trinity and the person of Christ. For example, they say that the words, "who eats my flesh," refer to the divine nature of Christ; also [they hold a different view] on original sin. Furthermore, they say that I do not understand purgatory correctly; they say the same thing about justification by faith.

Zwingli and *Oecolampadius* replied that they had the correct view in this matter, that they had always taught rightly, and that

---

[1] The date and exact time for the beginning of the debate are from Osiander's account. Cf. *WA* 30^{III}, 110, n. 1.

[2] Actually Luther was not present at Speyer, although Hedio's account seems to indicate this. In reality Luther subsequently approved of this plan, which was initially proposed by Landgrave Philip at the Second Diet of Speyer in 1529.

their books and the church bore witness to this fact. Nevertheless, they desired that first of all there be a discussion of the Lord's Supper for that was why this meeting had been arranged; after this had been finished all the remaining items could readily be discussed.

Luther agreed to this procedure, but protested that he did not agree with the writings of these people. He desired to indicate this disagreement so that people at home might not say that he was not allowed to speak freely. He went on to cite their basic principles:

(1) they desire to prove their case by way of logical conclusions;

(2) they hold that a body cannot be in two places at the same time and that it cannot be infinite;

(3) they appeal to natural reason.

I do not ask how Christ can be God and man and how these natures could be united, for God is able to do more than anything we can imagine. We must submit to the word of God. They themselves must prove that the body of Christ is not there [when Christ himself says]: "This is my body." He does not want to hear what reason says. He rejects entirely human arguments like the geometrical argument that a gate cannot fit into a doorway, nor can a post fit into a hole the size of a finger. Therefore, he requests a valid proof.

Oecolampadius, responding to the arguments of Luther, said: Chapter 6 [of St. John] explains the other passages of Scripture. Christ is not present there [i.e., in the sacrament] locally. He [Oecolampadius] did not want to appeal to reason or geometry, but because he possessed the fullness of faith he spoke on the basis of [such a] faith, for Christ has risen.[3] Our opinion is neither new nor profane.

Luther: Oecolampadius has enumerated many modes of speech in Scripture, e.g.: "I am the vine." (2) He admonishes us to understand the eating spiritually. (3) [He says,] "The fathers are on our side." [Luther] replied that it was not necessary to speak at length on the subject. He admits that there are many metaphors [in Holy

---

[3] Oecolampadius' argument about the impossibility of Christ's local presence in the sacrament is based on the conviction that Christ's body could no longer be present on earth because, after his ascension, his body was in heaven.

Scripture], but they have to prove that we have a metaphor here. They ought not to talk about what we already know; for, if he [Christ] had spoken in a demonstrative way when he said, "I am the vine," I would have believed it too. A general sentence allows a metaphor. Here we have a demonstrative [descriptive] sentence; therefore, you must prove that it is to be understood metaphorically.[4] So far no one has ever undertaken to prove this. Moreover [you must also prove] that spiritual eating excludes bodily eating so that there should be no bodily eating at all. (3) He [Luther] conceded that the fathers are to be interpreted in part in accordance with their views, if we accept their interpretation of them. Of what use would it be unless they can prove that "body" is here used instead of "figure of body"? He wants [them] to speak to the point without ambiguity.

Oecolampadius replied: "I am the vine" is also a demonstrative sentence. It is possible. How is it possible?

Luther: He does not deny that there are figures of speech, but he wants them to prove that this is the case here. He maintains that it is begging the question [to say] that because [in John 6 Christ][5] speaks of spiritual eating, therefore there cannot be bodily eating. You want me to edify the faith of my heart on this basis. That means you are not willing to produce any proof. Here my faith is strengthened because you do not prove yours. I have a clear and powerful text. Do justice to that text! What I have been waiting for all along is that you prove what you ought to prove.

Oecolampadius: I have said this: In the sixth chapter, [when Christ speaks][6] of spiritual eating, he separates it from bodily eat-

[4] By a general sentence Luther meant a statement that was made to illuminate a relationship or function. Thus when Christ said, "I am the vine, you are the branches" (John 15:5), he used this metaphor to shed light upon the relationship between himself and his disciples. On the other hand, a demonstrative or descriptive sentence has to do with a concrete situation in which a specific matter is stated. Luther believed the words of Jesus, "This is my body," to be a demonstrative sentence in the sense that they referred to the presence of Christ's body in the Holy Supper. Jesus' words here literally mean what they say. They are not to be taken as a general sentence that employs a figure of speech for clarification.

[5] These words, "in John 6 Christ" (*Christus in Ioh. 6*), are conjectures of the editor. Cf. *WA* 30^{III}, 114, n. 1.

[6] These words, "when Christ speaks" (*cum Christus dicit*), are conjectures of the editor. Cf. *WA* 30^{III}, 114, n. 2.

ing. Therefore, it is not the latter, for he advises against the bodily eating.

Luther: Your view is that through spiritual eating he [Christ] would deter us from bodily eating. To this I reply: He wanted to teach the Jews, the Capernaites, that he would not be eaten like bread and meat in a dish. If I eat Christ bodily in the bread, this is not something ordinary for the mind but a benefit of the Holy Spirit. Therefore, it is not ordinary or common but a sublime eating because man can believe those words that the body of Christ is there.

Oecolampadius said: They think it is faith because Christ is in the bread. This is an opinion, not faith. It is wrong to attribute too much to the element. Augustine [has dealt with this in his treatise] *On Christian Doctrine.*[7]

Luther: Again I refer to the words [of the Lord's Supper]. When I speak of the "body which is given for us," then this is not a base understanding of Scripture. If we had to deal with the bread only, even this would not be a low understanding of Scripture. But if I accept it [as God's word,] [even lifting up] a piece of straw [at God's command is something spiritual].[8] When we baptize with water we ought not to pay attention so much to what is said but to him who speaks; because God speaks, we must embrace the word. Take as an example a prince who gives orders to shoe a horse. The horseshoe is a lowly thing. There are [many] lowly things. To be hungry is also a lowly thing. [The command is:] "Baptize with water!" We attribute the washing not to the water but to the Holy Spirit. Concerning the element itself we are in

---

[7] Perhaps Oecolampadius read from *On Christian Doctrine* (*De doctrina christiana*), III, 5, 9 (*MPL* 34, 69), where Augustine, commenting on II Cor. 3:6, "The letter kills but the spirit gives life," says: "When a word that is meant figuratively is accepted literally, it is understood in a carnal way." Cf. Hermann Sasse, *op. cit.*, p. 235.

[8] The material in brackets here is inserted on the basis of Collin's account of this discussion (cf. below, p. 54). Luther used this same illustration more fully in his Septuagesima sermon in the Lenten Postil (1525), *WA* 17^{II}, 132, 16-21: "When God adds his word and sign to something it becomes a totally spiritual food and drink, no matter how external and physical it may be. If God would command me to elevate a piece of straw, there would immediately be spiritual food and drink connected with the piece of straw—not because of the piece of straw, but because of the divine truth and presence in the word and sign."

agreement. We do not ascribe dignity to the bread but to the word and to him who speaks it, Jesus Christ. Just as when a prince sends his servant to shoe his horse, the piece of iron is given dignity by being attached to the horse's foot. Give due honor to the cross, and it does many other things. As often as we speak of the body of Christ, we are speaking about his body which is at the right hand of the Father. We would readily accept your opinion, but [we cannot] because your understanding of Scripture is vague. He [Luther] asked the prince's [Landgrave Philip's] pardon. These words ["This is my body"] have taken me captive.[9] Now you speak.

Oecolampadius replied that he accepted the example brought forward. So far Luther's idea is that the word brings the body of Christ into the bread.

Luther answered: That is correct. For example, the prince furnishes a horseshoe and someone else fastens it, thus investing it with excellence.[10] We have previously spoken of Christ's intention.

Luther: Your argument implies this idea: Because we have a spiritual eating, there is no need of bodily eating. To this I reply: I am not inquiring whether or not it is necessary; that has not been entrusted to us. In that case I could neither be baptized nor believe in Christ.[11] Christ gives himself to us in many ways: first, in preaching; second, in baptism; [third,] in brotherly consolation; fourth, in the sacrament, as often as the body of Christ is eaten, because he himself commands us to do so. If he should command me to eat dung, I would do it. The servant should not inquire about the will of his lord. We ought to close our eyes.

Oecolampadius: Where is it written that we should go through the Scriptures with closed eyes, good Doctor?

Luther: If [we continued our discussion] for a hundred years,

[9] A marginal note indicates that these words were spoken to Oecolampadius.

[10] This illustration evidently has reference to the fact that Luther's opponents rejected his understanding of the presence of Christ's body in the bread as low or base and that they wanted to put something loftier in its place.

[11] Luther's emphasis is on Christ's word or command. We cannot question or debate what he has ordained. He has commanded the use of water in baptism and the use of the bread and the wine in the Lord's Supper. By faith these external matters become vehicles of Christ's saving power. Thus the outward (e.g., the spoken word, the water, and the bodily eating) is inextricably tied to the inward (e.g., the divine gifts received in faith).

still nothing would be proved. If you can do away with the text, I am satisfied. He who spoke in the sixth chapter of John has also spoken the words: "This is my body."

Oecolampadius: It is agreed that we should deal with the Scriptures in a clear way and compare one passage with the other. This is what Augustine does. Oecolampadius abides by what Christ has said.

Luther: I also abide by my text.

Zwingli: It is prejudice if he does not want to give up his opinion. He is not willing to give it up unless a passage is cited which proves that "body" means "figure of my body." This is the prejudice of heretics, for example, of Helvidius who denied that Jesus was the only son of Mary, because it cannot be proved from Scripture.[12] It is necessary to compare one Scripture passage with another. Even if we do not have [a passage that says], "This is the figure of my body," we do have [a passage] which leads us away from the bodily eating. It is the purpose of our meeting here to look at the passages, and we ought to consider the passage [in John 6] because it leads away from bodily eating. Hence it follows that in the Supper Christ did not give himself in bodily fashion. In fact, you yourself recognize that spiritual eating gives comfort. And since there is agreement on this point, which is the main one, he begs, for the sake of the love of Christ [that no one be accused of heresy on account of this dissension].[13] The early fathers, even if they disagreed, nevertheless did not condemn one another in such a way. He returns to the sixth chapter of John: "It is the spirit that gives life, the flesh is of no avail" [John 6:63]. He does not understand this to mean that the humanity of Christ is of no avail, because in the flesh he redeemed us. What a wonderful consolation; as often as I consider the fact that Christ had flesh like mine I am wonderfully comforted. You make it, he says, into something other than what the evangelist wanted; you make it unattractive with

[12] Helvidius denied the perpetual virginity of Mary (in Rome *ca.* A.D. 385). Jerome, repudiating his claims, upheld the perpetual virginity in his treatise *On the Perpetual Virginity of the Blessed Mary* and so established the doctrine for the Middle Ages. Cf. Sasse, *op. cit.*, p. 237.

[13] According to Scultetus' conjecture, this clause is to be added in order to complete the sentence.

unusual words like "dismembering" or "tearing apart." In what way does he give his flesh for eating? He reads these words[14] in Greek because he distrusts his memory. When I shall have ascended into heaven, then you shall see that I am not to be eaten bodily; this is Augustine's interpretation.[15] For Augustine did not want the body of Christ to be eaten essentially and bodily. It is the spirit that gives life; the antithesis of the spirit is the flesh. You have spoken of a base understanding. Some of your words pleased me, others displeased me because they seemed rather childish. The works which God commands he commands for our benefit. God is true and is light; he does not lead into darkness. Therefore, he does not intend to say [in a literal sense], "This is my body," for Scripture contradicts that. Oracles that are given are obscure. God does not act thus. The soul is spirit; the soul does not eat flesh, but spirit eats spirit. He begged them not to bear him any ill will; he desires their friendship and is not embittered. He likes to see the faces of Luther and Philip.

Luther promised that they would lay aside all passions for the sake of God and the prince. What is lost, is lost. Let us hope for the future. Even if they cannot agree on everything, they might discuss at the close of the colloquy whether or not they can regard each other as brethren.—As to the argument of Helvidius: It can be proved from Scripture that the word "brother" may be used for "cousin." But it cannot be proved that "This is my body" is a trope. What you call eating may do away with all eating; "flesh, flesh" means eating according to you. Form your own opinion, this has nothing to do with the matter itself; I would eat rotten apples or dried-up pears if God would place them before me. Where the word of God is, there is spiritual eating. Whenever God speaks to us, faith is required, and such faith means "eating." If, however, he adds bodily eating, we are bound to obey. In faith we eat this body which is given for us. The mouth receives the body of Christ, the soul believes the words when eating the body. If I receive the body of Christ into

[14] Zwingli probably read John 6:52, where the Jews ask: "How can this man give us his flesh to eat?"

[15] Augustine, *On the Gospel of John (In Ioannis evangelium)*, Tractate 27, 3 (*MPL* 35, 1616).

my arms, this would be for the purpose of embracing it. You have your interpretation and mean well; but this is of no consequence. Furthermore, when you say that God does not propose to us anything incomprehensible, I could not admit this.[16] [Consider] the virginity of Mary, the forgiveness of sins, and many similar matters. So also, "This is my body" [is incomprehensible]. "Thy path was through the great waters, yet thy footprints were unseen" [Psalm 77:19]. If we knew his ways, he who is marvelous would not be incomprehensible.

Zwingli: From Scripture it can be proved that the thing signified is used for the sign. Ezekiel [5:1 ff.] is ordered to cut off his hair. Then the passage continues: "This is Jerusalem"; i.e., this will happen to Jerusalem. The "is" means "signifies." The passover [Exodus 12:27] is according to the analogy a figure of Jesus Christ. He [Luther] does not want to acknowledge that such a mode of speech as occurs in other passages [is also to be found here in the Lord's Supper].[17] But there are many texts that prohibit a literal understanding. Such a passage is: "The elder [and honored man] is the head, and the prophet [who teaches] is the tail" [Isa. 9:14 ff.]. This was the customary way of speaking for the prophets, as it is in this prophetic word. Here Isaiah used "is" for "signifies." Therefore, comparison of Scripture with Scripture [necessitates][18] the acceptance of "is" for "signifies." Here he [Luther] employs all possible means of rhetorical extenuations. He puts forward strong arguments: "If God commanded"—you know very well that God commands those things. "If God commands us to eat his body in remembrance of him," etc., we know that we are pleasing God when we do this. Luther does not speak of the internal word but of the external word. We say that it is impossible to understand the words of the Lord's Supper literally because God has forbidden us to eat his flesh bodily. [Otherwise] we make the word ambiguous. Luther thinks that the word, when uttered, adds something to the bread and wine. Melanchthon agrees with Zwingli that words only signify

---

[16] The phrase *non concedo* is added here.

[17] The text is unclear; the material in brackets is conjectured on the basis of the parallel passage in the report of Anonymous. Cf. below, p. 40.

[18] The words *necesse est* are inserted.

something. The core or marrow of the word has meaning for us. He asks that they pay attention to the word; for they are equivocating. Take an example: If a papist hears the words, "The death of Christ is our justification," he does not therefore believe them, because he fails to grasp the core [of their meaning]. The sole purpose of these words [of the sacrament] is to make known the will of the Father. You reject our interpretation; we reject yours. "I will not be with you visibly," says Christ [cf. John 12:8]. It is not true that God places many incomprehensible matters before us. That Christ is true God and man is not unknown to the faithful. When Mary was told, "The Holy Spirit will come upon you" [Luke 1:35], she was satisfied because she knew that God's power was at work. But [in John 6] the disciples were doubtful about the carnal eating, so that Christ spoke to them of a spiritual eating, as is apparent. Concerning your statement, "Where the word of God is, there there is eating," [I say that] the pope, too, has that word. I believe that the words should be believed. Christ taught nothing about bodily eating. To teach otherwise is to understand him in another way. These words are for the intellect. Even if I would eat pure bread, says Luther [this would still be beneficial].[19] "When the word is added to the element."[20] Which word? If a papist speaks the word, it is no sacrament even if the word is added to the element. Thus the spoken words must be comprehended by my faith. Hence, the sacrament has an inner meaning, is a sign employed in an action. This makes it plain that it ought to be given to brethren who, by receiving it, testify that Christ died for them. I marvel greatly at your words that the body is eaten orally. If he is present, he is not there for the comfort of the body but of the soul. Would he ever join disparate things? What I say you will not refute either by philosophy or by rhetoric. Melanchthon has admitted that the Jews did not comprehend the spiritual understanding when Christ spoke of his body. Christ gave an answer that he might heal them, for

[19] These words have been added to complete the sentence.

[20] This may be a shortened reference to Augustine's statement in his commentary, *On the Gospel of John* (*In Ioannis evangelium*), Tractate 80, 3 (MPL 35, 1840): "When the word is added to the element a sacrament comes into being."

they were suffering from the disease of lacking understanding. For this reason I am speaking of understanding [the Lord's Supper] in a spiritual sense. If he [Luther] gives an ambiguous interpretation, he is then doing violence to Scripture. "The words that I have spoken to you are spirit and life" [John 6:63]. Here "words" refers to actions and not to the spoken word.

Luther: You deviate from the path. You accuse me of using rhetorical means and do not allow me to speak of straw as a simile. You say that the passages from Ezekiel [5:1 ff.] and the "passover" [in Exodus 12:27] are allegories. There are many passages in which "is" is used demonstratively. In such a case you cannot use the art of allegorical interpretation. I have not deliberately made the word ambiguous. As to [the efficacy of] the word, I want to state briefly: We do not say that the body is produced by our own words; rather, we are speaking of the institution by Christ; they are not our words but the Lord's. Take as an example the case of a servant who is leading horses to the pasture at the command of his lord. If I should say on my own: This is my body, then it would become the body of Luther. To the gallows with that! "Do this" [Luke 22:19]—this word causes the hand of a priest to become the hand of Christ. It is not my mouth, it is not my tongue, but both are Christ's. [This is true] even though I were a knave or a rascal. The same applies also to baptism. "Go and baptize" [cf. Matt. 28:19]—this is not my work, but God's. Let us take the example of a prince who beats his opponent. In that case the fists of all [the soldiers] are the fists of the prince. We do not regard these words as idle talk. [Christ says:] "If you will say to this mountain, ['Move hence to yonder place,'] it will move" [cf. Matt. 17:20]. I am not debating the "is," but I am satisfied because Christ says it. Even the devil is powerless over against these words. I do not want adherence to the words on my own authority, but on the authority and at the command of Christ. As to the other argument that Christ spoke in a well-ordered way [cf. John 6]: he intended[21]

[21] Reading the conjectured *intendit* instead of *indit* as found in the manuscript. Cf. *WA* 30^{III}, 122, n. 2. The purpose of Christ's words is to effect faith; but this does not preclude the possibility of talking about the devil in connection with Christ's words.

preaching to lead to faith; and yet I can in the course of preaching occasionally refer to the devil. – As to the soul's eating the body [of Christ,] it can be said: Where the word of God is, there must be spiritual eating because faith is required. If men do not do this [i.e., believe and eat spiritually], how can I help that? The body is present bodily in the word. The sum of faith is this: It does not behoove us to add marginal notes to what the word of our dear God says, unless an absurdity that contradicts the faith or articles of faith compels us [to do so]. When the blessed Virgin heard, "The Holy Spirit will come upon you" [Luke 1:35], Mary asked: "How can this be?" Even as in the case of Abraham, "in hope [he believed] against hope" [Rom. 4:18]. I do not understand it. I would fall from faith, if I tried to do so and would become a fool on account of it. If you make a trope here [i.e., out of the words of the Lord's Supper], why not make one out of this: "He ascended into heaven" [cf. Mark 16:19]? He [Luther] asks him to yield because his foundations are so weak and to give glory to God.

Zwingli: First, we, too, ask you to give glory to God and to stop begging the question.[22] Second, we ask, where do you prove your thesis? I shall diligently examine your words. Please do not be angry about this! Third, you want to divert me but I hold to this passage [John 6]. I do not think that you can divert me from it. You will have to change your tune.

Luther said that Zwingli was speaking spitefully.

Zwingli asks whether he [Luther] believes that Christ wanted to help the ignorant.

Luther: You want to win your case with bold words. *Luther:* You want to decide the matter. Allow others to do so also. "This is a hard saying" [John 6:60]; they are speaking about something which would be impossible and absurd. It is up to you to prove your point, not up to me.

Zwingli: The passage in John 6 does deal with bodily eating.

Luther: Your logic is very poor; it is the kind of logic for which a schoolboy is caned and sent to the corner.[23]

---

[22] *Petitio principii.*

[23] The Latin phrase, *a baculo ad angulum,* literally means "from the cane to the corner." In his treatise *Against Hanswurst* Luther, referring to the phrase

Zwingli: This passage is going to break your neck.

Luther: Don't boast too much. Necks do not break that easily here. You are in Hesse, not in Switzerland. Christ's body is death, poison, and the devil for those who eat unworthily. Death, dungeon, etc., are evil things; and yet, if the word is added, they are salutary, said Luther.

October 2, 2 P.M.

Zwingli: In Luther's postil [in the sermon] for Septuagesima Sunday [it is stated]: Christ spoke of himself when he said: "The flesh is of no avail" [John 6:63].[24] So, too, the words of Melanchthon are: "[By faith] in the word Christ is eaten, not in bodily eating, not in visible form, not in the sacramental sign."[25] Furthermore, it is to be noted that in your interpretation you are digressing from a particular concept to a general concept. That the body is eaten in a bodily way seems to us to be an unestablished statement. When the fathers say that the body of Christ feeds the soul, this is to be understood as referring to the resurrection. Luther states that the sentence, "Christ ascended into heaven," is as absurd as this one: "This is my body."[26] Luther asks how this is to be understood.

---

as one used by the Scholastics, elucidates its meaning in that context (*LW* 41, 246, n. 134; *WA* 51, 555, n. 3). The origins of the saying are obscure, and translators have handled it in different ways. Walther Koehler translates the phrase thus: "going no further than a stick in a corner"; Koehler, *Das Marburger Religionsgespräch*, p. 19. Hermann Sasse in his reconstruction of the debate omits the translation of the phrase; Sasse, *op. cit.*, p. 244.

[24] Sermon for Septuagesima Sunday (I Cor. 9:24-10:4), *WA* 17^{II}, 126-135. Zwingli is referring to a passage in the sermon (*WA* 17^{II}, 132) which reads: "If God's word and sign are not present or recognized, it would not help if God himself were there. For, as Christ says of himself in John 6 [:63]: 'The flesh is of no avail,' because they do not pay attention to the words that he speaks about his flesh. It is his words that make his body true food, when he says he is the living bread from heaven."

[25] Zwingli is referring to Melanchthon's commentary on the Gospel of John (1523). He was apparently quoting from memory. For the precise wording of Melanchthon's comments on the sixth chapter of the Gospel of John, see Walther Koehler, *Zwingli und Luther,* I, 192.

[26] Perhaps the meaning here is, the real presence is no greater mystery than the ascension of Christ. Both are articles of faith.

Finally, he thinks that if the words, "This is my body," are spoken, the body is there regardless of who the person might be who speaks them. Here he asks Luther to be careful, for in this way the papacy will be brought in. This does not agree with Melanchthon's statement in which he admitted that the words only "signify." Either I do not understand your words correctly, or what you have said is completely absurd.

Luther: As to my postil and Melanchthon – it is not a question of what we write or have written; rather, Oecolampadius and Zwingli should prove that in the Lord's Supper the body is not eaten in a bodily way. I admit that even if I shared your belief and would regard the body of Christ as being of no profit, these words can nevertheless not be refuted: "This is my body." No matter how many people have written against us, they have written as if we spoke of the sacrament without the word. We do not say that the body of Christ feeds our body as other food does; but we hold that the body of Christ is an incorruptible food which is not consumed but which he [Christ] may transmit to our body. As to the power of words: words merely signify, the human word is a mere sound. Emperor Maximilian is dead.[27] However, we add, when something is said by the Majesty on high, it does not become effective through our strength but through the divine power. When God says: Take, do that, speak these words–then something takes place. He speaks and it is done. We must distinguish between what we say and God's command. Nor does he [Luther] say that evil men should do this. Up to this day we do not know who believes and who does not believe. Even if Peter came and would celebrate the mass, I would not know whether he believes. Therefore, I say that the sacrament should be celebrated within Christendom. There God establishes the sacrament upon his word and not upon our holiness, as the Anabaptists and Donatists do. Baptism does not rest upon my faith but upon these words: "Go and baptize" [cf. Matthew 28: 19]. God, however, desires to make use of our ministry. We cannot prohibit a bad priest from celebrating the sacrament. Therefore, we cannot give or take away anything from the papacy; another way of

[27] Consequently, his words are no longer efficacious.

attacking the papacy must be followed. – Philip, you should speak; I am really tired. – When he asked today whether there could not be a trope in each of the two passages, "He ascended into heaven" and "This is my body," he [Luther] wanted to know whether in any passage the word "body" is to be understood figuratively. It would be easier in the case of "heaven"; for "heaven" would sooner permit a trope. He was taken into heaven and a cloud received him [Acts 1:9].

Zwingli: It would be an absurdity if the ungodly could do this [i.e., cause the body of Christ to be present].

Luther: This also is against you; otherwise you could not receive baptism, nor hear the word of God, nor receive the Supper, because you cannot know whether the minister is a godly one. He explained why Paul did not want to baptize others [I Cor. 1:14 ff.]. According to God's word the godly and the ungodly act as ministers. Matthew 23, which deals with the Pharisees, proves this. Judas was a traitor, and yet he held the apostolic office. Augustine says in opposition to the Donatists that the ministry must not be entrusted solely to the virtuous because the basis of our belief is the word of God.[28]

Zwingli: It makes a difference whether the Pharisees teach or whether a person does what Christ says. The ministry of preaching is greater than the ministry of baptizing. The words, "This is my body," belong to the ministry [of preaching].

Luther: Whether you accept them as words of teaching or as words of the sacrament, these words remain: "This is my body."

Oecolampadius: Up to this point I am not yet satisfied with our discussion of the sixth chapter of John. Oecolampadius desires that one ought not insolently to do violence to Scripture. He introduces the passage about Nicodemus in John 3.

Luther: Oecolampadius rightly has said that nothing should be added to Scripture. However, he must prove that we have added

---

[28] Augustine developed this specific teaching throughout his anti-Donatist writings. E.g., *Against the Letter of Parmenian* (*Contra epistolam Parmeniani*), II, 10, 22 (*MPL* 43, 65), and *On Baptism Against the Donatists* (*De Baptismo contra Donatistas*), IV, 3, 4 (*MPL* 43, 156). On the Donatists, cf. *LW* 35, 403, n. 78.

something. For in this matter [of adding to the Scriptures] we have wrestled with the pope. However, Oecolampadius inquires, by what means Christ, who ordained the Lord's Supper, here establishes faith. There are many such ways of establishing faith. For example, when we confess our sins to one another, and when we are being exercised [in our faith] in the word.

Oecolampadius: Oecolampadius' argument is: It is not proper that we connect our hope concerning the resurrection with the bread.

Luther: Luther replied that they were not doing this. For faith looks upon the body [of Christ] as present [in the sacrament] and upon the body which is in heaven.

Oecolampadius: Luther always impresses upon us the same thing, as if we had the bread without the word of God. The church is founded on the word, "You are the Son of the living God" [Matthew 16:16], and not on the word, "This is my body."

Luther: It displeases you that I always stick to the words: "This is my body." I am not doing this without a reason. "This is" is enough for me..You prove your point. I confess [that the body is] in heaven, I also confess [that it is] in the sacrament. Luther desires to stick to these words, that Christ is in heaven and in the Supper. He is not concerned about what is contrary to nature but only about what is contrary to faith.

Oecolampadius: In all things Christ has been made like us; as he is of one substance with the Father in his divinity, so he is of one substance with us in his humanity. In this there is agreement, that Christ is present; and as he is in heaven [according to his divinity and humanity], so he is in the Supper [according to his divinity].[29]

Luther: He acknowledges that he is in baptism, the Supper, and preaching until the end of the age, until he comes. Until his coming you may distinguish between his humanity and divinity; I am not concerned about this. "For you always have the poor with

[29] The parenthetical insertions here are based on Luther's reply to Oecolampadius, which shows that Oecolampadius did distinguish between Christ's humanity and divinity, and on the parallel account in Anonymous, cf., below, p. 45.

you" [Matthew 26:11]—this is the best argument which you have presented today. Christ is in the sacrament substantially as he was born of the Virgin. But he [Oecolampadius] does not want to allow that he is in heaven in the same way as he is in the bread. Here, said Luther, we have a most perfect analogy of faith because it is faith in things unseen and because there is the promise. "You will not always have me" [Matt. 26:11]; the antithesis to this is the poor whom we have visibly. You may wash their feet, since you will not always have me. He proves this meaning on the basis of a similar saying: "These are my words which I spoke to you, while I was still with you" [Luke 24:44]. Was Christ thus drawing us away from his humanity to his divinity?

[*Oecolampadius:*][30] We also say that we do not know Christ according to the flesh [II Cor. 5:16], for we know him, rather, according to the Spirit in the sacrament. Unless you are a new creature you know Christ according to the flesh only.

"Not according to the flesh," said *Philip* [Melanchthon], means "not according to our flesh."[31]

Oecolampadius:[32] At length Oecolampadius said: You do not admit a trope in the words of institution, and yet you make it a synecdoche. Thus you introduce a new meaning contrary to the understanding of the teachers of the church universal. Therefore [your interpretation is not tenable].

Luther: God will decide that. We compel no one but commit the matter to God. Synecdoche [is a form of speech, like] sword—sheath; mug—beer. Thus "This is my body" is an inclusive way of speaking: The body is in the bread as the sword is in the sheath. This figure [of speech] is in general use, and the text calls for it. A metaphor abolishes the content altogether: e.g., as when you understand "body" as "the figure of a body"; synecdoche does not do this. We admit the synecdoche in order to satisfy the sophists.

---

[30] Collin ascribes these words that follow to Oecolampadius.

[31] This is the only time that Melanchthon participated in the entire debate. Melanchthon's point is that II Cor. 5:16 is not referring to the flesh of Christ, but speaks of knowing Christ from a human point of view.

[32] Some reports, including the one by Anonymous, ascribe these remarks to Zwingli. However, Hedio's express reference to Oecolampadius militates against this assumption.

"He on whom you see the Spirit descend" [John 1:33]. . . . He [John the Baptist] saw the dove in which the Holy Spirit was. Your figure of speech does away with the kernel and leaves the shell. Synecdoche is not a comparison; it [says,] "It is there," and it is [actually] there. This also applies to the saying: "This is my body." Luther [said] to Dr. Philip. Why don't you reply? I am tired of talking.

Zwingli spoke next: Certain statements were made about Christ's body in heaven, but not enough has been said. Romans 8 [:29]: "Those whom he foreknew he also predestined to be conformed to the image of his Son." Also, Philippians [2:7]: "But emptied himself, taking the form of a servant" (Philip smiled at *schēmati*).[33] Hebrews 2 [:17]: "Therefore, he had to be made like his brethren in every respect," Hebrews 4 [:15], "yet without sinning." Christ therefore possesses a finite humanity. "As was the man of dust, so are those who are of the dust" [I Cor. 15:48]. Zwingli said that he would not allow these passages to be put aside. He answered all points [of the argument]. "If Christ's body is on high, it must be in one place," says Augustine.[34] He is saying nothing new; [see] Augustine and Fulgentius.[35] Luther has set forth the idea that the body of Christ is everywhere; hence it is something infinite. Zwingli concluded: The body of Christ is in one place, nor can it be in many places.

Luther: We shall find out to what extent you can boast about the fathers. You speak for your side, we for ours. As for Paul's saying, "like us in every respect" [Hebrews 2:17], Luther said: Therefore, one could conclude that Christ had dark eyes, a wife, etc. He does not want to consider mathematical similarities. I have written about mathematical similarities in my book.[36] You have read it, but you did not understand. I do not want to debate about

---

[33] Melanchthon smiled at Zwingli's pronunciation of the Greek word *schēmati* ("form").

[34] *On the Presence of God* (*De praesentia dei*) (*MPL* 33, 832 ff.).

[35] Fulgentius (467-532) was bishop of Ruspe in Numidia, North Africa. He defended Augustine's doctrine on grace. Cf. *Three Books to Trasimund* (*Libri tres ad Trasimundum*), Bk. II (*MPL* 65, 246 ff.).

[36] Luther is probably referring to his *Confession Concerning Christ's Supper* (1528), *LW* 37, 278 ff.

mathematics any more because I cannot define [the doctrine in terms of mathematics]. We must not search out what is in heaven in the same way as we investigate what is on earth. Christ is not in the Lord's Supper as if he were in one place. You want to argue from the unessential properties to what is substantive. This kind of argumentation is faulty; it is, says Luther, deliberately doing violence to Scripture.

Zwingli brought up additional passages.

Luther said: Read German or Latin, not Greek.[37]

Zwingli excused himself for employing the Greek Testament. He has used it for twelve years and has read the Latin Testament only once. "Form" [*morphē*] in Philippians [2] has two meanings. Christ is finite, as we are finite.

Luther admits that. There is Luther's well-known example of the kernel and the shell. So it is with regard to the body of Christ. God can cause his body not to be in one place, to be in one place and not to be in one place.

Sunday Morning, October 3

Zwingli began: Since the body of Christ is finite, it must therefore be in a certain place.

Luther: I have said that it can be in a place and not in a place. God can even arrange my body so that it is not in a place. In this text there is no room for mathematics. "Place" is a mathematical consideration. The sophists[38] have held that one body can be in many places; he does not want to deny this. Who am I to measure the power of God? The driving force of the universe is not in one place.

Zwingli said that Luther was arguing from what may be to what is. What he says about place applies also to an adverb of

---

[37] It is probable that Luther did not understand Zwingli's pronunciation of the Greek. He may also have felt that Zwingli was showing off his linguistic accomplishments, as the humanists of the day often did. Or Luther may have been aware of the fact that many of those present at the colloquy could not understand Greek. Cf. Sasse, *op. cit.*, p. 256, n. 97.

[38] I.e., Scholastic theologians. In his *Confession Concerning Christ's Supper* Luther appeals to the Occamist Scholastics in this matter. Cf. *LW* 37, 214 ff.

place. When Zwingli asked Luther to prove that the body of Christ can be in many places, Luther quoted the words: "This is my body." A passage in Fulgentius[39] reads that the body of Christ is in one place.—Zwingli objected that Luther had written: (1) Everything is filled with the body of Christ, and (2) If the divinity had not suffered in Christ, then it would not be Luther's Christ.[40]

Luther replied with regard to the passage in Fulgentius that it proves in opposition to the Manichaeans that Christ had a true body. Then he read another passage from Fulgentius concerning the Lord's Supper. He does not wish to reject what the fathers said, but he says that in the former passage Fulgentius was not talking about the Supper. It is a deficiency that the fathers say something in one place and leave it unmentioned in another.

Zwingli says that what he has quoted from Fulgentius is correct; it is not unknown. But "it is offered" means "remembrance of the sacrifice." This is the way Augustine in a letter to Boniface interprets it.[41] It is metonymy, a byname, like the saying: "Tomorrow is Ascension."

Luther: These are not proofs, but exaggerations. You are arguing with us about begging the question, and you beg the question. Note: he [Luther] does not want to accept "sacrifice" for "remembrance of sacrifice."

Zwingli regrets that he has written so much.

Osiander says: What if the fathers have erred in speaking of a sacrifice?

[*Luther*][42] replies to the passage from Augustine, as he did to the passage from Fulgentius; he brings up passages in opposition to them and permits us to retain our position. Luther's rule is: When the fathers speak, they are to be accepted in accordance with the canon of Scripture. Whatever they appear to write contrary to Scripture must either be interpreted or be rejected. "It must be in one place"—this word of Augustine from a collection of passages is

---

[39] Fulgentius in *MPL* 65, 266.

[40] Luther's *Confession Concerning Christ's Supper*. Cf. *LW* 37, 210 ff.

[41] Augustine, *Letter* 98, *To Boniface*, 9 (*MPL* 33, 363). Cf. *WA* 30^{III}, 140, n. 1.

[42] Parallel reports indicate that Luther is speaking here.

to be rejected or interpreted. He acknowledges that the body is not in the sacrament as in a place.

Oecolampadius concludes: Therefore, the body of Christ is not here in bodily fashion, in the flesh [*sōmatikos*], truly, physically, that is, in bodily fashion, with a true body.

Sunday Afternoon, October 3

Oecolampadius repeated: The body of Christ is not in the sacrament as in a place. Oecolampadius asks in all sincerity: How can he be there as a body?

Luther: At the beginning of our discussion we took Scripture as our basis. Scripture is not against us. You add the fathers; they are not against us either. Among them you have two, Augustine and Fulgentius, on your side; the rest are against you. Luther knows of no teacher who could bring about agreement among us, since none is aware of our situation. But I am wondering why we are having a dispute over "place" because the conclusion is accepted by the whole of Christendom that God can be at work outside of a place. He asks that we seek the middle ground on which we can agree so that there may be no dissension among the people and so that this very bad disagreement might be removed. – [We agree on] the cardinal points concerning the Trinity and concerning the signs wrought by angels and men. Luther cites a passage from Augustine: "I have seen the Lord our God"; that is what people say because of the words: "This is my body." – Luther admits that the sacrament is called a sign of a holy thing.[43] Luther admits that the sacraments are also sacred symbols and that as such they signify and represent something which is beyond them and which transcends the intellect. It is childish if a person, on seeing the bread, says: "I have seen the Lord." We must lift up our mind. But when a person says that it is a mere sign, this is hard for me to admit. There is a difference between natural signs and the signs instituted by God.

---

[43] Augustine, *City of God* (*De civitate dei*), *X*, 5 (*MPL* 41, 282).

Oecolampadius introduces a few passages from Augustine's *On Christian Doctrine* and also from his anti-Manichaean treatises: "The soul is the blood" [cf. Leviticus 17:11-14] and "The rock was Christ" [I Cor. 10:4].[44] Oecolampadius concedes: [The sacrament] is not a mere sign, but through faith the true body is there.

Luther: Augustine was a young man when he wrote against the Manichaeans and he had no reliable text. "The soul is the blood" [Leviticus 17:11]. Again he says, as [he said] earlier: It is necessary to subordinate the teachers to Christ.

Oecolampadius says that he cannot retract. Oecolampadius brings the matter to a conclusion.

Luther answers: [This is the case] because he cannot agree with our view.

Oecolampadius: Just as our text does not make you give in, so your exposition does not make us give in.

Luther wants to abide by his faith, nor can he yield. He commits us to God and his judgment. Luther then thanks [Oecolampadius] for having carefully explained his views in a friendly manner. He also thanks Zwingli, although he had spoken more sharply. He asks him to pardon his own sharp words if, yielding to flesh and blood, he had spoken such. He desires that their common cause unite them mutually.

Oecolampadius begs that the afflicted church be taken into consideration. This is his prayer to God.

Zwingli asks Luther to pardon his harshness, and says that he has always deeply desired his friendship and seeks it even now. Then he added, almost weeping: There are no men, neither in Italy nor in France, whom he would rather see.

Luther says: Pray God that you may come to a right understanding of this matter.

---

[44] Oecolampadius' reference is to Augustine's *On Christian Doctrine* (*De doctrina christiana*), IV, 21, 46 (*MPL* 34, 112), and to *Questions on the Heptateuch* (*Quaestiones in Heptateuchum*), III, 57 (*MPL* 34, 702, 703), where mention is made that the Rock is Christ and that the soul is the blood. Since Augustine did not write any specific treatises against the Manichaeans, Oecolampadius may have referred to anti-Manichaean remarks scattered throughout these various writings of Augustine.

Oecolampadius answers: You, too, should pray for this, for you have the same need.[45]

The Report of Anonymous

Before he began [the debate], *Luther* made certain prefatory remarks. He said that they had agreed to this colloquy reluctantly because each side had already presented in published books all of their arguments. Nevertheless, they could not but accede to the pious wish of the most noble prince. Therefore, they were ready to engage in the debate on this condition: Before the Eucharist is discussed, the opponents should explain their view of the other chief parts of Christian doctrine, since it is well known from published pamphlets that they disagree with us in many other important points. He was also informed by letter that some Strassburgers had said: [1] That Arius, [as could be shown] if his books were still extant, had taught the doctrine of the Trinity more correctly than St. Augustine or other orthodox fathers. (2) Also, [there seems to be an error] concerning the two natures in Christ, which certain persons distinguished in a way that they appeared to be making two persons out of one. (3) Concerning original sin, some deny that it can damn [a person]. (4) Concerning baptism, some teach that it is not a seal of faith but only the mark of external association [with the church]. (5) Concerning justification: they attribute it not to faith in Christ alone but in part also to our own abilities. (6) [There seem to be errors] concerning the spoken word and the ministry of the word. (7) The same is also true concerning purgatory and perhaps numerous other parts of Christian doctrine and religion; unless we first reach a common understanding on all these matters, we shall deal with the real dignity of the Eucharist in vain.

To this report by Luther, *Oecolampadius* replied that he was not aware of having taught, concerning the articles mentioned, any-

[45] In Hedio's *Itinerary*, from which this report of the colloquy is taken, there follows the account of Bucer's exposition of the teaching of the Strassburgers on the Lord's Supper and Luther's refusal to give his opinion with regard to their views, as well as an account of the negotiations of October 4.

thing in opposition to Luther's doctrine. The present colloquy had been called in order that they might confer with each other about their opinions on the Eucharist; so it appeared to him to be reasonable that this should be the first matter to be debated. If indeed it could be ascertained that certain persons somewhere had not taught correctly, it would seem right to him that each person should answer for himself.

Zwingli replied in almost the same way, alleging that he had conferred privately with Philip [Melanchthon] about these matters and that his view on justification was set forth in his treatise published under the title *Of the Clarity of the Word.*[46] Therefore, the Eucharist should now be dealt with.

Luther replied that he had said all this as a protest against their published writings; insofar as the aforementioned articles were concerned, he did not agree with them entirely. However, he would gladly engage in a debate about the Eucharist. He then quoted the Lord's words, "*This is* my body," saying: I cannot understand them in any other way than according to their literal meaning. Since they themselves want these words to be understood otherwise, it is up to them to show and prove this on the basis of clear testimonies from Scripture.

Taking up the subject first, *Oecolampadius* set it forth in this way: The matter under consideration indicates that Holy Scripture frequently employs figurative speech, metaphors, metonymies, and the like. In such cases words have a different meaning from what they say. Therefore, the words, "This is my body," may also be figurative speech, as in the expressions: "John is Elijah" [Matthew 11:14]; "The rock was Christ" [I Cor. 10:4]; "I am the true vine" [John 15:1]; "The seed is the Word of God" [Luke 8:11].

Luther replied: It is not enough to show that these words *can* be understood thus; but it is to be proved that they *must* be understood figuratively.

Then *Oecolampadius* [said]: Christ instituted [the Supper] in this way in order to prove that they *must* indeed be understood

---

[46] *Of the Clarity and Certainty of the Word of God* in G. W. Bromiley (ed.), *Zwingli and Bullinger, Library of Christian Classics* (Philadelphia: Westminster Press, 1953), XXIV, 49-95.

figuratively. In John 6 Christ spoke of the eating of his flesh and the drinking of his blood to the Jews as well as to his disciples. When they, understanding it as a carnal eating, shuddered, he answered: "It is the spirit that gives life; the flesh is of no avail" [John 6:63]. From this it can be understood that he rejected once and for all a carnal eating of his body. And it should follow that he would not and could not from then on institute what he had here once rejected.

Luther replied: Not the eating in itself but the carnal understanding or signification concerning the method or manner of eating is reproached by Christ. For the Jews understood that Christ would be cut into pieces or would be torn asunder like the flesh of oxen or of swine.

Then *Oecolampadius,* on the basis of Luther's reply, himself began to discuss the twofold understanding or signification. There is a difference between a base and carnal understanding of the words of God and a sublime and spiritual one. It is an altogether base understanding of eating Christ's flesh upon which Luther insists but which is emphatically repudiated by Christ. In reality, Christ commanded that the sublime, or spiritual, meaning, which they themselves teach, be accepted.

Luther replied that he has heard a great deal about the distinction between a twofold understanding of the words of the Lord's Supper. It is true that one neither can nor should permit it that they want to relate the words of the Supper to a carnal understanding, without the testimony or authority of Holy Scripture. However carnal the words may seem to them, they are, nevertheless, as no one can deny, the words and deeds of the highest Majesty and in no way carnal or insignificant because indeed forgiveness of sins, life eternal, and the kindom of heaven are attached to these insignificant and, as it would seem, carnal things by the word of God. Therefore, they should by no means be disparaged or be held in contempt as insignificant but should be held in highest esteem and regarded as sublime and spiritual.

Oecolampadius again stated that the spiritual eating of Christ in John 6 was the only thing that was commanded and was sufficient for salvation, and that the bodily eating was neither prescribed nor useful.

Luther replied: We do not deny this spiritual eating in the least; on the contrary, we teach and believe it to be altogether necessary. But from this it cannot be proved that the bodily eating is either useless or unnecessary. Christ himself instituted it (that it was Christ cannot be denied) and commanded it, saying: "Do this!" It is agreed that all pious hearts should obey his command and not debate in any way whether it is useful, since his command stands quite firm. His words, wherever they are found, are the words of eternal life. Let this suffice then: He himself has said so [*autos epha*].

At this point Zwingli began his conversation with Luther. After the preliminary discussion, Zwingli stated in advance that he did not wish to speak harshly against Luther or call to mind what had been written in a more acrimonious way by the one against the other. He desired only to give himself to the task so that, as much as would be feasible, the truth might be rescued from darkness. At the same time he begged that no one should censure the other with the reproach of heresy. Then he put forward the argument from the sixth chapter of John in this fashion: Christ desired to reply to a misunderstanding of the Jews. The error of the Jews concerned the eating of the flesh of Christ. Therefore, Christ's reply, "The flesh is of no avail" must necessarily refer to the eating of Christ.

Luther replied: If this argument were completely valid, it would only prove that the flesh of Christ which is eaten is of no avail; that is something which can be readily admitted, if the unbelievers and impious eat it. However, it is not only this one sacrament, but also the word or gospel of God, yes, God himself who becomes for the unbelievers death and ruin according to the word: "a fragrance from death to death" [II Cor. 2:16]. But, even if one admits the same thing about the eating of believers, which he is not at all willing to do, one cannot prove from it that Christ's body is not present in the Supper, and that therefore the words of the Supper *must* be interpreted figuratively. This is what they themselves have to prove.

After this *Zwingli* brought up the passage from the fifth chapter of Ezekiel [Ezek. 5:1 ff.] concerning the division of the hair and the beard into three parts, particularly these words: "This is Jerusalem" [Ezek. 5:5]. For in this sentence the substantive verb "is" *must* be understood as "signifies." On that basis Zwingli desired to prove that also in the sentence, "This is my body," the "is" *ought* to be interpreted similarly.

Luther replied: This is a clear allegory by the prophet. It is not in any way to be compared with the words of the Supper, unless they have previously proved that here the words must also be understood allegorically.

Zwingli, continuing to speak, said that the Supper must of necessity be understood in this way. Christ himself established this; for when he commanded spiritual eating in the sixth chapter of John, he seems to have repudiated the carnal eating.

Luther replied that he has already confessed several times that not only does he not despise or deny such spiritual eating, in fact, he both says and believes it to be particularly necessary. What he is saying, however, is that from this it does not follow that the bodily eating, instituted and commanded by the Lord Jesus Christ, is useless, especially to believers who eat not only spiritually but also bodily. Still less does it follow, yes, the conclusion is quite impossible, that the true body of Christ cannot be bodily present at all in the Lord's Supper. It is there, and it is useful. For even if the spirit itself does not eat the body of Christ in a bodily way, it nevertheless believes that it is eating it under the bread and wine in the word which the spirit itself hears.

As both sides had argued sufficiently about this matter, they departed for lunch.

After Lunch

When *Zwingli* again met with Luther, he repeated the very same arguments from the sixth chapter of John in a verbose manner and with remarkable variations, pitiably urging and twisting the word "eating."

He said: It is written: "How can this man give us his flesh to eat?" [John 6:52]. [It says,] "to eat," not to dismember or to tear in pieces. Christ's sermon here, since it deals entirely with spiritual eating, makes it clear enough that he roundly rejected carnal eating. After Zwingli had sufficiently belabored the point in a long and verbose argument, he finally made the charge that Luther in his own postil for Septuagesima Sunday did not interpret the words of Christ, "The flesh is of no avail," in a carnal sense but as dealing with Christ's own flesh.[47] Philip [Melanchthon] has also written about the same passage, saying that Christ is to be eaten only [by believing] in the word.[48]

Luther replied that what either he or Philip has written is not to be attacked here. In fact, they will not defend anything of theirs here except insofar as it agrees with the word of God. What they [the opponents] have to prove is why Christ's body cannot be in the Supper.

Even though Luther as well as Philip wanted by all means to have the words about eating refer to Christ's flesh, *Zwingli* nevertheless again alleged that the orthodox fathers [had referred them] to the resurrection, not to the food.

This *Luther* in fact conceded willingly. On the basis of this he concluded and pointed out that it does not therefore follow that the flesh of Christ or the food is not present or is useless. Rather, the food is truly there and most useful; but it cannot be digested as is other bodily food by those who eat it.

Zwingli: Philip admitted that the words have no other meaning than "signify." If this is true, from where, then, does the body of the Lord come in the Supper?

Luther replied: Of course this is true, but when the words are spoken at the command and in the name of God, then they not only signify but also at the same time effect and offer that which they signify. Then the words are not only the sound of a man who speaks them but of God who conveys [something] to the person who eats the bread. It is the same in baptism: The minister does not administer the word and sign on his own but does so in the name

---

[47] Cf. above, p. 26, n. 24.

[48] Cf. above, p. 26, n. 25.

of God; therefore, it is not the person of the minister who speaks that ought to be considered but the power of God who gives the command to perform this act.

Zwingli: The word of an evil priest cannot effect the presence of Christ's body. In what way therefore can it be there in the Supper?

Luther replied: The word of God is efficacious and true, no matter who proclaims it, according to the passage: "The scribes and the Pharisees sit on Moses' seat," etc. [Matt. 23:2 ff.].

Zwingli did not want this to be understood solely concerning their teaching.

Luther admitted that the ministry of the word and the ministry of the sacrament are identical [in purpose], and to whom the ministry of the word is entrusted to him also the administration of the sacraments is given according to the passage: "For the Lord did not send me to baptize," etc. [I Cor. 1:17].

Zwingli repeated: If the person who officiates is not to be taken into account at all, so that, even if he as an ungodly person in the assembly of the ungodly recites the words of the Supper, his words are nevertheless efficacious, then it must be admitted that the papacy is thus again raised up and strengthened.

Luther replied that he is not saying anything about the assembly of the ungodly, but only this: Since no one can be sure about the faith of ministers in the church, not even in the case of godly and faithful men, the power of *God*'s word must be taken into account rather than the faith of its ministers. For of the latter no one can be sure, but the former [i.e., the power of God's word] no one can really doubt.

At this point *Zwingli,* interrupting the order of the debate, again charged Luther with making contradictory assertions about one and the same thing. For he said at one time that eating the flesh of Christ was useful and again, at another time, when it pleased him, that it was useless.

Luther replied that he has said so and says so even now that the flesh of Christ, eaten by unbelievers, is not only unprofitable but is both poison and death, just as the word of God or God himself is. Furthermore, as it is unprofitable and death-dealing for unbelievers, even so it is profitable for believers, a medicine and eternal life. But even if the flesh of Christ were in itself unprofitable and pernicious, as indeed it is not, it would nevertheless become salutary through the word of life connected with it.

Zwingli insisted that there must be a *trope* in the words of the Lord's Supper; what it is can be demonstrated at any time. It is like the article of the Creed which also demands [a trope]: "He ascended into heaven and sitteth on the right hand of God the Father." Otherwise it would be a great incongruity if, when Christ says he is in heaven, we should seek him in the Supper. For one and the same body can in no way be in several places at the same time.

Luther replied by inquiring: And why should one not rather assume a trope to be in this sentence, "He ascended into heaven," and leave the text of the Supper as it is? For the figure of speech could much more conveniently be found in the word "heaven," which indeed continues to be used in Scripture in various meanings.

Zwingli replied that this sentence does not require a figurative understanding.

Luther retorted that the other one did not either.

Since Zwingli was tired, Oecolampadius took his place. In John 3 Christ teaches Nicodemus that the one and only way of entering the kingdom of heaven is through regeneration. Since this is sufficient, it is not necessary and therefore is without benefit that the body of Christ be eaten in a bodily way in the Supper.

Luther replied: God has many ways and means of creating, supporting, and increasing faith in us: When we hear the word publicly or privately, when we are baptized, when we are nourished with the body of the Lord, etc. But which one of these he employs and how he employs so many and diverse ones, is none of our business. He himself knows what is profitable for us. Therefore, it is foolish and wrong to conclude: Regeneration opens heaven; therefore, the body of Christ is not in the Supper or is unprofitable. But, to be sure, for that kind of eating an altogether new and regenerated person, who can believe and truly eat, is required.

When with all these arguments *Oecolampadius* could not prove anything, he brought forward some more Scripture passages.

First, [he cited] the one in John 16: "I came from the Father and have come into the world; again, I am leaving the world and going to the Father" [John 16:28]. This passage, he said, excludes the presence of Christ's body from the Supper and *compels* us to admit a trope in the Lord's words.

Luther, however, in opposition to that passage quoted the words of Christ in Luke 24 [:44]: "These are my words which I spoke to you while I was still with you." From this sentence it can be readily understood what Christ meant when he spoke of "leaving the world."

Oecolampadius brought forward another passage: "It is to your advantage that I go away; for if I do not go away, the Counselor will not come to you," etc. [John 16:7]. From this he concludes the following: Since Christ says that it is expedient that he go away, there is no doubt that, if he did not go away, his presence would not only be useless to us but even a hindrance as he himself says: "If I do not go away, the Counselor will not come to you," etc. Similarly he said much more about our hope [for life] after the resurrection on the basis of this passage in Romans 8 [:11]: "He who raised Christ Jesus from the dead will give life to your mortal bodies also." He said that this hope is completely taken from us and destroyed if we say that the bread is the body of Christ.

Luther replied to the contrary that this hope is not at all taken away and destroyed for us by the presence of Christ's body; but much rather is it supported and confirmed, since his gracious word of promise is connected with it. He began to formulate a conclusion in this manner: Most certainly we hold strongly to the flesh of Christ as being indeed altogether useful; no Scripture passage, no exposition, no human reason can wrest this from us by force. If you hold the flesh to be useless, you have my permission for that; we rely on the word of God. The word says, first, that Christ has a body. This I believe. Furthermore, it says that this body ascended into heaven and sits at the right hand of the Father. This I also believe. The word likewise says that this same body is in the Supper and is given to us to be eaten. This I also believe because my Lord Jesus Christ can easily do this if he desires to, and in his words he testifies that he does desire to do it. On these words I rely steadfastly until he himself by another word of his says something different.

But when with all these [passages] nothing was accomplished (nor could they cite any passages from Scripture which testified that a trope was contained in the words of the Supper), arguments from reason were finally admitted, and *Oecolampadius* began a discussion about the circumscription and finitude of human bodies, saying: A body must necessarily be in one place only. And so he dealt with this subject at great length.

Then *Luther* replied that he does not want to hear about mathematical distinctions in this connection. God, as the Aristotelian philosophers also concede, can cause one body to be only in one place or in several places at the same time, or outside of every place; [he is even able to bring it about that] several bodies are simultaneously in one place. For this reason he does not want to discuss anxiously the manner of his presence, whether the body of Christ is in one place or outside of one place, because such views are of no consequence in the discussion. Therefore, he does not demand rational arguments of this kind but clear and sure words from Scripture. Nevertheless, if it is generally desired, he is willing at an appointed hour to discuss mathematics with them to their heart's content. Still, he predicts here and now that nothing will be accomplished in this matter by such discussions; here we need the testimonies of Scripture.

Thereupon *Oecolampadius* brought forward this passage of Scripture from Matthew 26 [:11]: "For you always have the poor with you, but you will not always have me," inferring this from it: According to his divinity, grace, and power Christ is present to all always and everywhere. But since he said he would be absent, he must necessarily be absent according to his humanity. If he is in truth absent according to his humanity, he is consequently not able to be present bodily in the Supper.

Luther replied: This one argument among the many that have been brought up has a certain attraction. If this passage [Matthew 26:11] actually appears to our adversaries to be in conflict with the words in the Supper, why then do they not look for a figure of speech in the former rather than in the latter [the words of institution]? To him [Luther] the real meaning of this passage appeared to be this: Christ simply did not want to be present to us so as to be in need of our services in the same way as he stood in need of them then, but he wanted to give us the poor upon whom we could in his name bestow our benefactions. This, he alleged, was also what Christ meant [in this passage]: "These are my words which I spoke to you, while I was still with you," etc. [Luke 24:44].

At this point *Oecolampadius* began to admonish Luther not to cling to the humanity and flesh of Christ but to lift up his mind to his divinity. Thus he detracted from Christ's humanity more than was proper.

Luther answered that he could hardly put up with such remarks. For he did not know or worship any God except him who was made man; nor did he want to have another God besides him. And besides him there was no other God who could save us. Therefore, we cannot suffer his humanity to be thus curtailed and minimized.

Then *Oecolampadius* also [said] that he does not know any other God, nor is there another besides him who was made man. Nonetheless, even though he is himself true God and man, he is not to be known according to the flesh in consonance with the passage in II Corinthians 5 [:16]: "Even though we once knew Christ according to the flesh, we know him thus no longer."

Luther answered: Neither do we know him according to the flesh. Truly, it would be according to the flesh to know him externally, [that is,] without the Spirit and without faith. However, we know him according to the Spirit in such a way that we are certain by faith that Christ has come for us and has done and suffered all for us.

Oecolampadius: When Christ gave us his body, he indeed gave the kind of body he had; but he had a body capable of suffering and death. If this is so, surely that body cannot be profitable, but spiritual eating is required.

Luther replied: It is plain that the eating of Christ's body is profitable because it is connected with the promise of the forgiveness of sins. Because every promise requires faith, faith is a spiritual knowledge. Therefore, the bodily eating itself, when it takes place in faith, must also become a spiritual matter. It is sufficient for me that such a profitable body be set before me to be eaten. Whether the body is mortal or capable of suffering—mortality and passibility are accidentals—I do not care any more about that than I would care about the garment in which Christ was dressed at the Last Supper.

Zwingli[49] *again [began to debate] with Luther:* Why do you not want to admit that there is a trope in the words of the Supper when you yourself are nevertheless compelled, whether you want to or not, to admit synecdoche, [that is,] a figure of speech?

Luther replied: This form of speech is to be found not only in Holy Scripture but is also frequently used in everyday language so that we cannot do without it. But it is [synecdoche] when the containing vessel of which we speak includes the content and vice versa. For example, when a king tells his servant, "Bring me my sword," in which case he wants the servant to bring the sheath at the same time even if he did not in so many words command him to do so. So also this form of speech is to be allowed in the sacrament when at times it is called the bread and when nevertheless the body [of Christ] is also meant, and vice versa.

Then *Zwingli* set forth these Scripture passages: [1] Romans 8 [:29]: "Those whom he foreknew he also predestined to be conformed to the image of his Son." [2] Philippians 2 [:7 f.]: "He emptied himself, taking the form [*morphēn*] of a servant. . . . And being found in human form [*schēmati*]." [3] Hebrews 2 [:16-17]: "He took upon himself the seed of Abraham. Therefore he had to be made like his brethren in every respect." [4] I Corinthians 15 [:48]: "As was the man of dust, so are those who are of the dust; and as is the man of heaven, so are those who are of heaven." Then he drew this conclusion: If Christ's body is in various places, and if we must become like him, then our bodies ought also simultaneously to be in many and various places. If in every way his body is like ours and he has also assumed our nature, and we cannot be in various places, then neither can he, since his existence is truly like ours.

[49] Some of the reports, including the one by Anonymous, attribute the words that follow to Zwingli. However, Hedio's report ascribes these remarks to Oecolampadius with a great degree of certainty.

Luther replied: This conclusion from the "conformity" or "likeness" [between Christ's body and our bodies] is not cogent with regard to the undertaking at hand. It is again an argument which deduces what is essential from what is accidental.[50] Even if it were completely valid, it would prove nothing except that the form of our bodies will be similar to that of Christ's body. At the same time it would by no means follow that also with respect to power we would in the future have bodies similar to his body, unless God himself according to his extraordinary counsel and purpose wanted to arrange it thus. As to the second argument, which likewise consists of deducing what is essential from what is accidental, Luther said that, if they wished to draw their conclusions in this way, they could also easily prove that Christ had a wife, dark eyes, etc., because to be in one place is an inconsequential matter.

Then *Zwingli* spoke several times about the sacramental presence of Christ's body as signifying that his body is in the Supper in a representative way.

Luther replied to this: Those who make an effort to speak of the permanent presence of Christ's body in such a way take away the substance of the body from the bread, leaving us only crusts and empty chaff. However, the words of Christ sound altogether different. He then showed them the very words [of the Lord].

Several times *Zwingli* and *Oecolampadius* admitted that it was certainly possible for God to cause a body to be in different places; but they demanded genuine proof that this took place in the Supper.

At this point *Luther* set forth the words of the Testament, *Hoc est corpus meum*, rendering them in German in this way: My dearest sirs, since the text of my Lord Jesus Christ reads *Hoc est corpus meum*, I cannot pass over it but must confess and believe that the body of Christ is there.

Then *Zwingli* jumped to his feet and said: Thus you also, Doctor, assume that the body of Christ is locally in the Supper, for

[50] *Argumentum ab accidente ad substantiam.*

you say: The body of Christ must be there. There, there—this is certainly an adverb of place.

Luther replied that he had simply quoted the words of Christ, and did not in any way expect false conclusions of this kind. But if they want to deal cunningly with one another, then he testifies here, as he has before, that he will have nothing whatever to do with mathematical reasons and that he completely rejects and repudiates the adverb of place in connection with the words of the Supper. The words are "This is," not "There is my body." Whether it is there locally or not locally, this he would rather not know, since God has not yet revealed anything about it and no mortal man can prove it one way or another.

Sunday Morning, Zwingli and Luther

Zwingli again began to put forward the words "form" [*morphēn*] and "likeness" [*schēmati*] from Philippians 2 [:7], and did so in an extraordinarily verbose address. It [the body of Christ] must occupy a certain space and must exist locally.

To this speech *Luther* replied briefly as follows: He has mentioned before in the dispute that he rejects mathematical reasons, since it is not only possible but also an easy matter for God to make one body present in many places or many bodies in one place. He can also maintain a body in no place at all. If God is able to do this with all kinds of things, how much more can he do it with the body of Christ. The sophists[51] have also admitted this.

Zwingli said that Luther was arguing from what may be to what is. Furthermore, nothing would be more difficult to prove than what he had said, namely, that one body is actually in various places.

Luther answered that he had on several occasions already proved it with the Lord's words: "*This is my body.*"

After this, when they were totally unable to accomplish anything either by the use of Scripture or reasonable arguments they

[51] Cf. above, p. 32, n. 38.

testified that they were not the authors of this doctrine but that in times past the oldest teachers of the church had both thought and taught thus. And so *Zwingli* brought up a passage from Augustine in a sentence something like this: "Whatever exists in a certain place is a body."[52]

To this *Luther* replied: It is indeed true that whatever is contained in a place is a body; nevertheless, the contrary does not follow from it, that whatever is a body must itself always be contained in a place.

Zwingli then advanced another passage from Augustine in different words, to be sure, but in a sentence something like this: "Take away space from bodies and you will have taken away the bodies."[53]

Luther replied: According to the general rule it is by and large true that bodies are contained in places, but God can easily maintain bodies outside of any place.

Then *Zwingli* brought forward another passage from Fulgentius' *To King Trasimund,* from the latter part of the second book, *On the Immensity of God*: "Since one and the same Son of God," etc.[54] It is quite clear from this passage that nearly all his arguments have been placed on my side.

Luther replied: Fulgentius did not say these things about the Lord's Supper but against the Manichaeans and other heretics who denied the humanity of Christ, and he did this to prove that Christ had a real body. He sought to convince them with this argument: Because he was in a certain place, this was characteristic of a body. But Luther adduced another passage from Fulgentius which clearly

---

[52] Augustine, *Sermon* 52, 5,15–7,18 (*MPL* 38, 360 f.).

[53] Augustine, *On the Presence of God* (*De praesentia dei*), 6, 18 (*MPL* 33, 838-839).

[54] Fulgentius, *Three Books to Trasimund* (*Libri tres ad Trasimundum*), II, 17 (*MPL* 65, 264-265). The passage continues as follows: ". . . true God, born of God the Father, has become true man for us from human seed (for 'he is of the seed of David according to the flesh' [Rom. 1:3]), he has a true divine and a true human nature. He has not lost the marks of true divinity, and he has accepted the marks of true humanity. He is one and the same who was born according to the flesh of his mother in time, and who remains according to his divinity from the Father eternal. He is one and the same person who is a man locally circumscribed according to his human origin and who is immeasurable God according to his divine origin."

testified that the body and blood of the Lord are offered in the Supper.[55]

Zwingli, desiring to nullify that passage, interpreted it thus: The word "offer" ought to be understood in a figurative sense as meaning "to celebrate the remembrance"; therefore it would be in agreement with the words "body and blood" which are also to be understood in a figurative way. It is the same as we are accustomed to say "Today is the Ascension of the Lord," when in reality it is not the Ascension but only the remembrance of the Ascension.

Luther replied to both interpretations.

Indignantly *Zwingli* accused Luther of speaking as if he wanted again to re-establish the sacrifice of the mass and to revoke all his pious and learned writings against that sacrifice.

To this *Luther* [replied] that he is bound and held captive by the words of the Lord and he cannot accede to their opinion on the basis of their explanations of them.

Zwingli then begged the question: In what way is the sentence, "*This is* my body," to be understood in a literal sense?

Luther replied: Every article of faith is a principle in itself and does not need to be proved by a similar example.

Oecolampadius read certain passages from Augustine's *On the Gospel of John,* chapter 6, where [Augustine explains] these words: "It was not Moses who gave you the bread from heaven" [v. 32].[56] He replied that the body of Christ in which he rose must be in one place.

Luther: I say to this passage from Augustine, as I did about Fulgentius before, that it has nothing to do with the Lord's Supper. In his letter to Januarius, Augustine, in words something like this,

---

[55] Luther may have quoted a passage from Fulgentius' *Fragments Against Fabian* (*Contra Fabianum fragmenta*), Fragment 28 (*MPL* 65, 789): "Therefore acknowledge what happens in offering the sacrifices so that you might then understand why the coming of the Holy Spirit is demanded. Namely, this is fulfilled in offering the sacrifices because the blessed apostle, testifying that our Savior himself has commanded it, says: Our Lord Jesus Christ on the night when he was betrayed, took bread, and when he had given thanks, he broke it, and said, 'This is my body which is for you' [I Cor. 11:23-24]. Therefore the sacrifice is offered so that the death of the Lord might be proclaimed and that there might be a remembrance of him who laid down his life for us."

[56] Augustine, *On the Gospel of John* (*In Ioannis evangelium*), Tractate 25, 13 (*MPL* 35, 1602-1603).

speaks about the Lord's Supper, emphasizing that the body and blood of the Lord ought to be received by disciples who had fasted.[57] In another letter Augustine establishes the rule[58] that the readers of his books, of whatever nature these books may be, should measure everything by the standard of Scripture. Whatever did not agree with Scripture was to be accommodated through interpretation if this could be done adequately, or, if this proved impossible, it was to be completely rejected.

Oecolampadius brought up another passage from Augustine on the basis of which he wanted to prove that Christ had a body which had to be in a place.[59] A true body is locally circumscribed; Christ's body is a true body. Therefore, it has to be locally circumscribed.

Luther replied that he has already replied to this argument more than enough. If they have more convincing arguments than these, they should advance them now. On the basis of these arguments he cannot be compelled to embrace a different understanding of the text of the Lord's Supper.

Then *Oecolampadius* said: If you refuse to be moved by those arguments, it would be in vain for us to bring forward a thousand passages from the fathers. Therefore, it seemed more advantageous to him that both sides cease the discussion. So it ended.

The End of the Disputation

The Report of Collin

Before the colloquy began, and as he was about to debate with Zwingli and Oecolampadius, *Luther* had written on his table, "This is my body," in order that he might not allow himself to be diverted from these words. Then in a long speech he testified in advance that he disagreed with the persons of the opposing party and that

[57] Augustine, *Letter 54, To Januarius,* 6, 8 (*MPL* 33, 203). Cf. *WA* 30^{III}, 141, n. 4.

[58] Augustine, *Letter 148, To Fortunatianus,* 4, 15 (*MPL* 33, 628 f.).

[59] The exact source of Oecolampadius' quote has not been located. Augustine deals with this question in some of his sermons. Cf. *Sermon 75,* 7, 8 (*MPL* 38, 477); *Sermon* 237, 1-2 (*MPL* 38, 1122); *Sermon* 238, 2 (*MPL* 38, 1125).

he would continue to do so, since Christ has said most clearly: "Take, eat, this is my body." Here, he said, it must be shown that the body is not the body. He cited the opinion of his opponents, but would allow no questioning on such a clear text. He excluded all rational understanding and common opinion. He rejected carnal or mathematical arguments, saying that God is above and beyond mathematics and that the words of God are to be honored and spoken of with awe. God, however, commands: "Take, eat; this is my body."

Oecolampadius replies to Luther's arguments and proposes that the sixth chapter of John be dealt with because in it the other passages of Scripture are explained. To the saying, "This is my body," he relates, "I am the true vine" [John 15:1]. He does not deny the divine possibility here. He proceeds from the bodily to the spiritual eating. He says his own opinion is neither meaningless nor godless, for it is based on faith and Scripture.

Luther acknowledges that there are metaphors. "This is my body" is taken to be a demonstrative sentence: for [only] a general sentence permits a metaphor. Then he asks in what way spiritual eating excludes bodily eating. He concedes that the fathers would be partly on his [Oecolampadius'] side if his interpretation of them were admitted.

Oecolampadius: "I am the true vine" is also a demonstrative sentence. It is possible. How is it possible?

Luther does not deny that there are figures of speech, but he wants him [Oecolampadius] to prove that here [in the Lord's Supper] it [the argument] results from begging the question: When Christ said, "This is," the close connection is required.

Oecolampadius reads from the sixth chapter of John and afterwards proves that Christ is dealing there with spiritual eating and is directing attention away from the bodily eating. Therefore, it is not a bodily eating.

Luther repeats the quotation from the sixth chapter of John and says: You think that the spiritual eating is to be separated from the bodily eating. The Jews held that Christ was to be eaten as bread and meat are eaten in a dish, or like roast pork.

Oecolampadius replied: This is a base understanding, on which there has been a lengthy dispute and contention on both sides.

Oecolampadius [added]: To believe that Christ is in the bread is an opinion, not faith. It is dangerous to attribute too much to the elements.

Luther: To pick up a piece of straw at the command of the Lord is a spiritual act. He explains the example of the horseshoe at length. One must look not so much upon what is said but, rather, upon who says it. When God says something, we poor, weak humans should listen. When he commands something, the world must obey, and all of us should honor his word; for there is nothing to which we should be more attentive.

After this argument *Oecolampadius* said: Since we have the spiritual eating, what need is there for bodily eating?

Luther: I care not what is necessary, but since it is written, "Take, eat," etc., it is to be done and to be believed altogether. One must do it. Luther urged this again and again. If he should command me, he said, to eat dung, I should do so, knowing full well that this is salutary for me.

Oecolampadius quotes the passage from the sixth chapter of John: "The flesh is of no avail" [v. 63]. If the flesh, when eaten, is of no avail, but the Spirit is, then we must look to that which is of avail, and pay close attention to the will of God.

Finally both men [Oecolampadius and Luther] testified that they would persevere in their opinion, since neither of the two had convinced the other.

Zwingli begins to accuse Luther of prejudice because he [Luther] testifies that he is unwilling to abandon his view. In the same way Helvidius, with reference to the word "brother," could prove [that Jesus had brothers], since it is clearly written "his brothers" [John 7:3]. We should compare one passage of Scripture with another. Therefore, if we do not have a passage which says, "This is the figure of my body," we nevertheless have a passage which leads us away from bodily eating. For that reason [it follows] he did not give his body physically in the Supper.

They were of one mind on the cardinal point, namely, the spiritual eating.

Then he [Zwingli] treats the sixth chapter of John, especially these words: "The spirit gives life, the flesh is of no avail" [John 6:63]. He deals with Christ's humanity which suffered; for that was a salutary act. By the logic of his words he proves in a most powerful manner that the flesh which is eaten does not avail in any way. He accuses Luther of trickery in the use of the words "tearing apart" and "lacerating," since the word "to eat" [*esthīein*] is the same as to eat, to eat up, or to manducate.[60] "When I shall have ascended into heaven," then you shall see that I am not to be eaten bodily, essentially, etc. Spirit and flesh are opposed to one another. He renews the argument about a base understanding and says: Some things were excellently spoken by you, others were childish, namely: "If God would command us to eat dung," etc. For what God does command, he commands for our good and our salvation. God gives light and he does not spread darkness. Therefore, he does not say, "This is my body," essentially, really, and in a carnal way, since Scripture opposes this. The oracles of the demons are obscure, not the words of Christ. The soul "eats" spirit; therefore [it does] not [eat] flesh.

Luther proves from Scripture against Helvidius that the word "brother" can be used for "cousin." But it cannot be proved that "This is my body" is a trope. If God told me to eat a crabapple, I would eat spiritually. For wherever the word of God is, there is spiritual eating. Therefore, since he added the bodily eating by saying, "This is my body," it is to be believed. By faith we eat this body which is given for us. The mouth receives the body of Christ, the soul believes the words that it is eating the body.

Zwingli: From Scripture it can be proved that the thing signified is often used for the sign; in Ezekiel [5:1 ff.], in the "passover" [Exodus 12:27]. Since in passages of Scripture which are uncertain a comparison is demanded, passages similar to them are to be believed.

He accuses Luther of rhetoric and fictitious arguments when the latter says: "If God would command those things or such mat-

---

[60] Zwingli uses three Latin synonyms which mean "to eat": *edere, commedere, manducare.*

ters"; for we know that God does not command those things or such matters. The word, he said, is made ambiguous by you.

Words only signify to us the will of God. God does not set before us incomprehensible matters. That Christ is true God and man is not unknown to the believer. We have the example of Mary who asked: "How can this be?" [Luke 1:34]. When she had become more certain through inquiry she then believed. But here in chapter 6 the disciples expressed doubt about the carnal eating because he himself [Christ] taught a spiritual eating. – As to your words, "The word of God is the eating," I do not deny this; but the word is to be believed.

Luther: The passages from Ezekiel and the "passover" [in Exodus 12] are allegories. But allegory or signification has no meaning in this case. As to the efficacy of the word, we do not say that the body is produced by our words, but rather, we are speaking of the institution of Christ. These are not our words but the words of the Lord.

"Do this," etc. [Luke 22:19]–this word causes the hand of the priest to be the hand of Christ. It is not my mouth, it is not my tongue, but both are Christ's. [This is true] even though I were a knave or rascal. The same applies to baptism. Let us take the example of a prince who defeats the enemy and puts him to flight. In that case the hands of all [the soldiers] are said to be the hands of the prince. "If you will say to this mountain, ['Move hence to yonder place,'] it will move" [Matt. 17:20]. I am not debating whether the "is" may be "signifies," but I am satisfied that Christ says: "This is my body." Even the devil is powerless over against these words. This is what I want: The words are not to be dependent on my power but on the power and command of the Lord. The soul eats the body [of Christ]. The body is also present bodily in the word. If I question it, I would fall from faith and would become a fool on account of it. Why do you not also make a trope out of, "He ascended into heaven" [Mark 16:19]? Therefore, believe the plain words and give glory to God.

Zwingli: We, too, ask you to give glory to God and to stop begging the question. Where do you prove your thesis? I am not going to abandon this passage [from John], which is unassailable and which you treat so lightly. You will have to change your tune.

Luther: You are speaking spitefully.

Zwingli asks whether he believes that Christ in the sixth chapter of John wanted to help the ignorant.

Luther: You want to win your case with bold words. "This is a hard saying," etc. [John 6:60]; the Jews are speaking about something which is impossible and absurd. But we will pass over that text because it does not deal with the matter at hand.

Zwingli: No, no, this passage (meaning John 6) is going to break your neck.

Luther: Don't boast too much. You are in Hesse and not in Switzerland. Necks do not break so easily here. On account of this statement other accusations were made and there was much shouting. Yet Luther used a similar phrase in his book *Against the Heavenly Prophets,* where he says: "Let us take the rogue," meaning Karlstadt, "by the throat." (Jena Edition of *Luther's Works,* 3, 84)[61]

Zwingli apologized for having used an expression common among his people. Recognizing that there were diverse manners of expression, the prince with a nod of his head and an oral statement accepted the excuse.

Zwingli cited Luther's postil in which he had written that Christ had said of himself: "The flesh is of no avail" [John 6:63].[62] Then he introduced Melanchthon's remarks about the same passage. That the body is eaten in a bodily way is not established in his statement. When the fathers said that the body of Christ feeds the soul, I understand this to mean the resurrection.

Luther: I do not care what we have written. Prove that "This is my body" is not his body. The body [of Christ] nourishes man's body for eternity. When the mouth receives the body, a person acquires a kind of immortality. For the word on the basis of God's command supplies strength. God says, "Take, do," and so it comes to pass. He speaks and it is done. There is a difference between our speaking and God's command. If St. Peter were present, we

[61] Cf. *Against the Heavenly Prophets,* LW 40, 209. The reference to the Jena Edition was a later insertion into the text, since this edition of Luther's works first appeared in 1560.

[62] Cf. above, p. 26, n. 24.

would not know whether he believes. Consequently, God does not establish the sacrament upon our sanctity but upon his word. The worst priest can celebrate the sacrament.

Zwingli: It would be an absurdity if the impious could perform this sacred act.

Luther: It is not in the least absurd, for a bad person may baptize. The ungodly minister on the basis of the word of God. "For they [the scribes and the Pharisees] sit on Moses' seat" [Matthew 23:2 ff.]. Augustine says against the Donatists that the ministry must not be entrusted solely to the virtuous and godly because our accomplishment is dependent on the word of God.[63]

Zwingli: It makes a difference whether the Pharisees teach or whether a person does what Christ says. The ministry of preaching is greater than the ministry of baptizing. The words, "This is my body," belong to the ministry of preaching.

Oecolampadius again takes up John 6. He also brings up the passage about Nicodemus and explains it [John 3:1 ff.].

Luther: Faith looks upon the body [of Christ] as present [in the sacrament] and upon the body which is in heaven.

Oecolampadius: Luther always impresses upon us the same thing, as if we had the bread without the word of God. The church is founded on the word, "You are the Son of God" [Matthew 16:16], and not on the word, "This is my body."

Luther: I am not adhering to this passage without a reason. "This is my body" is enough for me. I confess that the body is in heaven, I also confess that it is in the sacrament. I am not concerned about what is contrary to nature but only about what is contrary to faith.

Oecolampadius: In all these things Christ has been made like us. As he is like the Father in his divinity in every respect, so he is like us in his humanity in every respect.

Luther: We are to partake of the Supper "until he comes," etc. [I Cor. 11:26]. You are distinguishing between his humanity and his divinity; I am not concerned about this. "For you always have

---

[63] Cf. above, p. 28, n. 28.

the poor with you, not me," etc. [Matthew 26:11]. This is the best argument you have presented today. Christ is thus in the sacrament substantially, as he was born of the Virgin. Here the analogy of faith is demanded according to the definition of faith in Hebrews 11 [:1].

Oecolampadius: We do not know Christ according to the flesh.

Philip [Melanchthon]: That is according to our flesh.[64]

Oecolampadius: You do not admit a trope in the words of institution, and yet you understand them as synecdoche. This is contrary to the understanding of the teachers of the church universal.

Luther: May God decide that question! We have synecdoche in sayings like the sword with the sheath, a mug with beer; it is therefore an inclusive way of speaking. "This is my body"; here the body is in the bread, even as the sword is in the sheath. The text demands this figurative form of speech; but the metaphor does away with the content altogether, as when one says "body," that is, "figure of the body." Here is an example: "On whom you see the Spirit descend" [John 1:33]; the Holy Spirit was in the dove.

Oecolampadius laid hold of this example [from John 1:33] and related it to his view in a most excellent way.

Zwingli: Romans 8[:3]: "God . . . sent his Son in the likeness of sinful flesh." Philippians [2:7 f.]: "He emptied himself. . . . [And being found] in human form . . . ." Hebrews 2 [:17]: "Therefore he had to be made like his brethren in every respect." Consequently, he had a finite humanity. If Christ's body is above, it must be in one place as Augustine, Fulgentius, and others state. The conclusion of the matter is: The body of Christ is in one place; therefore, it cannot be in many places.

Luther, repeating [the passage, i.e., Phil. 2:7], said "powers" [*hexeis*], "form" [*schēmati*]. To be like us in all things would mean that he had a wife, dark eyes, etc. As to the body being there locally, I have told you before and I make it known now that I

[64] Cf. above, p. 30, n. 31.

do not care about mathematics. I have often repeated this. How he is in the Supper and how he is in a place, we do not care.

Zwingli quoted Paul in Philippians 2 [:7 f.]: "Who, though he was in the form of God" [*Hos en morphē theou huparchōn*] and "taking the form of a servant" [*morphēn doulou labōn*].

Luther: Read Latin or German, not Greek.[65]

Zwingli: He excuses himself in Latin [and explains] that he has used nothing but the Greek New Testament for twelve years. Continuing, he said: Christ therefore is finite, as we are finite.

Luther: I admit that. We have the illustration of the kernel and the shell. So it is with the body of Christ. God can cause the body of Christ either not to be in a place or to be in a place. There followed a considerable controversy concerning "place."

When *Luther* had conceded that the body of Christ was finite, *Zwingli* wanted to conclude that it was therefore in a place. If it was also in a certain place and in heaven, it could not be in the bread. Then *Luther*, not wanting to hear anything more about place or locality, said: I do not want this matter discussed. I do not want these expressions used. – *Zwingli:* Must everything then be done according to your wishes?

Supper was ready and the debate was interrupted.

Zwingli: The body of Christ is finite, therefore it is in a certain place.

Luther: The body is not in one place when it is in the sacrament. It can either be in a place or not be in a place. God can arrange my body so that it is not in one place. For the sophists[66] also say that one body can be in various places; I do not reject this argument. For example, the universe is a body; nevertheless, it is not in one place.

Zwingli: You are arguing from what may be to what exists. Prove that the body of Christ can simultaneously be in various places.

Luther: "This is my body."

Zwingli reads a passage from Fulgentius, stating that Christ

---

[65] Cf. above, p. 32, n. 37.
[66] Cf. above, p. 32, n. 38.

is in one place. He objects that Luther has written: "Everything is filled with the body of Christ," and "If the divinity had not suffered in Christ, then it would not be my Christ."[67]

Luther: Fulgentius is not speaking about the Lord's Supper but against the Manichaeans. Luther brought up a passage in Fulgentius concerning the Lord's Supper in which mention of the sacrifice is made.[68]

Zwingli: "It is offered" means "the remembrance of the sacrifice is celebrated."

At this point *Luther* called into question [this interpretation of] "sacrifice" so that he would not have to abandon his point of view. But when *Zwingli* opposed him he again allowed the use of the expression. *Luther* again sought to prove that the body of Christ is in many places by the words: "This is my body." Here *Zwingli* caught him [in a contradiction]. *Luther* repeated his words: I leave it to God whether the body of Christ is in a place or not. For me this is enough: "This is my body." *Zwingli* said repeatedly: You are begging the question. In the same way a quarrelsome person could say: John was the son of Mary, for Christ said, "Behold your son!" and he would keep on repeating, "Christ said, 'Behold your son, behold your son!' " [John 19:26].

Luther: We are not begging the question, for one article of faith is not proved by another.

Zwingli: Scripture passages ought to be compared with one another and to be explained by themselves. Tell me, is the body of Christ in a place? *Brenz:* It is not in a place. *Zwingli:* Augustine says it must be in one place.

Luther: Augustine is not talking of the Lord's Supper.

Luther at length admitted that the body is not in the sacrament as in a place.

Oecolampadius drew this conclusion: Therefore, it is not here corporeally, with a real body.[69]

Oecolampadius repeated: They had conceded that the body of

---

[67] Cf. above, p. 33, n. 40.
[68] Cf. above, p. 50, n. 54.
[69] According to Hedio's account this is the point at which Saturday's discussion ended.

Christ is not in the sacrament as in a place and so he inquired in all sincerity: In what way then is the body there? He reads from Augustine and Fulgentius.

Luther: You have Augustine and Fulgentius on your side, but the remaining fathers are on our side.

Oecolampadius asks them to bring up the fathers who are on their side; but they refuse.

Luther admits that the sacrament is a sign of a sacred thing; he further concedes that the symbols are sacred and as such they signify something which is beyond them and represent something that transcends the mind. They agree concerning the differences between natural signs and signs instituted by God.

Luther, among other things, rejected Augustine because he had written his work against the Manichaeans as a young man and because as an author he was obscure and out of date. He concludes.

Oecolampadius says that they quote the fathers for this reason, lest theirs appear to be a new and unheard-of opinion. So he, too, concludes.

Zwingli did the same. *Bucer* gave his testimony along with Zwingli.

The Report of Osiander[70]

Sagacious, honorable, wise, gracious, dear lords! Among other things, Mr. Martin Pfinzing[70a] has notified me, in accordance with the order which you, honorable and wise sirs, gave him for me and of which I learned with particular pleasure and thankfulness, that you, honorable and wise sirs, desire a brief report concerning the proceedings at Marburg. The following is my report to you, honorable and wise sirs.

---

[70] The account in *WA* 30^{III}, 144 ff., is taken from Johann Bartholomäus Riederer, *Nachrichten zur Kirchen-, Gelehrten- und Büchergeschichte: aus gedruckten und ungedruckten Schriften gesammelt* (4 vols.; Altdorf, 1764-1768), II, 110-121.

[70a] Martin I. Pfinzing (1490–1552) was a Nürnberg patrician. He was elected to the city council in 1523, and was put in charge of the Nürnberg soldiers in the war against the Turks in 1532 and 1542. Cf. Gerhard May, ed., *Das Marburger Religionsgespräch 1529* in *Texte zur Kirchen- und Theologiegeschichte,* edited by Gerhard Ruhbach, Heft 13 (Gütersloh, 1970), p. 51, n. 280.

When Dr. Stephan (namely, Agricola) of Augsburg, John Brenz of Hall,[71] and I arrived at Marburg on Saturday afternoon and our presence was announced at the court, we were immediately sent for and brought into the prince's chamber where Luther was already debating with Zwingli and Oecolampadius. We were seated with Dr. Martin Luther and Philip Melanchthon in order to listen to the debate and, if necessary, also to take part in it. Dr. Martin Luther, Philip Melanchthon, Justus Jonas, Frederick Myconius, and Caspar Cruciger had arrived from Wittenberg Thursday forenoon. Martin Luther spent Friday engaging in a special private colloquy with Zwingli and Oecolampadius; but, as he said, nothing profitable was achieved. For this reason early Saturday morning at about six o'clock a public, friendly, nonargumentative colloquy (as it was called) was undertaken. The prince was personally present from the beginning to the end, as were the courtiers and the preachers of Hesse who had come for the occasion. And we who had been especially called upon by the prince for this event were also there. Beyond this no one else was permitted to attend, possibly because of deaths [resulting from a plague], for the English sickness[72] was widely prevalent then, as we first learned at the time of our departure. By diligently inquiring of others we ascertained that on Saturday morning prior to our arrival the following matters were transacted. First, the prince's chancellor explained why the prince had called them together. He reminded them of what was at stake and implored them that, more than anything else, they should seek God's glory, the benefit of all Christendom, and brotherly unity.

Thereafter Luther briefly explained how the opposition had undertaken to prove that the words of Christ, "This is my body . . .

[71] Schwäbisch-Hall.

[72] The reference is to the "English sweat," an epidemic which first appeared in England in 1485 and recurred sporadically until 1551. The most severe onslaught of this disease took place in 1529 when it spread to the continent of Europe by way of Hamburg. On October 4, 1529, Luther wrote to his wife from Marburg: "All of us are still hale and hardy (in spite of the 'English sweat' which has been responsible for fifty cases of sickness and one or two deaths), and are living like princes" (*WA*, Br 5, No. 1476, 24 f.). This plague caused Philip of Hesse to curtail the colloquy. He himself left the castle early on Tuesday, October 5. Cf. Sasse, *op. cit.*, p. 218, n. 43; Koehler, *Zwingli und Luther,* II, 131 and 139.

this is my blood" [Matthew 26:26 ff.], permit and demand an interpretation other than what we believe and teach. When they acknowledged this, Luther continued that he wanted a proof from them, since so far none had been offered. He believed that it could also not be offered in the future. Yet he desired to hear their proof and, wherever he would find it deficient, he would indicate this amicably and briefly. Then, for his own benefit, he wrote the text, "This is my body," etc., on the table with a piece of chalk.

Thereupon Zwingli and Oecolampadius attempted to prove their position with the sacred and divine Scripture and the clear sayings of the fathers. But Luther implored them, rather, to do this in an orderly and kindly way. They should not mingle the two sources, but refrain from mentioning the fathers until the sacred and divine Scripture had first been dealt with. They agreed to this procedure and adhered to it.

Then Zwingli began. He cited the passage from John 6 [:63]: "The flesh is of no avail." With it he intended to prove that, since the flesh of Christ is of no avail, Christ did not give it to be eaten. When Zwingli wanted to talk about the whole chapter to bolster his argument, even as he had done extensively in his books, Luther observed that this would result in long, unnecessary, useless, and irksome chatter. He told Zwingli he was surprised that he brought up this passage, since he knew full well that Christ was not talking about the Supper there, but about faith. For this reason the passage was of no use in the present controversy. Zwingli replied that this was true; nevertheless, he still wanted to use it to prove that the flesh was of no avail in the Lord's Supper. He was not surprised that Luther disliked hearing the passage, for it (he said this with great defiance and boastfulness) would eventually break Luther's neck. After that Luther admonished Zwingli in a friendly manner that they did not desire a contentious disputation but, rather, a friendly colloquy. In addition, he begged him to forgo the use of his proud and defiant words until he had returned to his Swiss people. If he would not comply, then Luther would be well able to reply so brusquely that Zwingli would regret that he had provided a reason for it and had begun the whole affair.

Luther made additional comments. Following this, Zwingli became silent and reserved.

Now when Zwingli had expounded the passage, "The flesh is of no avail," in his own way, even as he had done in all of his books, Luther replied to this opinion diligently and without malice. First, he in no way admitted that Christ was here speaking of his own flesh, but of our sinful and carnal being, as is generally customary in Scripture and as he had painstakingly taught and proved in his book.[73] – Second, even if Christ had spoken of his own flesh, he did not admit that it follows from this and could be rightly concluded that the flesh is of no avail, and that therefore it is not present. If this were true he could also deduce, contrary to Zwingli's opinion, that the bread is of no avail and that therefore it is not present. Likewise it could be said of baptism: The water is of no avail; therefore it is not there. Zwingli himself would have to perceive that this was not a sound conclusion, but that the word, comprehending flesh and blood, was instituted and commanded the eating. The word makes everything useful which would otherwise be useless if the word were not connected with it, and which would remain useless, if one does not give attention to the word or does not believe it, etc.

Thus a half day was spent dealing with this passage and, according to the judgment of many, even according to the judgment of the opposing party, it was argued successfully by Luther that the passage did not apply in this dispute and that the opposition could not prove anything with it.

However, after lunch, when we were also present, Zwingli brought up the passage from Hebrews 5 [4:15], "who in every respect has been tempted as we are, yet without sinning," and supplemented it with the passage from Romans 8 [:3], "sending his own Son in the likeness of sinful flesh." The passage from Philippians 2 [:7-8], "taking the form of a servant, being born in the likeness of men. And being found in human form," was also quoted.

[73] Presumably Luther was referring to passages in his treatise *That These Words of Christ, "This Is My Body," etc. Still Stand Firm Against the Fanatics*, *LW* 37, 78 ff. and 100-102.

From these he wanted to draw the conclusion that Christ became like us in every respect, except that he was without sin. But our bodies are only in one place; therefore, the body of Christ must also be limited to one place and cannot be in many places in the Lord's Supper.

Thereupon Luther, laughing, answered thus: "If the word 'likeness' or 'form' can be broadened so that it includes everything except sin alone, I would find that very strange indeed. For I have a wife, this is no sin; then Christ must also have had a wife, etc. However, I'll let that go by the boards and simply reply: Even if it were true that Christ had to become like us in all things, with the exception of sin, I will nevertheless not concede that our body would have to be in one place alone, for God is almighty. He is well able also to keep my body outside of a place so that it is really in no place. He is also well able to keep a body in more than one place, in one place, or without a place, just as he wishes." Then he earnestly pleaded with Zwingli not to regard or talk of the divine majesty and omnipotence in such a childish way. For God "calls into existence the things that do not exist" [Romans 4:17], etc.

In his reply Zwingli confessed that God was indeed able to do such things if he desired; but he did not do them. He proved this thus: Holy Scripture portrays Christ as being at all times in a particular place, as for example, in the manger, in the temple, in the wilderness, on the cross, in the grave, at the right hand of the Father. For this reason he was of the opinion that he must always be in one particular place. In answer to this I said:[74] "With these passages one can prove no more than that at certain times Christ had been in certain places; but that he was always and eternally in one particular place or certain locality, indeed, that he had to be there and could not be outside of a place or in many places in a natural or supernatural way, as they allege, this can never be proved from these passages," etc. After this Zwingli said: "I have proved that Christ was in one place; now you in turn prove that he is in no other place or in many places." Luther replied: "At the

[74] Osiander's participation here is not mentioned in any of the other accounts.

outset you volunteered to prove that it [the real presence] was impossible and that our interpretation was false. You are obligated to prove this and cannot demand proof from us, for we do not owe you a proof."

Zwingli said that it was a disgrace that we upheld, taught, and defended such a difficult article of faith and still were unable and did not wish to cite Scripture in support of it.

At this point Luther removed the velvet cloth and showed him the passage, "This is my body," which he had written for himself on the table with chalk, and said: "Here is our Scripture passage. You have not yet wrested it away from us, as you volunteered to do. We have no need of another passage."

Zwingli asked whether he had no Scripture passage, argument, or testimony other than this one alone.

Luther answered: "Indeed I have others, which you will hear after you have succeeded in taking this one away from me; since I have a sure word of God which no one can wrest from me, why should I let go of it and look about for another? Overthrow this argument, then you can expect to hear what additional arguments I have."

To this extent and no more, Zwingli and Oecolampadius presented testimony from the sacred Scripture; but they went ahead and tried to explore by the use of reason how a body could be in many places or even in no place. Luther did not want to permit this and said: "Reason, philosophy, and mathematics have no place here, for even if we concluded that a body must be only in one place, we would simply be saying that a body must be only in one place according to the common course of nature. However, it could never be the case that God's almighty word would not have the power to do something other than occurs in ordinary nature. Therefore, this approach cannot serve the purpose here." He offered, since this kind of argumentation is so important to them, to discuss the matter with them, apart from this disputation, for an hour or two, a day or two, or even a whole month. They asked where God had ever put or contained a body outside of a particular place. To this Luther replied: "God maintains the very greatest body, in which all other bodies are contained, namely, the whole world, outside of a place. Therefore, the world has no place in which it is." In the face of this statement they all were silent.

Consequently they did not introduce any further passages out of Scripture. We were very surprised at this and did not doubt that it happened because they knew what kind of an answer they would receive, namely, that it would bring more disgrace upon them than their silence. For if they would have brought up the Scripture passage, "he sits at the right hand of the Father" [cf. Mark 16:19], and other passages with which they have hoodwinked and misled the common man, they would have received a skillful reply because then we would have been consulted about the matter, and would thus have trapped them in their answers. This would have been of no advantage to them. However, they prevented this from happening and themselves confessed that the right hand of God was not in a particular place or locality but that it signified the omnipotence of God. From this it can certainly be seen just how conscientious they are in their negotiations.

Sunday morning and afternoon Zwingli and Oecolampadius brought forward passages from the fathers, namely, one from Fulgentius and several from St. Augustine.[75] These passages stated that a body had to be in a particular place and that the bread in the Lord's Supper was a sign of the body and blood of Christ. We listened to them practically the whole day on this matter, as they searched for, read, and translated the passages. Listening to them was quite tedious.

Finally, Luther answered in this way: "That St. Augustine calls the bread a sign of the body of Christ is nothing extraordinary, since we cannot know from this whether his opinion was that the body was present or not. We ourselves consider and call it a sign and nevertheless hold that the body is there. When he speaks about a body having to be in one place alone, he is writing about other things and does not refer to the Lord's Supper at all. But when he speaks about the Lord's Supper, he calls it the body and blood of Christ just as we do." Luther demonstrated this in several passages

[75] Cf. above, p. 31, n. 35 and p. 31, n. 34.

and said: "Now why should we dismiss the passages of Augustine in those sections where he deals with the Lord's Supper and direct our attention to those which do not deal with the Lord's Supper at all? Besides, even if I were certain that Augustine had in mind what you assert, why should we depend on Augustine here and not rather, on Cyprian, Cyril, Ambrose, Jerome, and many others who have given our interpretation in the clearest possible way? And even if all the fathers would agree with our interpretation, how could we arrive at the point where for the sake of the fathers we would abandon God's word and depend on them? Follow the example of St. Augustine himself![76] One ought to read his books, even as he read the books of others; for he did not believe what someone said simply because he said it, no matter how respected he might be, but only if the author proved his case from Holy Scripture. Let us gladly do the dear fathers the honor of interpreting, to the best of our ability, their writings which they have left for us, so that they remain in harmony with Holy Scripture. However, where their writings do not agree with God's word, there it is much better that we say they have erred than that for their sake we should abandon God's word."

Then Oecolampadius said: "Very well, we have nevertheless shown this much that we did not come to hold this view lightheartedly or without reason or without great effort."

To this Luther replied: "We know full well that you have had an important reason for your interpretation, but the cause is none the better for it."

After this they were asked whether they had anything further to bring forward. They said no. Since what they had previously said was not accepted, they could indeed infer that what they would subsequently say would be even less acceptable. Then Luther said: "You have still not proved anything. To this your own consciences must bear witness."

The chancellor interrupted, saying that they should seek ways and means to come to an agreement. Luther said: "I know of no other means than that they give the glory to God's word and be-

[76] Cf. above, p. 52, n. 58.

lieve as we do." In reply to this they said that they could neither comprehend nor believe that the body of Christ was present. Luther said: "Consequently we are also ready to let the matter rest and commend you to the just judgment of God. He will indeed know who is in the right." Oecolampadius replied: "We commend you to the same judgment." But Zwingli shed tears so that everyone noticed it.

At the beginning, Luther had said among other things: "If we are to be of one accord, we shall have to deal not only with the sacrament but also with other doctrines, for those who oppose us do not even teach one cardinal point of Christian doctrine rightly; this is particularly true of the men from Strassburg," etc.

Because of these remarks Jacob Sturm arose and pointed out that he was sent to see to it that the discussion about the sacrament would be resolved, etc. He had come with the understanding that the matter concerned only one controversial article of faith. However, if more controversial articles would be discovered and if he should report this at home, he would fare badly, etc. His request that they listen to the teachings of his preachers and certify where they taught correctly or incorrectly was granted. Bucer gave an account for all of them, but not accurately, particularly with regard to baptism. He desired that Luther certify that they were teaching correctly. But Luther replied: "No, I cannot depend on you. I am neither your lord nor judge. Since you do not want to accept me or my doctrine I cannot allow you to be my disciples. Indeed, we have previously noticed that you desire to spread your teaching in our name. I hear what you say now, but I do not know whether or not you also teach the same way at home, etc. That is why I shall not testify on your behalf. You do not need it either, for you boast everywhere that you have not learned the teaching from us. What need do you have of our testimony? It is all too obvious that you have not learned anything from us. We would dislike having such disciples."

Then Bucer desired that he [Luther] should point out what he did not like about their teaching. Luther said: "I am not your master, not your judge, and not your teacher either. Our spirit is different from yours; it is clear that we do not possess the same spirit, for it cannot be the same spirit when in one place the words of Christ are simply believed and in another place the same faith is censured, resisted, regarded as false and attacked with all kinds of malicious and blasphemous words. Therefore, as I have previously stated, we commend you to the judgment of God. Teach, as you can account for it before God."

When it became apparent that they did not want him [Luther] to help or counsel them with regard to the chief article concerning the sacrament, the prince expressed his thanks that we had come there to please His Grace, and entreated us to stop [the debate] at this time. If His Grace should summon us again, together or individually, we should not be inconvenienced. His Grace would take further counsel; for we ought not to take leave of one another in this spirit, etc. After this he sent for one person at a time, asking for counsel and means of reaching agreement and whether concessions could be made. He found among all of us the view that if the opposing party would confess that the body of Christ was in the Lord's Supper, not only in the memory of man, we would be willing to drop all other questions and not at all insist [upon such details] as to whether the body was there corporeally or spiritually, naturally or supernaturally, in a place or outside of a place. In this way we could accept them again as brothers and do everything to please them.

However, (strange as it may sound) they refused.[77] The prince invited all of us, from both parties, to a meal.

On Monday we were told to negotiate among ourselves. Consequently, Luther and Philip negotiated in secret with Zwingli and Oecolampadius, Brenz and I with Martin Bucer and Hedio. We brought Bucer to the point where he admitted that Christ's body was in the Lord's Supper and was given to believers in and with the bread; but [he said] it was not given to unbelievers, for this reason: Christ called only the bread which he gave to believers his body and did not at all mean the bread given to unbelievers. At this point we said that in this way a new controversy would arise, yet not as vehement as the previous one. We expected that because of this

[77] For an assessment of Zwingli's position here, cf. Oskar Farner, *Huldrych Zwingli*, IV, 374.

debate we would perhaps still reach an agreement. However, Bucer, after he joined his companions, was dissuaded from his point of view and again apostatized.

Luther also negotiated diligently, but achieved nothing with regard to the sacrament. However, they had begged us for God's sake to regard them as brothers and to permit their party to receive the sacrament with us. They also would do the same [for us]. But this request was denied them for important Christian reasons. After that they desired that there should be agreement about the other differences. This pleased Luther and he made the attempt. It was decided that Luther should list the chief articles of faith. Whatever did not please them they would report. If agreement were reached, everyone should subscribe to them. For this reason Luther was very apprehensive. He would have been happy to spare their weakness but he did not want the true, saving Christian doctrine to suffer any injury. However, at last he said: "I will formulate the articles of faith in the best possible way; they will not accept them in any case." So he formulated them, as I have had them printed.[78]

Thus in this negotiation it became apparent that our opposition became more aloof and more apprehensive with regard to their teaching, as time went by. They falsely condemned and slandered us as eaters of human flesh, Capernaites and Thyesteans,[79] and as worshipers of a God of bread, a baked God, a God who devours food and drinks to excess. They indulged in additional words of slander, even though they entreated us to receive them as brothers. Yet they did not prove worthy of it, for if we were the kind of people they accused us of being in their slandering and lying, they should not accept us as brothers, even if we would entreat them to do so. Besides, it became apparent that they were having doubts about their teaching, because they did not bring forward the bulk of it, for fear that it could not stand the test. It also became ap-

---

[78] Osiander had the articles of faith, which Luther had drawn up, printed by Frederick Peypus in Nürnberg. Cf. *WA* 30^{III}, 104.

[79] The word "Capernaites" refers to the people at Capernaum who falsely interpreted the eating of Jesus' flesh in a crassly materialistic way (John 6:52). The expression "Thyesteans" derives from the Greek legend which tells of King Atreus of Mycenae who, feigning reconciliation with his brother Thyestes, slew three of Thyestes' sons and served them in a banquet to their father, who unwittingly ate their flesh. Cf. *LW* 37, 93, n. 153, and *LW* 37, 138, n. 237.

parent that they had erred, because in the agreement they secretly repudiated five articles of the faith which they had previously held, taught, and put in writing, namely, concerning the indivisible union of the divine and human nature in the one person of Christ, original sin, absolution, the fruits and benefits of the office of the ministry, baptism, and the Supper of Christ our Lord. Everyone, who has read their writings extensively, knows about this.

Finally, at the time of their departure, they desired that the vehement and sharp polemics against one another should be discontinued and avoided. This wish was granted to them insofar as they would carry it out and would see to it that their own followers would refrain from [such polemics]. We, too, would then deal with them only in a friendly way.

Early on Tuesday the prince departed. We, too, got underway that afternoon. Tuesday and Wednesday we accompanied Luther on horseback, taking the road that led to Schlaitz, in order to consult him about several problems, like the unnecessary parts of the mass and other ecclesiastical usages. Early on Thursday we took the shortest road to Nürnberg.

This, honorable, wise, gracious, and dear lords, is approximately what happened at Marburg. As much as I have been able to retain in my memory I have sought to relate to you, honorable and wise sirs, according to your wish. I herewith humbly commend myself to you, honorable and wise sirs.

Your obedient servant,
Andreas Osiander

The Report of Brenz[80]

I received your letter, requesting an account of our colloquy at Marburg. However, there is no account of this colloquy which would enable me to describe all things in order, just as they were spoken in the course of the discussion. No shorthand secretary was present to record in his notes the course of the argument; nor was

[80] Brenz's report is based in part on a letter of November 14, 1529 to Hans Schradin, a pastor at Reutlingen in the southern part of Germany. The letter appears in *Huldrici Zuinglii Opera* (Zurich, 1832), IV, 201-204. In addition to this letter, the report is supplemented by part of Brenz's treatise, *The*

any one of the auditors allowed to jot it all down with a pen. Therefore, there is nothing that can be repeated by anyone about that colloquy except what has been securely retained in his memory. At first Luther and Oecolampadius alone, and then Philip and Zwingli alone, after all witnesses had been removed, discussed the arguments pertaining to the sacrament among themselves for several hours. After nothing at all was achieved by that discussion, a public colloquy took place; it was public in the sense that at the most only a small number were admitted. The prince of Hesse was present throughout, as were several of his councilors, several noblemen and men of rank, and several scholars; there were at the most fifty or sixty people present at the colloquy. Everything was transacted in a most courteous manner and with utmost decorum except that Oecolampadius, of whom everyone expected a milder manner, at times appeared to be quite obstinate, although not insulting. Even Zwingli repudiated the obstinate nature of his speech. You would have heard no other appellations than these: Dearest Sir, Your Grace, and similar expressions. No mention of either schism [*schismatos*] or heresy [*haireseōs*] was made there; you would have alleged that Luther and Zwingli were brothers, not opponents. At the beginning, Luther, our chief spokesman, quoted the words of the Supper, "This is my body," asserting that he was compelled by these words to confess the presence of Christ's body in the bread. If the opponents would not accept this understanding of the words, it was up to them to prove from Scripture that this interpretation was not to be admitted. Replying to these words, Zwingli opposed them with his old song: "The flesh is of no avail" [John 6:63]. Luther, however, refuted the argument by saying that Christ was not talking about his flesh, or even if it could be understood as referring exclusively to his own flesh, it would nevertheless not be possible to refer it to the sacramental eating. He mentioned three kinds of

---

Foundation in Holy Scripture Which Was Treated Somewhat in the Colloquy at Marburg in Dealing with the Sacrament (*Grundt der hailigen geschrifft, darvon ungeverd in dem gesprech zu Martburg in des Sacraments sach gehandelt worden* (1529). Cf. Theodor Pressel, *Anecdota Brentiana, Ungedruckte Briefe und Bedenken von Johannes Brenz* (Tübingen: J. J. Heckenhauer, 1868), pp. 69 f. We are following the procedure of the editor of *The Marburg Colloquy* in *WA* 30III, 152-156, in presenting this material by Brenz.

eating: the spiritual kind, which is faith; the Capernaitic kind, which is described in John 6; and the sacramental kind instituted in the Supper. This sacramental kind of eating gives us the basis for saying that the body of Christ, present in the bread, is truly eaten, but not torn in pieces, as the Capernaites understood it. In the face of Luther's attitude the opponents replied with practically the same arguments which they had previously published in their writings. At noon there was a cessation in the dialogue and they dispersed in order that the decision might be left to the auditors as to which party had won.

Afterward our opponents brought up the article of faith: "He ascended into heaven." If, they said, Christ is in heaven according to his body, how can he be present with his body in the bread? In what way can one single body be in various places? Rejecting this line of reasoning, Luther said the body of Christ is in the bread, not as if it were in a place but present in a manner which God knows. Nevertheless, the body is truly present. To this Zwingli said: If the body is not in a place, it is not a body. Take away the place, he said, and you do away with the nature of a body. This objection by Zwingli Luther refuted so admirably that the opponents did not dare to open their mouths for even a syllable [*gru*] in rebuttal. Luther said: God is omnipotent and can maintain a body without a location; he is not only able to do this, but in fact he actually does it. The universe, he said, is the greatest of all bodies and yet, even according to the view of science, it is not in a place because outside of the universe there is neither place nor time. Even the Aristotelians declare that the most distant planet is not in a place. Luther added: The debate concerning space and its nature belongs to the realm of mathematics; theology, however, deals, rather, with the omnipotence of God which is above all mathematics. Therefore, he did not wish to dispute about mathematical concepts in this place and in a theological argument that has to do with divine omnipotence, although he would not refuse to engage in a debate of this kind in private at some other time.

In the face of these words the opponents became silent, for what could they say in reply? They brought up the saying of Paul: "Now we do not know Christ according to the flesh" [II Cor. 5:16]. Luther gave this interpretation with perfectly clear reasons, even as he had explained at great length in his writings: "According to the flesh" in Pauline usage is not to be understood as referring to the bodily flesh of Christ but to carnal desires. When in this point, too, the opponents had given in, they took refuge in this scriptural passage, as though it were a sacred anchor and place of safety, as it is written in Hebrews 2 [:17]: "Therefore he had to be made like his brethren in every respect," and Romans 8 [:29]: "For those whom he foreknew he also predestined to be conformed to the image of his Son." If, they said, Christ had to be made like us in everything, except without sin, and we are to be conformed to Christ, it must follow that, as we are in one place only, so Christ ought also to be only in one place; or that we, too, are outside of a place or also simultaneously in many places. But Luther replied: In these passages Paul is not speaking about a likeness in every respect between us and Christ; otherwise Christ would also have had to take a wife, or would have needed a permanent home in Germany like us; but [Paul is talking] about the likeness or similitude of suffering and being glorified. In the face of these arguments the opponents were again silent. Therefore, they appealed to the ancient fathers whose interpretation, they said, was that the body of Christ was not in the Supper, but in heaven; they mentioned Augustine more than the other ones. However, Luther denied that this was the intention of the fathers. Indeed, even if it were Augustine's understanding, which is not the case, he still could not pass judgment on the word of God, inasmuch as he forbade the reading of his books as if they were canonical. Only the Holy Scripture possesses canonical authority.

[There[81] were several arguments which were pointed out particularly to Oecolampadius.

From what we could understand of what Oecolampadius said, [it is evident that] he was caught up in this error when he came to deal with the matter of the sacrament: No body can be at two places; therefore, since Christ's body is in heaven, it could not be in the Lord's Supper on earth.

He received this answer to his argument: First, before God's countenance places or localities are like time because place and time

[81] The bracketed material which follows here is taken from Brenz's treatise, *The Foundation in Holy Scripture,* cf. above, p. 73, n. 80.

are conceptions of the same kind, namely, of continuous magnitude and possess a nature of the same kind. For this reason it is written: "If I ascend into heaven, thou art there; if I descend into hell, thou art there" [Psalm 139:8]. Just as before God a thousand years are only a moment, yes, even less, as Peter writes, II Peter 3 [:8], "a thousand years are as one day," so a thousand places before God must also be as only one place, yes, less than one place. Since Christ has ascended to another world with his heavenly Father, outside of this world in which places have their meaning, even though in particular he is in heaven and on earth, he is consequently not in two places but only in one place because heaven and earth are only one place before God, and it is only in our finite view that they are separated so far from one another. According to man's perspective here on earth, Basel and Marburg are about two hundred miles apart; but in the sight of God, who looks at things from a true and absolute perspective, the two places are closer to one another than are man's hand and flesh.

Second, Paul writes in II Corinthians 12 [:2] that he "was caught up to the third heaven"; and in I Corinthians 15 [:8] he states that Christ appeared to him. He could not truly say whether this trance occurred out of the body or in the body. Now if Christ had to be in a particular place in heaven and could not at that time be on earth, why did Paul have to harbor doubt? But because he was in doubt as to whether his trance had occurred in the body or out of the body, he would have us understand that Christ, though he is indeed in heaven, could also be on earth and did not have to leave heaven to do this. – Third, it is written in Ephesians 4 [:10] that he "also ascended far above all the heavens, that he might fill all things." If he has ascended far above all the heavens, he did not remain in heaven but proceeded outside of heaven and therefore did not have to remain in a particular place in heaven. – Fourth, Jerome writes in *Against Vigilantius*[82] thus: "It is written concerning the saints that they follow the Lamb wherever he goes. Since the Lamb is everywhere, one would have to believe that those, who are with the Lamb, would be everywhere. Since the devil and wicked foes roam about in the whole world and with quick tricks are

[82] Jerome, *Against Vigilantius* (*Contra Vigilantium*), I, 4-6 (*MPL* 23, 342-345).

present everywhere, should the martyrs, after shedding their blood, be locked up in a box without permission to leave?" These are the words of Jerome. If, therefore, according to the opinion of Jerome the martyrs are everywhere with Christ, how is it that Christ should be unable to be everywhere according to his humanity?]

After they had dealt with these concerns in this way, Luther, observing that the opponents were becoming more and more obdurate, concluded the colloquy. He thanked Oecolampadius and Zwingli for having dealt with the subject so courteously. But since they did not wish to give up their view, he would in turn leave them to the divine judgment and would pray that the Lord might illumine them and bring them back into the way of truth.

Then Bucer stood up there and presented a summary of the teaching of the churches of Strassburg. For Luther had said at the beginning of the debate that at Strassburg, if what he had learned through the letters of friends was true, many errors were being taught, particularly with reference to the Trinity. And after Bucer had presented the summary, he requested a testimony by Luther as to whether they were teaching what was true and right. Luther did not wish to give his approval or disapproval, asserting that he was not their judge, nor had he heard their sermons, and that therefore he would leave them to the divine judgment. And indeed Luther acted wisely, since on the basis of Luther's testimony they would have been able to defend all their errors among their people in Strassburg. After the meeting had been dismissed, the prince left no stone unturned in determining whether some way of agreement among us could be found, urging, begging, suggesting, admonishing, and demanding from each one of us separately, apart from our own judgments, that we consider the cause of the Christian commonwealth and remove the discord from our midst. However, we who affirm the presence of the body of Christ would have gladly received our opponents into fellowship with us if they had turned away from their error. Since no kind of an agreement could be reached with them, we decided unanimously that they were outside of the fellowship of the Christian church and that we would not recognize them as brothers and members of the church. This decision seemed so harsh to our opponents that the negotiations almost ended in strife; for surprisingly enough they wanted to have us as brothers. We were amazed at the changeableness of those men who a little earlier in their wailings had ridiculed us as worshipers of a God made of bread and who now sincerely sought our fraternity and fellowship, but we did not abandon the view which we had once and for all decided to uphold. But when our attitude also seemed harsh to the prince, we tempered our view in this way, that we were indeed willing to acknowledge our opponents, Zwingli and Oecolampadius, as friends, but not as brothers and members of the church of Christ. What, my Schradin, do you think of that remarkable changeableness of our opponents? Because they solicited our fellowship, should they not, in that case, have confessed that the church of Christ is in our midst? Should they not in this case confess that our view relative to the sacrament is not wrong? Or if it is wrong (I speak as they do), surely it is not fatally wrong, deadly wrong, and mortally wrong, but tolerably wrong? Are they not, in this case, giving away their own perversity because they are committing a most grievous sin when they cause so great an offense in the church of Christ on account of an opinion which even according to their own view is tolerable? Otherwise they would not have desired to have us as brothers. Dearest brothers in Christ, I wanted you to know this especially so that you might perceive how the Swiss stand on this issue. At last Luther was given the assignment of drawing up those articles [of faith] about which we agreed and disagreed, so that we might not appear to have accomplished nothing. However, he drew up those articles of faith to which you hold and which, without having to be persuaded by any argument, our opponents accepted, a fact which astonished us greatly. Naturally we knew that they had for a long time previously taught otherwise concerning original sin, baptism, the ministry of the word of God, and the profitable use of the Eucharist than that which they now willingly confessed. — Here I appeal to your trustworthiness, brothers, that what I am writing might not be divulged in print. I was not given the assignment of making these matters known.

In a rather hasty report by Justus Jonas,[83] who attended the colloquy, little was said about Oecolampadius, and really nothing

[83] Letter by Justus Jonas to William Reifenstein in *C. R.* 1, 1095-1098. Cf. *S-J* 2, 497-499.

about Zwingli except a few personal views such as: "Zwingli is somewhat boorish and presumptuous; in Oecolampadius there is a wonderful gentleness of spirit and kindliness; Hedio is no less refined and broadminded; Bucer possesses the craftiness of a fox, making a perverse pretense of shrewdness and wisdom. They are all scholars, of that there can be no doubt; the papists are no opponents at all compared with them; but Zwingli seems to have occupied himself with writing when the Muses were angry and Minerva was unwilling."

Rhapsodies on the Marburg Colloquy

Luther said that the true body of Christ is there bodily under or in the bread. The three evangelists and Paul are witnesses of this teaching.

Oecolampadius: Most of the time the words [regarding the Lord's Supper] seem to be clear, but they are obscure for him who does not understand them.

Luther would not allow a figure of speech in the words of the Eucharist, unless this could be proved to apply here. He also stated: It does not follow [to argue]: It is enough to be refreshed spiritually; therefore, it is not necessary or it is useless for the body of Christ to be given or taken in the Supper. It has not been entrusted to us to decide whether it is profitable or unprofitable. It is the same as when a prince orders his servant to take the horse to the blacksmith to be shod.[84] So, for example, Abraham was given orders to sacrifice his son and Adam was given instruction about the tree [cf. Genesis 22; 2:16-17].

Oecolampadius decided to abide by his belief that spiritual eating alone is sufficient.

Luther: Abide in your belief in God's name. I will let it go at that. Nevertheless, you have been admonished with well-chosen words so that you might come to your senses.

Oecolampadius: Christ wanted his body in the sacrament to be received sacramentally through faith.

---

[84] Cf. above, p. 18.

Luther replied: Christ is our Master. We must leave it to him. We must interpret the signs to be what he wants them to be, even as he did this with regard to the bread and the wine: "This is my body." If Augustine or other teachers also want to interpret these signs, then they should follow Christ and interpret as he interprets. If they do this, we can depend on them and believe them. If not, we must let go of these teachers and believe Christ and not consider them to be right just because they are teachers. In short, Zwingli and Oecolampadius are of the opinion that God's word is profitable and good when pious and holy persons use it. However, God did not base his sacraments on our worthiness or unworthiness. They are founded on his word. They said that this is foolishness; they oppose the statement that Christ ascended into heaven and yet is in the bread. *Luther* said that there is no trope in the words of the Supper. Why should there not, rather, be a trope in the statement: "He ascended into heaven," since heaven is variously interpreted in the Scriptures? *Zwingli* said that it is absurd for evil priests to effect the presence of Christ's body through the word. *Luther* said: They "sit on Moses' seat" [Matthew 23:2] whether rightfully or as opportunists.

Oecolampadius emphasized that in the Scripture passage from John 3 [:3], Nicodemus was instructed by Christ concerning the coming of the kingdom of heaven. Therefore, there is no need of other ways [of establishing faith].

Luther replied that not one but many ways have been prescribed for establishing faith, such as through the preached word, through baptism, through the Eucharist; but why such a variety of ways has been instituted we should not try to find out. God knows what is profitable and good for us. Among other things God has also said that the flesh of Christ is profitable for us. If you regard it as useless, I cannot help that. The word says that Christ has a body. This I believe. The word says that the body of Christ ascended into heaven and sits on the right hand of God. This I also believe. The word says that this same body is in the Supper, and I believe this. Why should I discuss whether it is outside of a place or in a place? This is a mathematical argument. The word of God is above it, for God created mathematics and everything. He commands us to have faith in this matter. For Luther absolutely opposed mathematical argumentation in divine matters. He also said that if they discussed this for many months, it would nevertheless be altogether useless.

Oecolampadius: "The poor you have always" [Matthew 26:11].[85] *Luther* replied that he understood the passage to mean that Christ left to us the performance of charity.

Oecolampadius said that we ought not to adhere to the humanity of Christ so closely but be lifted up to his divinity. *Luther:* I know of no God except him who became man. Therefore, I also desire to have no other God.

Oecolampadius: Christ has given his body. What was its nature, that is, was it capable of suffering and useless? *Luther* replied: It is useful because the remission of sins is promised by it. Where the promise is, there faith is established; but faith consists of spiritual knowledge.

Zwingli insisted that it was a trope in the Lord's Supper in accordance with the principle of synecdoche [*kata tēn sunekdochēn*]. *Luther* answered that synecdoche [*sunekdochēn*] is very frequently employed in Scripture, such as when the prince gives orders that his sword be brought to him, the sheath is also to be brought. So in the words [of institution] a person receives the bread and Christ gives his body at the same time.

Zwingli made much of the passage from Romans 8, [saying] that we should "be conformed to the image of his Son" [v. 29]. But this [similarity] is something which cannot occur in many places. *Luther* replied: I have said it a thousand times and I still say, I will not admit a mathematical approach in the understanding of Holy Scripture because God is above all mathematics. Christ can keep his body outside of a place as well as in a place; nor is this argument from the accidental to the substantive valid: The body of Christ is not in a place, therefore, it is not the body of Christ. It is not white, therefore, it is not bread.

Oecolampadius and *Zwingli* conceded that God could make it possible for a body to be in many places; but they demanded that

---

[85] Oecolampadius wanted to point out that the disciples would not always have Christ's bodily presence among them.

it be proved. *Luther* said that it was proved by these words: "This is my body."

Zwingli brought up a passage from Fulgentius[86] which he used to prove that Christ's body is in a certain place. *Luther,* in his response, produced another passage from Fulgentius[87] in which he writes that the body of Christ is offered in the bread and the chalice to those who commune and receive it.

Zwingli wished to interpret the word "offer" as "to signify [an offering]," as is done in ordinary speech. *Luther,* however, proved that the words of Christ give what they signify.

Conclusion: Oecolampadius and his followers said that they wanted to adhere to their view. Luther commended them to God's judgment and illumination.

M[artin] L[uther]

O dearest Spalatin, open your gates to me;
And receive me and my companions with hospitality.

Summary Report Concerning the Marburg Colloquy[88]

October 3, 1519[89]

These words were written down at the time when negotiations with Dr. M. Luther took place at Marburg in Hesse on October 3, 1519.

M. Luther:

The body is eaten orally; the soul does not eat the body.

Answer by H. Zwingli:

Then it is food for the body, and not food for the soul. At this

[86] Cf. above, p. 50, n. 54.

[87] Cf. above, p. 51, n. 55.

[88] From the manuscript by Heinrich Utinger which is found in the archives of the City Library of Zurich. Heinrich Utinger was canon and curator of the Great Minster at Zurich and a close friend of Zwingli. He evidently took down these notes from a sermon in which Zwingli, shortly after his return from Marburg, reported at some length on the colloquy there. Cf. Oskar Farner, *op. cit.*, IV, 56 and 379.

[89] The date 1519 is mistakenly given twice as the year when the colloquy took place.

point Luther was hard put to it so that soon thereafter he spoke as follows.

M. Luther:

I have said and I still say it: The body is eaten bodily by our body; nevertheless, I shall reserve judgment as to whether the soul eats it also.

Answer by H. Zwingli:

All this is said apart from Scripture. Besides, you previously rejected the idea that the soul does not eat the body. Now you want to withhold your judgment.

M. Luther:

That is deceitful. You are trying to trick me.

Answer by H. Zwingli:

No, but you are speaking about matters that contradict one another. So we must nonetheless point out the truth.

Luther:

I concede that the body of Christ is finite, insofar as "finite" is understood as "being limited."

Answer by Zwingli:

If it is finite, it is not everywhere. However, you taught previously that the body of Christ is everywhere like the Godhead. H. Zwingli reminded him three times of this. This, too, he brought to his attention three times that M. Luther had grossly belittled the Godhead when he said that it had suffered, something which no teacher has ever said. But he [Luther] did not reply to this at all, except to say that they were trying to catch him [in a contradiction].

M. Luther:

The Scholastics also taught that a body which is finite could be in many places simultaneously.

Answer by Zwingli:

So Luther is returning again to his state of doubt in Egypt,[90] for, like the sophists, he wants to have the body present in many places simultaneously.

---

[90] The allusion is to the desire of the Israelites to return to Egypt and their former bondage, when they were wandering in the wilderness under Moses' leadership (Exod. 16:1-3). Reverting to the speculative Scholasticism of the medieval teachers would amount to returning to bondage in the church.

Luther:

Christ's body is in the Lord's Supper, but not as though in a place.

Answer by Zwingli:

Since Christ's body is acknowledged as being finite by you, dear Doctor, and since everything which is finite is in one place, and since Christ's body is not there as in a place, therefore, it is not there.

Luther:

I am not against the fact that it [the bread] is taken to be the sign of the body of Christ. Luther tried [to prove] this, although few people treat the matter in this way.

Luther also said: When the words [of institution] are spoken over the bread, the body is there, God willing, no matter how evil the person who speaks them may be.

Answer by Zwingli:

In this way you are establishing the papacy, for as little as the preacher, when he preaches, effects faith in those who hear him, so little does the person who speaks these words effect anything.

These are the words that were spoken in the colloquy of H. Z[wingli] with M. Luther.

THE MARBURG ARTICLES

The undersigned have agreed to the articles given below at Marburg on October 3, 1529.

First, that we on both sides unanimously believe and hold that there is only one true, natural God, Maker of all creatures, and that this same God is one in essence and nature and triune as to persons, namely, Father, Son, and Holy Spirit, exactly as was decided in the Council of Nicaea and as is sung and read in the Nicene Creed by the entire Christian church throughout the world.

Second, we believe that neither the Father nor the Holy Spirit, but the Son of God the Father, true and natural God himself, became man through the working of the Holy Spirit without the agency of male seed, was born of the pure Virgin Mary, was altogether human with body and soul, like another man, but without sin.

Third, that this same Son of God and of Mary, undivided in person, Jesus Christ, was crucified for us, died and was buried, rose from the dead, ascended into heaven, sits at the right hand of God, Lord over all creatures, and will come to judge the living and the dead, etc.

Fourth, we believe that original sin is innate and inherited by us from Adam and is the kind of sin which condemns all men. And if Jesus Christ had not come to our aid by his death and life, we would have had to die eternally as a result of it and could not have received God's kingdom and salvation.

Fifth, we believe that we are saved from such sin and all other sins as well as from eternal death, if we believe in the same Son of God, Jesus Christ, who died for us, etc., and that apart from such faith we cannot free ourselves of any sin through any kind of works, station in life, or [religious] order, etc.

Sixth, that such faith is a gift of God which we cannot earn with any works or merit that precede, nor can we achieve it by our own strength, but the Holy Spirit gives and creates this faith in our hearts as it pleases him, when we hear the gospel or the word of Christ.

Seventh, that such faith is our righteousness before God, for the sake of which God reckons and regards us as righteous, godly, and holy apart from all works and merit, and through which he delivers us from sin, death, and hell, receives us by grace and saves us, for the sake of his Son, in whom we thus believe, and thereby we enjoy and partake of his Son's righteousness, life, and all blessings. [Therefore,[1] all monastic life and vows, when regarded as an aid to salvation, are altogether condemned.]

[1] This last sentence of the seventh article is found only in the Zurich manuscript. See *WA* 30^{III}, 164.

Concerning the External Word[2]

Eighth, that the Holy Spirit, ordinarily, gives such faith or his gift to no one without preaching or the oral word or the gospel of Christ preceding, but that through and by means of such oral word he effects and creates faith where and in whom it pleases him (Romans 10 [:14 ff.]).

Concerning Baptism

Ninth, that holy baptism is a sacrament which has been instituted by God as an aid to such a faith, and because God's command, "Go, baptize" [cf. Matt. 28:19], and God's promise, "He who believes" [Mark 16:16], are connected with it, it is therefore not merely an empty sign or watchword among Christians but, rather, a sign and work of God by which our faith grows[3] and through which we are regenerated to [eternal] life.

Concerning Good Works

Tenth, that such faith, through the working of the Holy Spirit, and by which we are reckoned and have become righteous and holy, performs good works through us, namely, love toward the neighbor, prayer to God, and the suffering of persecution of every kind.

Concerning Confession

Eleventh, that confession or the seeking of counsel from one's pastor or neighbor should indeed be without constraint and free. Nevertheless, it is very helpful to consciences that are afflicted, troubled, or burdened with sins, or have fallen into error, most especially on account of the absolution or consolation afforded by the gospel, which is the true absolution.

Concerning Governing Authorities

Twelfth, that all governing authorities and secular laws, courts, and ordinances, wherever they exist, are a truly good estate and

[2] Headings for the articles appear here for the first time. There are no headings for the thirteenth and fourteenth articles.

[3] The various manuscripts have both *gefurdert* and *gefoddert*, which can mean either "to promote, grow" or "to demand." Zwingli understood the latter meaning. Luther used the word in both of its meanings. See the note to the ninth article in *WA* 30^III, 165 f. Cf. Sasse, *op. cit.*, p. 271.

are not forbidden, as some papists and Anabaptists teach and hold. On the contrary, [we believe] that a Christian, called or born thereto, can indeed be saved through faith in Christ, just as in the estate of father or mother, husband or wife, etc.

Thirteenth, that what is called tradition or human ordinances in spiritual or ecclesiastical matters, provided they do not plainly contradict the word of God, may be freely kept or abolished in accordance with the needs of the people with whom we are dealing, in order to avoid unnecessary offense in every way and to serve the weak and the peace of all, etc.

[Also,[4] that the doctrine forbidding clerical marriage is a teaching of the devil.]

Fourteenth, that baptism of infants is right, and that they are thereby received into God's grace and into Christendom.

Concerning the Sacrament of the Body and Blood of Christ

Fifteenth, we all believe and hold concerning the Supper of our dear Lord Jesus Christ that both kinds should be used according to the institution by Christ; [also[5] that the mass is not a work with which one can secure grace for someone else, whether he is dead or alive;] also that the Sacrament of the Altar is a sacrament of the true body and blood of Jesus Christ and that the spiritual partaking of the same body and blood is especially necessary for every Christian. Similarly, that the use of the sacrament, like the word, has been given and ordained by God Almighty in order that weak consciences may thereby be excited to faith by the Holy Spirit. And although at this time, we have not reached an agreement as to whether the true body and blood of Christ are bodily present in the bread and wine, nevertheless, each side should show Christian love to the other side insofar as conscience will permit,

---

[4] This sentence of the thirteenth article is found only in the Zurich manuscript. See *WA* 30^{III}, 168.

[5] The Zurich manuscript contains this additional statement. See *WA* 30^{III}, 169.

and both sides should diligently pray to Almighty God that through his Spirit he might confirm us in the right understanding. Amen.

Martin Luther
Justus Jonas
Philip Melanchthon
Andreas Osiander
Stephan Agricola
John Brenz
John Oecolampadius
Huldrych Zwingli
Martin Bucer
Caspar Hedio[6]

[6] The Zurich manuscript lists the signatures in this order: John Oecolampadius, Huldrych Zwingli, Martin Bucer, Caspar Hedio, Martin Luther, Justus Jonas, Philip Melanchthon, Andreas Osiander, Stephan Agricola, John Brenz.

ADMONITION CONCERNING THE SACRAMENT OF THE BODY AND BLOOD OF OUR LORD

1530

Translated by

Martin E. Lehmann

INTRODUCTION

During the fateful days of the Diet at Worms in 1521 Luther had courageously journeyed to that city along the Rhine in order to obey the summons to appear before the emperor, Charles V, the estates of the realm, and the official representatives of the Holy Catholic Church. It was one of the most decisive moments in the life of the Reformer when he took his stand there upon the word of God and refused to recant.

Nine years later another diet was convened by the same emperor, this time at Augsburg in southern Germany. But Luther was not privileged to appear at the Diet of Augsburg. His ruler, Elector John of Saxony, had hoped to take Luther with him as far as Nürnberg in order to have him fairly close by for counsel while he was attending the diet. However, Luther was still under the imperial ban and the Nürnberg authorities deemed it unwise for the Reformer to venture beyond Electoral Saxony. Understandably, Luther was quite disappointed when his elector decided that he should remain at the Coburg, a castle which lay in the southernmost reaches of his ruler's territory.

Luther's sense of frustration, in the face of not being allowed to go as far as Nürnberg, found expression in a brief letter to his friend Wenceslaus Link, written from the Coburg. "Although my good friends may follow the Elector to Augsburg," he stated, "he is determined that I shall remain."[1] Still, Luther speedily adjusted to his new circumstances, thus making his six-month stay at the Coburg from April 16 to October 13, 1530, like his previous ten-month sojourn at the Wartburg Castle, a period of amazing and brilliant literary productivity.

"We have at last reached our Sinai, dearest Philip," he told Melanchthon in a letter of April, 1530, "but out of Sinai we shall make a Zion and build three tabernacles there: one to the Psalter, one to the Prophets, and one to Aesop. But time is needed for this.

[1] *WA*, Br 5, 282.

This is a most pleasant place, most suitable for study, only I miss you very much."[2]

Just when Luther began to write his *Admonition Concerning the Sacrament of the Body and Blood of Our Lord* during his stay at the Coburg is not known. Early in September, in a letter to his "beloved housewife, Katherine Luther, at Wittenberg," he speaks of his extensive literary work despite hostile rumors that he was sick. "I cannot understand who told you I was ill—just look at the books I am writing. I have translated all the prophets except Ezekiel; I am working on him at present, as well as on a treatise on the Sacrament, not to speak of letter writing, etc."[3] In these words we have Luther's first mention of the *Admonition*. He evidently finished writing this treatise before October 17, for on that date George Rörer of Wittenberg was able to report to his friend Stephan Roth at Zwickau that the local printer would soon be publishing Luther's exposition of Psalm 111 and his *Admonition Concerning the Holy Eucharist*.[4] By the end of October, however, these two pieces of writing had not yet come off the press, causing Luther to complain to Amsdorf about the slowness of the printers. "They still have in the press two treatises which I wrote long ago."[5]

On November 23, 1530, Melanchthon informed Frederick Myconius, a pastor at Gotha, that he was sending him a printed copy of the *Admonition*.[6] It is therefore generally assumed that the treatise appeared in print for the first time around the middle of November.[7]

The work circu'ated quite widely, finding ready acceptance even in Switzerland among the Zwinglians. This favorable reception is somewhat surprising. It was only a year earlier—at the Marburg Colloquy—that the Zwinglians and Lutherans had failed to reach an agreement on the Lord's Supper. Yet in December of 1530

---

[2] *WA*, Br 5, 285.
[3] *WA*, Br 5, 608.
[4] *WA* 30^{II}, 589. For Luther's treatment of Ps. 111, cf. *LW* 13, 351-387. Here, too, Luther deals quite extensively with the significance of the Lord's Supper for believers.
[5] *WA*, Br 5, 665.
[6] *C. R.* 2, 445.
[7] Kurt Aland (ed.), *Luther Deutsch: Die Werke Martin Luthers in neuer Auswahl für die Gegenwart* (10 vols.; Stuttgart, 1957-1969), VI, 320.

Ambrose Blaurer of Constance, after a perusal of the *Admonition*, commended it to Bucer of Strassburg in these words: "Luther has come out with a splendid book on the sacrament, which certainly pleases all our Zwinglians extremely well. They are manifestly satisfied that he talks in this way about the presence of the body of Christ. Luther has also published an excellent book on Psalm 111 about giving thanks for the sacrament."[8]

The *Admonition* deals in a detailed and impressive manner with the Lord's Supper and its central meaning in the faith and life of the Christian community. The place of the sacrament within the context of infant baptism, preaching, and worship is clearly set forth. In the course of the argument Luther sharply takes issue with the then current concept in the Roman Catholic Church which interpreted the sacrament as a sacrifice and a good work offered to God by the priest both for himself and for others. By contrast, Luther sees participation in the Eucharist as an act of remembering Christ's death on the cross and of thanksgiving to God for his gift of forgiveness and love in Christ. It is a communion in which the believer shares with others the gift of the body and blood of Christ.

Affirming the necessity of communing under both kinds according to the New Testament mandate, he regards the increase of faith in God, of love toward one's neighbor, and of patient bearing of affliction and suffering as a fruit of faithful participation in the sacrament. The treatise is a moving testimony to Luther's deep appreciation of the Lord's Supper as Christ's gift of his body and blood to his people.

The translation presented here is based on the printed version in *WA* 30^{II}, 595-626, entitled *Vermanung zum Sacrament des leibs und bluts unsers Herrn.* This version was compared with the one that appears in Johann Georg Walch (ed.), *D. Martin Luthers sämmtliche Schriften, St. L.* 10, 2170-2209. The treatise is also printed in a somewhat abbreviated form in volume 6 of Kurt Aland's ten-volume edition, *Luther Deutsch.* In addition, the complete text is given in *EA* 23, 162-207.

[8] *WA* 30^{II}, 589-590, n. 9.

ADMONITION CONCERNING THE SACRAMENT OF THE BODY AND BLOOD OF OUR LORD

It seems to me to be the result of God's special counsel and providence that we baptize infants in all of Christendom throughout the world and do not wait until they grow up and reach the age of discretion. If we were now to baptize them as grownups and older persons, I am certain that a tenth of them would not let themselves be baptized. Indeed, if it were up to us, we would surely long, long ago have become nothing but Turks. For those who were not baptized would not go to church and would despise all its doctrine and practice because the church seeks to make them holy, godly people. In fact, this is what they are doing now, although they have been baptized and claim to be Christians. If such an unbaptized multitude would gain the upper hand, what could the result be but a Turkish kingdom or heathenism? Even though there would be a few among them who would go to church, they would nevertheless postpone baptism until the hour of death, as is done now with respect to repentance and amendment of life.

Indeed, I am willing to make a substantial wager that the devil, through the activity of the factious spirits and the Anabaptists, has all this in mind so that he might put an end to infant baptism, and would want only adults to be baptized. His ideas are surely these: If I could do away with infant baptism, then I could probably deal with the adults in such a way that they would delay and postpone baptism until they had had their fling or until the hour of death. In addition to (encouraging) such postponement, I would discreetly keep them from going to church so that they would neither learn about Christ and baptism nor value them in any way. So I would hold up before the great masses in the world powerful examples like the Turks, Persians, Tartars, Jews, and heathens so that finally people would become indifferent and say: Why bother with baptism? Why become Christians? I, too, want to belong to the majority. Do you think that God will condemn the entire world for the sake of three or four Christians? Why should I live among those few despised beggars and miserable persons?

St. Augustine[1] writes concerning himself that his mother and other good friends delayed his baptism and did not want him to be baptized in his youth so that he might not thereafter fall into sin; they wanted to wait until he had left his youthful years behind and might adhere to his baptism more securely. The result of this good intention was that the longer St. Augustine waited the further away from both baptism and the gospel he came to be, until he fell prey to the Manichaean heresy and made a mockery of both Christ and his baptism up to his thirtieth year. It was only with extreme difficulty that he returned from heresy to Christ. His mother shed many a bitter tear over this matter and in this way had to atone for the good intention and devotion by which she had aided in delaying her son's baptism.

The devil indeed observes that even without such a delay people are so coarse and godless that a tenth of them do not inquire about the meaning of baptism; they simply never think about it nor thank God that they have been baptized. Much less do they care about their baptism and live according to it by their worthy conduct. What would happen if they would not be baptized at all and would not go to church? As it is, it is difficult to be and remain a Christian even though we daily teach, pray, and practice baptism. However, such baptism and teaching constitute a great advantage and a strong admonition which ultimately ought to cause some to exercise greater foresight than an unbaptized heathen.

Anyone can readily observe and understand all of this when he sees how people now regard the holy sacrament of the body and blood of our Lord so lightly and assume an attitude toward it as if there were nothing on earth which they needed less than just this sacrament; and yet they want to be called Christians. They imagine, because they have now become free from papal coercion,

[1] Augustine, *Confessions* (*Confessionum*), I, 11, 17-18 (*MPL* 32, 669).

that they are no longer obligated to use this sacrament but may well do without it and freely despise it without sinning at all. And if this sacrament were never used or were lost, it would not matter to them. In this way they indicate and acknowledge by their deeds with what great devotion and love they previously partook of this sacrament when they were compelled to do so by the pope and what fine Christians they had been. We also learn from this in what a refined way people can be forced to become Christians and pious folk. This is what the pope presumed to do with his laws; as a result only false hypocrites, unwilling and coerced Christians were produced. A person, compelled to be a Christian, however, is a very joyous, acceptable guest in the kingdom of heaven. God is especially pleased with him and will certainly place him at the head of the angels in the deepest part of hell!

I am uneasy and am convinced that a large part of all this is the fault of those of us who are preachers, clergymen, bishops, and spiritual advisers. For we have allowed the people to go their own merry way without amending and changing their lives. We do not admonish, do not urge, do not persevere, even as our office demands. Rather, we snore and sleep as securely as they do, and do not reflect on the matter any more than this: Whoever comes [to the Lord's Table] will come; whoever does not come, let him stay away. Thus we deal with both kinds of Christians, although better things should be expected of us. We know that the abominable Satan and prince of this world does not take a vacation but roams about day and night with his angels and assails both us and the people, detains, hinders, and makes us lazy and sluggish for every kind of worship. Where he is unable to suppress them completely, he tries at least to weaken baptism, the sacrament, the gospel, and all divine order. Since we are familiar with these tactics we should remember that we are the angels and watchmen of our Lord Christ who should daily guard the people against such angels of the devil. By means of unceasing activity, teaching, admonitions, inducements, and enticements, as St. Paul commands his dear Timothy [I Tim. 4:13; II Tim. 4:2], let us fight boldly so that the devil cannot exercise his mischief so securely and without resistance among Christians.

Therefore I am writing this treatise with diligence, complete earnestness, and in a brotherly spirit, as a plea both to myself and to all pastors and preachers that they, together with me, would diligently look after the people whom God has purchased as his possession through the blood of his Son and has called and brought to baptism and into his kingdom. He has entrusted them to us and will demand a strict accounting from us, as we well know. For if we, who have the office and the mandate, are sluggish and lazy in carrying them out, we will have to wait a long time before the people admonish themselves of their own accord and come [to the Lord's Table], since they hardly come even when we are most persistent in our pleas. For, as has been said, the devil is present with his angels and offers resistance. Even so the people must look to us and hear our word and we contrariwise must not look to them and their behavior. Of what use would the office of preaching and the ministry be if the people could teach and admonish themselves? Christ could just as well have kept it and not purchased it so dearly. And why do we hold such an office if we do not want to carry on with teaching and admonishing? By such conduct we would not be any better, and we might even be worse, than the popes, bishops, clergymen, and monks have been until now. They, too, did not show any concern for the people with respect to either teaching or admonishing them.

Although I know that some persons are so wicked and obdurate that they do not care at all for any teaching or admonition, how should we correct this? We are not going to fare better than Christ and his apostles and all the prophets. Christ says in Matthew 11 [:17] that his fellow Jews did not want to dance or mourn if one piped to them or wailed for them. And St. Paul says, II Timothy 4 [:3]: "The time is coming when people will not endure sound teaching." Even so he commands that one should not therefore desist but should confidently continue whether they like it or not. For we know that teaching and admonishing are based on God's word, office, and divine mandate; and we also know, as Isaiah 55 [:11] says, that they cannot be without fruit, even if we should win only a Zacchaeus or a tax collector or a thief on a cross. There will indeed be some, when they hear the admonition, who will remember their baptism and will not want to despise, like non-Christians, their sacrament which Christ has so richly bestowed and purchased so dearly. Their example will have its effect on the uncouth, vulgar, wanton Christians, as one knife sharpens another,[2] so that eventually perhaps they will mend their ways.

My intention in writing this is not that people ought to be driven to the sacrament at certain times and seasons, as the pope has ordained.[3] For thereby the pope has provided for himself and the clergy lazy and secure times during which they do not have to labor with teaching and urging toward participation in the sacrament. Rather, he captured and coerced the consciences so that the people participated in it without joy and free will, without benefit and salvation; he has made of it not a sacrament of faith but a work of merit. Certainly the devil could not have thought up a better or more powerful trick with which to destroy the sacrament than with such laws. The appearance and the shell remained, but the kernel and the power were taken away so that no one noticed it. Nevertheless, they called it a sacrament of Christ, even though they had made of it simply a sacrifice and work of men. God has not instituted the office of the ministry that it might produce for him secure, lazy preachers and unwilling, coerced Christians. Whoever is not willingly and gladly a Christian or does not go to the sacrament in that frame of mind let him remain far away from it and go his own way. God does not want compulsory service as Paul says in II Corinthians 9 [:7]: "God loves a cheerful giver." Rather, the sacrament has been instituted to attract, entice, and draw the people, so that they might come willingly and gladly, yes, so that they might afterwards run with might, wrestle, and strive, as Christ says in Matthew 11 [:12]: "The kingdom of heaven has suffered violence, and men of violence take it by force." He does not want the weary, bored, satisfied souls, but the hungry and thirsty who press forward and struggle for it, as he says in Matthew 5 [:6]: "Blessed are those

---

[2] Proverbial German expression. Cf. Ernst Thiele, *Luthers Sprichwörtersammlung* (Weimar, 1900), No. 188.

[3] Cf. the statement of the Fourth Lateran Council (1215) that Christians should receive the Eucharist at least at Easter. H. Denzinger and A. Schönmetzer, *Enchiridion Symbolorum* (34th edition; Freiburg, 1967), No. 812.

who hunger and thirst for righteousness, for they shall be satisfied."

Therefore in this treatise I would like to provide clergymen and preachers with the reasons to be used in admonishing their people and attracting them to the sacrament. I want to point out, as I did previously in the Catechism,[4] certain things which can be used to move them to go to the sacrament willingly and without human compulsion and to receive the same with joy. Those pastors who are able to do this in a better way than I have no need of this discourse. It is enough that they have been admonished thereto. However, the others who are not able to do it better may want to take note of several points or read it word for word to the people, if they so desire, so that this sacrament might not be completely neglected and despised. And I want to give the reasons in two parts. The first part concerns Christ himself, the second part concerns us who want to be Christians.

Part One

It is reasonable to expect that a Christian should be aware of the fact that this sacrament is not a human fabrication or invention but has been instituted and established by Christ himself on the basis of the will and command of God his Father. It has also not been ordained and appointed to be used for dogs, pigs, wood or stones, but for us human beings and in particular for us Christians, out of great affectionate and boundless love. If the heart of a Christian ponders this, how is it possible that it should not be moved with devotion to seek and desire the sacrament willingly, with joy and love, and without any kind of compulsion and laws? If, however, the heart is not moved by it, then there is no spark or drop of a Christian spirit in that heart and it is doubtlessly an unchristian, Turkish, heathenish heart which assuredly does not believe that Christ has instituted this sacrament and commanded that it should be used. Much less does such a heart believe that Christ has ordained this for us out of fathomless, sincere love, for where

[4] Cf. the Large Catechism, *The Book of Concord*, ed. by Theodore G. Tappert (Philadelphia: Fortress Press, 1959), pp. 451 ff.

any of this is truly believed a heart cannot comport itself so sluggishly, lazily, and contemptuously.

Therefore, let everyone look at himself and examine his own heart: First, whether he believes that Christ, God's Son, has instituted and bequeathed to us human beings such a sacrament; second, whether he believes that Christ, out of fathomless love, was so sincerely and faithfully concerned about us. If you do not believe these things, you should know that you are no Christian but an apostate, condemned heathen and Turk. For you have regard neither for Christ nor for his command, neither for his love nor for his faithfulness toward you; rather, you act as if it were all untrue and sheer tomfoolery. However, if you believe it, then the same faith will preach the following sermon in your heart and say: "You want to be a Christian and know that it is Christ's command and ordinance to use this sacrament, but you put it off a half a year, a whole year, three years and even longer." Are you listening, dear young fellow? How does this agree with being a Christian? What do you want to bet that such a sermon will make you ashamed and fearful of yourself? If such preaching does not take place in your heart, then you do not have the faith that holds that this sacrament is Christ's institution, and your mouth is lying when it says that you truly believe this. You are twice as much a heathen and worse than any Turk, for you do not believe (this is one thing) and, in addition, are lying by saying that you do believe.

Consequently you see and must confess that all lies, hypocritical life, contempt of the divine mandate, sluggishness, laziness, and indulgence with respect to the sacrament, in addition to ingratitude and forgetfulness of such unspeakable love of Christ for us, originate entirely as a result of unbelief. That is, the heart does not believe that this sacrament is Christ's precious and true ordinance. For whatever the heart does not believe it cannot respect, honor, love, or praise. If a person despises, ignores, or forgets something, that is a sure sign that he thinks nothing of it, believes nothing about it, and does not concern himself with it. On the other hand, if a person believes and is sure of something, he cannot despise it whether it be good or bad. If it is good, the heart loves and desires it; if it is evil, the heart is afraid of it and abhors it. We see the latter taking place in the case of a false faith and an erroneous delusion where a person is afraid when there is nothing to be afraid of or is glad when there is no reason for joy. Faith is such an active and busy thing.

Therefore, the pastors should make the first reason [for going to the sacrament] quite clear to the people so that they might understand, and indeed believe, that this sacrament is God's gracious and fatherly ordinance, instituted for us human beings. We are here compelling no one to believe. But we are indicating what the nature of faith is; whoever wants to be a Christian should know what and how he should believe, in order that he might not deceive himself because of his Christian name and appearance and regard himself as a Christian even though he is a non-Christian and a heathen, yes, even worse than a heathen and a non-Christian. If anyone, in spite of this, wants to deny Christ, be a non-Christian, and remain unbelieving, we will willingly let him go his own way. We will not bother him except to say to him: "He who does not believe is condemned; he will indeed meet his judge and the one who has the power to compel him." We are excused and have done our part. For it was no jest or idle plan of God when he established and instituted this sacrament for us human beings. Therefore he does not want to have it despised, neglected, or not used; much less does he want us to regard it as an unnecessary and insignificant matter. Rather, he wants us to exercise ourselves in its use faithfully.

What if it were such an insignificant sacrament that was neither beneficial nor necessary,[5] that granted neither grace nor help, but was a mere command and law of God, which he required us to carry out on the basis of his divine power to which we are subject and obedient? For the sake of the command itself, we should be sufficiently impelled and stirred up so that we do not despise it or regard it as unnecessary or insignificant. Rather, with all earnest and faithful obedience we should fulfill it diligently and honor it greatly, since there can be nothing greater and more glorious than

[5] Luther is here referring to the sovereign freedom of God, holding that he has the power to command whatever he wills, even if we as human beings may not comprehend his command or may regard it as "neither beneficial nor necessary" (*weder nutz noch not*). Cf. below pp. 108-109; 110-111; 115-116.

what God commands and orders in his word. However, it is not just an insignificant sacrament, a mere naked command, which we must fulfill without benefit and necessity, as the Jews had to observe their sacrifices and external conduct without benefit and necessity, solely as a burden and obligation by which they were coerced and held captive like bondmen or serfs in a worldly government. Rather, this is a sacrament rich in grace; it is full of benefit and salvation, as well as innumerable and unspeakable blessings. Therefore not only ought it not to be despised and not forgotten; rather, it ought to be honored in the highest degree and used most diligently.

In order that we might point this out in part, let us consider first of all that he has instituted this sacrament in his memory, as he says: "Do this in remembrance of me" [I Cor. 11:24]. Carefully ponder and consider this word "remembrance"; it will say much to you and will appeal to you greatly. But I am not now speaking of any benefit or necessity which we may look for in the sacrament but of the benefit which accrues to Christ and God himself and how necessary it is to his divine glory and service that we use and honor it diligently. For here you learn that he invests this sacrament with his divine glory and ministry so that we should thereby remember him. But what does it mean to remember him other than to praise, listen to, proclaim, laud, thank, and honor the grace and mercy which he has shown us in Christ? Upon this Christ he has directed and concentrated all his glory and worship so that he does not wish to know of any glory or worship apart from Christ, yes, he does not even acknowledge it. Nor does he want to be anybody's God apart from Christ. He has moreover also condemned and annulled his own ancient worship, given in the law of Moses, along with all forms of worship in the whole world, no matter how great, beautiful, ancient, or glorious they might be.

Now because everyone wants to be reverent and devout, in order to honor Christ's sufferings and to worship God, one person undertakes this, another that, one person goes to Rome, another becomes a monk, a third person fasts. Who can enumerate all the forms of divine worship which we have up till now instituted and observed on the basis of the devil's inspiration and our own devotion? Because of them we have obscured and forgotten this lofty, beautiful worship, namely, his remembrance and the glory of the passion of Christ, which worship God himself established and to which he bore witness that he was indeed well pleased with it. He has established it in such a way that it can never be exhausted or observed enough, for who remembers God sufficiently? Who can praise him too much? Who can thank him too much? Who can honor Christ's passion too much? Why then have we mad saints raved so shamefully, as if there were no worship for us in this sacrament or as if we had long ago performed it and completely exhausted it? Above and beyond this, we have initiated a much more disgraceful, abominable, and odious worship of our own devotion and self-chosen works and have filled the world with it. Besides, we have denied, disgraced, and reviled this true worship. Now if you want to engage in a marvelous, great worship of God and honor Christ's passion rightly, then remember and participate in the sacrament; in it, as you hear, there is a remembrance of him, that is, he is praised and glorified. If you practice or assist in practicing this same remembrance with diligence, then you will assuredly forget about the self-chosen forms of worship, for, as has been said, you cannot praise and thank God too often or too much for his grace revealed in Christ.

Such remembrance may appear to be an insignificant worship because there is not much external display with vestments, gestures, buildings, and so forth, that the eyes and the ears might have their fill; rather, it is accomplished solely by the spoken word which has a lowly appearance for eyes here on earth. But no eye can see nor ear hear nor heart comprehend how lofty and glorious it is for God and his angels! God's words and works are initially always of a lowly appearance. For this reason they have to be considered with diligence and earnestness. Whoever does that, discovers how great they are. He himself says, Psalm 50 [:23]: "Thanksgiving honors me." Is that not the same as saying: Thank offering confers upon me my divine glory; it regards me as God and lets me remain God? On the other hand, sacrifices of human works rob him of his divine glory, make an idol out of him, and do not let him remain God. For whoever does not give thanks but wants to earn merit has no God; rather, internally in his heart and externally in his works, he makes a different God out of the true God, and he does this in the name of the true God. God often complains about this in Isaiah and other prophets and strictly forbids it in the First Commandment, saying that we should not devise other gods, and should not make him other than he is.

If you want to be a maker of God, come here and listen. He wants to teach you the art so that you do not err and make an idol but make the true God as he really is. Not that you are to create his divine nature, for it is and remains eternally uncreated; rather, you are to make him God for you, so that he might also be for you a true God, as he is for himself a true God. The art of doing this is set forth briefly and surely in these words: "Do this in remembrance of me." Learn to remember him, that is, as has been said, by preaching, praising, honoring, listening, and giving thanks for the grace revealed in Christ. If you do that, behold, you are confessing with heart and mouth, with ears and eyes, with body and soul that you have given nothing to God, nor are able to, but that you have and receive each and every thing from him, particularly eternal life and infinite righteousness in Christ. When this takes place, you have made him the true God for yourself, and by means of such a confession you have upheld his divine glory. For this is a true God who gives and does not receive, who helps and does not let himself be helped, who teaches and rules and does not let himself be taught or ruled. In short, he does and gives everything, and he has need of no one; he does all things freely out of pure grace without merit, for the unworthy and undeserving, yes, for the damned and lost. This kind of a remembrance, confession, and glory he desires to have.

It is true that such worship takes place devoid of all splendor and does not appeal to the eye according to the flesh; but it fills the heart, which otherwise neither heaven nor earth could fill. If the heart is filled, then also eyes and ears, mouth and nose, body and soul, and all members must be filled. For the way the heart behaves, so all the members behave and act, and each and every thing you do is nothing but an expression of the praise and thanks to God. That is then a different ornament and embellishment from the golden chasubles, yes, from imperial, royal, papal crowns; the ornaments and glitter of all churches and all the world are as refuse compared with this glorious remembrance of Christ. A single expression of this divine worship rings clearer, sounds better, chimes further than all drums, trumpets, organs, bells, and whatever else on earth may produce sounds even if they were all in one place and would all simultaneously ring out with all their might. That is indeed a different sound and song from all songs and sounds on earth, and yet it sounds insignificant as it enters the ears; but coming from within, from the heart, it sounds so mighty that you think all living creatures are making the same sound and all external human song is by comparison altogether silent.

However, that praising and thanking God is the same as adorning and decorating God is plainly written in the Song of Moses, Exodus 15 [:2]: "This is my God, and I will praise him, my father's God, and I will exalt him." See, there you are told how you can make your God beautiful, embellish, adorn, and paint him in the nicest way, place a wreath and crown upon him, deck him out with brooches and chains, and you need no money or bronze for it; but you must believe with your heart and praise him with your mouth, listen to his praise and grace with your ears, and whatever else has been said above. What will happen to the person who does not want to grant such adornment and embellishment to his God? No doubt he will become blind and mad, and in the devil's name he will proceed instead to adorn images of wood and stone, paint tablets and walls, embellish altar and churches, clothe the sacrificing priests with gold and silk, and use all his belongings and power for religious foundations, cloisters, pilgrimages, and many other types of false, condemned self-worship. Not that I reject entirely external adornment; but it should not be called a divine worship, much less should it hinder or obscure this one true worship. But, if a person desires to be of service, he should demand and promote the worship of thanksgiving or he will be condemned together with all other works and merits with which one desires to win or to purchase God's grace.

Now if you had no other reason or benefit in this sacrament than such remembrance alone, should you not be satisfied with such urging and enticement? Should not your heart say to you: Although I receive no other benefit from it, I still want to be present to the praise and glory of my God; I want to help in upholding his divine glory and also have a share in making him into a true God? If I cannot or must not preach, I still want to listen; whoever listens also assists in thanking and honoring God, since, where there are no listeners, there can be no preacher. If I cannot listen, I nevertheless want to be among the listeners; at least I want to be present there, with my body and its members, where God is praised and glorified. Even if I could do no more, I still desire to receive the sacrament for this reason, that by such reception I might confess and bear witness that I also am one who would praise and thank God, and therefore desire to receive the sacrament to the glory of God. Such reception shall be my remembrance with which I think of and thank him for his grace shown me in Christ.

For it is not a small thing when someone is gladly in the midst of the multitude among whom God is praised and thanked; it is something for which the ancient fathers longed with deep sighs, as Psalm 42 [:5] says: "I would gladly go with the multitude and go with them to the house of God, with the sound of praise and thanks among the multitude keeping festival"; and in the beautiful *Confitemini*[6] [Psalm 118:15] we read: "Hark, glad songs of victory in the tents of the righteous"; and many similar passages. For whoever belongs to the multitude, if he is not insincere, has a part in all the honor and thanks which are rendered to God there. Since you can render such service to God and can show him such great honor, which costs you neither money nor great effort, and which you can accomplish by listening willingly or by receiving communion with a thankful heart, you would have to be a desperate knave if you did not want to do this for your God. In fact, you should be quite willing to walk to the end of the world if you knew you would find there such a multitude among whom God is praised and glorified and you could thus share in the sacred fellowship. Remember how, previously, you ran to see the graves of the saints,

[6] This was Luther's title for his exposition of Ps. 118. Cf. *LW* 14, 46.

their clothes, and their bones? Do you recall how eagerly pilgrimages were made to Rome, to Jerusalem, to St. James,[7] only to see a stone, a bone, wood, and earth, and nothing was thought of Christ? And here in your city or village, in front of your door, Christ himself is present with his body and blood, with his remembrance, alive to receive praise and glory, and you do not desire to go there and to assist in giving thanks and praise? You are surely not a Christian, not even a human being, but a devil or the devil's servant.

It would be wrong if such scorners and disloyal Christians were not possessed, betrayed, and misled by the devil as punishment for their disgraceful ingratitude. In this way they would never again hear or learn anything about the sacrament. Let them have papists and enthusiasts as teachers. The enthusiasts make mere bread and wine of the sacrament, peel out the kernel, and give them the husk; the papists, on the other hand, make a sacrifice and commercial business of it in order to forgive sins and to rescue from every need. After that they place the host in the monstrance and pyx, form a procession, and bear it about as a spectacle and perform nothing but jugglery with it. They even retain only one form of the sacrament, and yet it is fruitless and does only harm. In return for this they are supposed to give money and means until they make emperors, kings, and princes out of these teachers of theirs. All this is supposed to be perfectly lawful. As Psalm 18 [:26] says: "With the crooked thou dost show thyself perverse." Why have they despised this worship and thereby the remembrance of Christ, for it is so glorious, beautiful, and great, and they could have it without price and trouble? All right then, let them have the husks of it with all damage to body and soul, goods and honor. They will get what they desire!

But whoever holds to the understanding of Christ's remembrance, as stated above, and honors his suffering, he is secure and free from all error and the deceit of all devils. He does not need to expend any cost or labor for the sacrament and effects innumerable

---

[7] St. James of Compostella in Spain. According to Spanish tradition St. James was martyred here in A.D. 44. Cf. Acts 12:2.

benefits besides; for he performs for God two great divine services, two great honors. The first is that he does not despise God's institution and ordinance but uses it submissively and readily. This honor doubtlessly pleases God, since he has not instituted this sacrament in vain but for use and has no pleasure in it when it is neglected and not used. For in the latter case one almost acts as if one regarded God as a fool who establishes unnecessary ordinances and does not know what he should institute for us, or as if he were a peddler who was carrying about and offering us worthless, unfit merchandise. Who can calculate what dishonor is done to God and our Lord Christ in this matter when we permit his sacrament to be so despised, neglected, and unused, and still we claim that we are not papists but evangelicals? Whoever does away with this kind of dishonoring and helps to abolish it, whoever adheres to this dear sacrament and honors and uses it as God's institution, God will in return honor him, as is written in I Samuel 2 [:30]: "Those who honor me I will honor, and those who despise me shall be lightly esteemed."

The second honor is that one keeps Christ in remembrance and assists in preserving such remembrance. This is done by preaching, praising, and thanking God for the grace of Christ shown to us poor sinners by his suffering. God instituted this sacrament chiefly for the sake of this remembrance, and this is the honor that he seeks and demands in it, for in Christ he wants to be acknowledged and regarded as our God. What great honor and glorious worship that is has been said above, namely, that the divine glory is upheld and God is made to be the true God. In return, God will doubtlessly bring that person to divine honor and as a result make him a god and a child of God. Who can even estimate what good things such honor and worship of God produce? For thereby a person thanks and praises not only God in Christ, which is the peculiar function of this divine institution, but he also confesses his Lord Christ openly before the world and confesses that he is a Christian and wants to be one. Simultaneously, he carries out the highest office of a true priest in a twofold way: By thanking, praising, and glorifying God he performs the most beautiful sacrifice, the supreme worship of God, and the most glorious work, namely, a thank offering. With his confession before men he does as much as if he preached and taught people to believe in Christ. Thereby he assists in augmenting and preserving Christianity, in confirming the gospel and the sacrament, in converting sinners and in assaulting the devil's kingdom. In short, he assists in whatever the teaching of the word accomplishes in the world and participates in the same work. But who can relate what great benefit results here?

On the other hand, however, we should consider what unhappy people they are who despise the sacrament and are so lazy and sluggish in using it. For these people do the exact opposite of honoring God and, therefore, their vices can be enumerated and calculated. First, they dishonor God himself in his ordinance and regard him as a fool for ordering such unnecessary worship. Indeed, because they do not believe that a worship service is his divine ordinance and gracious institution, in their unbelief they revile him as a liar and good-for-nothing. For unbelief is nothing other than blasphemy of God, according to which he is regarded as a liar. In addition, they also despise the remembrance of Christ which God has instituted in this sacrament and which is preserved in it. They fail to give honor to the suffering of Christ; they do not thank him for it at all; rather, they commit the most horrible sin of ingratitude. Besides, what is even worse, they act as if they dislike hearing about giving thanks for and honor to Christ's suffering or as if they do not like to be present when honor and thanks are given for it. In this way they take from God his divine glory and impede and check it so that he can neither be their God nor be acknowledged as God in Christ, as stated above. If they had their way they would desire that both Christ's suffering and all divine glory would count for nothing in the world and would be completely nullified and devils themselves would become our gods. For they do not inquire how Christ's suffering might be honored, his remembrance preserved, his word preached, or God known. This is much worse than if someone would throw dirt at God's image or would dishonor Christ himself.

Besides, in this way, they give others a bad, offensive example and are to blame for all those who, following their example, also abandon and despise this sacrament so that, as much as it lies in their power, Christ's remembrance is forgotten, his suffering is entirely in vain and useless, and finally the Christian faith perishes. This is to say nothing about the good they abandon and thwart, so that they bring no thank offering to God, do not confess their Lord Christ, do not teach, encourage, and improve their neighbor by deed and example, but deprive God of a thank offering, deny Christ, and mislead their neighbor. Dear fellow, would it be any wonder if God permitted nothing but devils to rage among us with daily plagues, war, famine, murder, and distress? Here the Turk, Tartar, and all devils do not suffice to punish such malice, since not only great, horrible dishonoring and despising of God, but also such shameful and damnable ingratitude toward Christ, are present in an excessive measure in the midst of Christian people.

The Jews had to give praise, glory, and thanks in a magnificent fashion each year for their exodus and redemption out of Egypt and their passage through the Red Sea. Nowhere could the dear prophets sufficiently extol and adorn this miraculous work of God. Moreover, we heathen, who otherwise were in bondage to the devil and were not worthy of knowing or possessing anything of Christ, have attained to such grace and honor that we have come to share in the salvation of Christ. He has not redeemed us out of Egypt and the Red Sea but from sins, death, hell, the devil, God's wrath, and all misery, and has brought us not into the physical land of Canaan but to an eternal righteousness, life, heaven, grace, and to God himself. All this he did, not through Moses nor through angels, but by himself. To do this he endured much toil and moil, sweat blood, had his heart melt like wax, permitted himself to be killed on the cross, wept and groaned for us, allowed himself to be reviled in the most disgraceful manner. Oh, what tongue, what heart is capable of considering or speaking of such love, grace, and mercy?

In return for all that, he is supposed to have merited no more from those for whom he did this than such thanks and honor that they do not want to remember him, hear anything about him, nor be among those who observe his remembrance and give thanks. They do not want to use his sacrament to his honor but let him sit there uselessly with his sacrament and summon us in vain to attend, even while they proceed to eat and drink excessively or do something worse. It is a wonder that the sun has not long ago become black as coal. No leaves or grass ought to grow, no drop of water or air should remain in the world in the face of such inhuman ingratitude. The Jews, who crucified him, were wicked; but we heathen are much worse, for we despise his suffering so disgracefully and are so thankless for it and do not even out of love and respect for him partake of this sacrament and help to observe the remembrance of him. O pope, O bishops, O sophists, O monks, O clerics, what have you done that you are to blame for all this and the cause of it all? You have made this sacrament a sacrifice of the mass and a work; thereby you have obscured it for the people and robbed them of the right usage, honor, and thanks. For they have sought nothing else in it but their own work, obedience, and merit. This you have taught them, and made laws to compel them to engage in such a work, and nonetheless have taken away the one element [the wine].

You, who strain out gnats and swallow camels [Matt. 23:24], have pretended to bestow great honor upon the sacrament by placing it in a golden, exquisite monstrance, by saying that it should be handled in golden chalices and patens and by especially anointing the fingers of the priests with ointment; you have used costly corporals, eucharistic vestments, and altar cloths, a tablet, candles, and flags along with various processions and songs, as if much depended on these. In order that people might indeed be impressed with the great and splendid seriousness of it, you have decided that one should drink out of the chalice with a small tube so that the blood of Christ might not be spilled.[8] Certainly you scrutinized the

---

[8] Concern about spilling the consecrated wine led, as early as the ninth century, to the use of a glass or fine metal tube which the deacon offered to communicants as they partook of the wine from the chalice. At solemn masses the pope continued this practice of partaking of wine from the chalice by means of such a tube. In certain instances individual churches that embraced the Reformation upheld this custom of having communicants receive the wine in this manner. Cf. Albert Hauck (ed.), *Realencyklopädie für protestantische Theologie und Kirche* (3rd edition; Leipzig, 1896-1913), VI, 413.

Withholding the chalice from the laity in the Western Church was a later practice which established itself in the twelfth century. It is of interest that the laity, not the clergy, were primarily responsible for this development.

faith very closely and commanded that one should believe the entire Christ to be present under either form. But, on the other hand, you made the precious sacrament into a sacrifice and a work so that you might purchase for yourselves the entire world's goods and honor. What has happened to the teaching concerning the remembrance of Christ? When have you instructed the people that they should use this sacrament out of love, honor it as God's institution, glorify, praise, and thank Christ through it, receive it in honor of his suffering, and acknowledge his grace, bestowed upon us apart from our work and merit? Contrary to such remembrance, you have taught them to perform their work and to believe in the freedom of the will; you have even made a work of the sacrament itself and have turned everything upside down. Nor do you want to repent of this action; rather, you even defend it. O scorners, O charlatans, O hypocrites, O blasphemers! O my Lord Christ, come soon from heaven with fire and brimstone and put an end to such mockery and blasphemy! How they do everything in excess in quite an intolerable and repulsive way!

However, in order that I might finally get beyond this point, let me give you a mighty and splendid argument which should induce you to go to the sacrament, so that your heart may exhort you in this manner: Yes, I want to go to the sacrament, not that I would thereby do a good work or achieve merit, also not for the sake of obedience or for the sake of the law of the pope or of the church, but to praise and glorify my God who has established it

---

Though they were opposed by the theologians, the laity in their superstitious fear of not wanting to spill the precious blood of Christ began to refuse to drink wine from the chalice. Looking with favor upon the Eastern Church's practice of intinction which consisted of dipping the bread in the wine and giving it to the communicants on a spoon, they felt justified in their refusal to receive the wine at the Eucharist. Increasingly therefore it became the custom in the Western Church to withhold the chalice from all except the celebrant of each mass. Cf. Friedrich Loofs, *Leitfaden zum Studien der Dogmengeschichte* (4th edition; Halle, 1906), p. 504; and Hermann Sasse, *This Is My Body* (Minneapolis: Augsburg Publishing House, 1959), pp. 69-70. In 1415 at the Council of Constance (1414-1418) the practice of withholding the cup from the laity was at last officially sanctioned. The council decreed that the laity and also the clergy, when not celebrating the mass, should receive only the bread in the Eucharist, Cf. H. Denzinger and A. Schönmetzer, *op. cit.*, Nos. 1198-1200.

for my reception and out of love and thanks to my Lord and Savior who has instituted it in honor of his suffering in order that I might use it and give thanks for it. For I want to be one of those who thanks him for his suffering and I do not want to be found among those who despise it and are ungrateful. I also do not want to give others a bad example and become an offense and thus make myself a partaker of their contempt and ingratitude; but, much rather, I want to set a good example and attract others to it so that they, too, may glorify and praise it and also assist in observing and strengthening the remembrance of the suffering of Christ. At the same time, as a Christian I want to confess my Lord before the world. Such a thank offering I want to perform for him, even if I should not obtain any other benefit from it; for it is supposed to be my thanks to the Lord for his bitter suffering which he endured for my sake.

But I hope there is no need to teach at great length here what Christ's remembrance means. We have taught about it repeatedly on other occasions, namely, that it does not consist of meditating on his suffering, with which some have sought to serve God as with a good work and to obtain grace, going about mourning on account of the bitter suffering of Christ, etc. Rather, this is the remembrance of Christ when we teach and believe in the power and fruit of his suffering. This means that our work and merit are nothing, that the free will is dead and lost; it means that we are free from sins and become righteous only through Christ's suffering and death and that it is a teaching or remembrance of the grace of God in Christ and not a work accomplished by us before God. The entire papacy with its religious foundations, cloisters, and its special works struggles against such teaching and faith. Besides, they have also made of the sacrament the most common and greatest work, even though this is just the place where our works should least be mentioned and the whole thing should be seen as sheer grace. Thus they have subordinated Christ's remembrance to everything else and have perverted this institution of God, so rich in grace, into such a fearful abomination. Watch out for this and seek to do no more here than to thank your Lord Christ for his suffering and God for his grace and mercy! As a sign and confession of such thanks and praise receive the sacrament with joy.

If, on the basis of my discourse, the papists would quibble here (as they are accustomed to do) and boast in opposition to me that I am here making a sacrifice of the sacrament, even though I have hitherto firmly maintained that the mass is no sacrifice, you should speak thus in reply: I am making neither the mass nor the sacrament a sacrifice; rather, the sacrifice is the remembrance of Christ, which consists of the teaching and faith concerning grace in opposition to our merits and works. And it is a sacrifice of thanksgiving, for by this very remembrance we confess and thank God that we have been saved and become righteous and blessed by sheer grace through Christ's suffering. But the papists have rejected, condemned, and blasphemed such remembrance, and still condemn it today. For they want to defend their works and merits, retain cloisters and sacrificial masses, which contradict such remembrance of Christ. We know that they sell their works and masses and impart them to their founders and brothers so that their works, when they have too many for themselves and have them left over, are supposed to assist other people to obtain grace. They dispose of them in a way which, after all, Christ alone can do by virtue of his suffering. They take over Christ's office and work, saying: "I am the Christ," Matthew 24 [:5]. This is one thing against which I have fought.

In the second place, they have not only suppressed such a sacrifice of thanksgiving or remembrance, but have fabricated another sacrifice in its place. They made the sacrament which they should accept from God, namely, the body and blood of Christ, into a sacrifice and have offered it to the selfsame God; and if they had not fabricated the sacrifice, I do not think that they would have turned out to be such lords. Furthermore, they do not regard Christ's body and blood as a sacrifice of thanksgiving but as a sacrifice of works in which they do not thank God for his grace but obtain merits for themselves and others and, first and foremost, secure grace. Thus Christ has not won grace for us, but we want to win grace ourselves through our works by offering to God his

Son's body and blood. This is the true and chief abomination and the basis of all blasphemy in the papacy. I have fought against such blasphemous sacrifice and am still fighting against it, so that we do not want to permit the sacrament either to be a sacrifice or to be called a sacrifice, but a sacrament or institution of God given to us.

With our arguments we have achieved this much, that they themselves now sense that they are in the wrong and that the mass cannot be a sacrifice; but they do not want to retract their error nor repent and so they begin to look for loopholes. They would like to adorn themselves with the interpretation that the mass or sacrament is a *misteriale* or *memoriale sacrificium,* that is, an interpretative or memorial sacrifice by means of which one interprets or recalls the sacrifice of Christ which he effected on the cross. But who possesses a seal or a letter indicating that such an interpretation pleases God? Who will assure us of that? This interpretation also becomes a shameless, palpable lie when they appeal to the seals and letters of religious foundations and cloisters on the basis of which they sell to those who wish to endow them, masses and vigils for both the living and the dead as a sacrifice of works or achievement. Their books and writings, which are still extant, give the same testimony. Since they neither retract nor repent of these false interpretations but defend them, we can assume that they plan to use them to confirm the same old abomination. St. Gregory[9] writes in this vein that he had the sacrifice of the mass offered for thirty days for a dead person. But of what use is it thus to confirm with manifest lies the ancient abominations in opposition to the clear truth? It does not mean that one evil effectively cancels out the other.

Such an interpretation also does not help in the matter at issue. For although they thus want to call the sacrament an interpretative or memorial sacrifice, yet they make it a work which we do for God for the sake of merit. As a result our work for God is glorified

---

[9] Luther is here alluding to the story about a monk, Justus, who owned some property (contrary to his monastic vows) and was, therefore, deprived of the intercession of his brothers after his death until Pope Gregory ordered that for thirty consecutive days a mass should be said for him (Dial. IV, 55, in *MPL* 77, 421). See *WA* 30^{II}, 611, n. 3.

in it and not God's grace toward us. In the same way up till now some persons have had the passion depicted and read for them out of books, and have attributed great honor to such a work, in accordance with the teaching of Albertus that a single contemplation of the suffering of Christ even in a superficial way was better than if one fasted for a whole year, prayed the Psalter every day, and flagellated oneself until one bled.[10] The sacrament was also made into that kind of a work when it was called an interpretative or memorial sacrifice according to which one merely contemplated the history of the suffering of Christ. Such a work an impious person and the devil can also perform. Therefore, Christ has not instituted the sacrament for that purpose, but for his remembrance so that we might rightly teach, believe, love, and praise his grace, which work no impious person is able to do. Therefore, the papists do not mean well with their interpretation but want to preserve their sacrifice of the mass with cunning and with stealthy, deceptive tricks; they are not concerned about or interested in the sacrament at all, but in their belly and mammon.

This should also be noted: They, as priests, desire to possess something distinctive, loftier, and better with regard to the sacrament, above all other Christians; for even though all of Christendom uses, receives, believes in, and gives thanks for the sacrament, in this connection it must not be called a sacrifice, and no one can use or deal with the sacrament for someone else, but everyone must do it for himself alone. But when the clerics deal with it, then it is a sacrifice which they bring not alone for themselves, also not for the purpose of thanksgiving, but for all other Christians in order to obtain grace and help for them. Do you not see and comprehend that the words of Christ do not make a sacrifice out of the sacrament and that it is in itself also no sacrifice? But when the chasuble and the tonsure supervene, then it becomes a sacrifice. For even if the entire, holy body of Christians deals with the sacrament, with hands and mouths, with chalices and with linens, with faith and love, with praise and thanks, yes, even with all angels in heaven,

[10] This saying is not found verbatim in the writings of Albertus Magnus, the medieval Scholastic; but it is often cited, for example, in a document of Bishop John VI of Meissen, Stolpen, January 14, 1502. See *WA* 30^{II}, 611, n. 4.

it is still not a sacrifice; but when the tonsured priests at the altar deal with it, then it is a sacrifice. Such a powerful effect the consecration of both the person and the altar has! Dear fellow, ask them for me, why the sacrament is not also a sacrifice when the laity uses and receives it, or whether they have a different sacrament from the laity.

So now the churches of the papacy have a twofold Sacrament of the Altar: The ordinary Christian has no sacrament of sacrifice but the plain sacrament, even though only half of it. The priests have a sacrament of sacrifice and have it complete. They get along in a brotherly spirit, and have neatly divided it up. However, Christ gave and left behind for all his Christians alike, one baptism, sacrament, and gospel, and did not want to have a distinction made between persons. Where does this distinction arise that our precious, comforting treasure becomes a sacrifice in the hand and mouth of the priest and in our hands and mouths cannot be a sacrifice but must be an ordinary sacrament, and yet they are both one and the same sacrament? Indeed, it comes about in this way: *Sic volo, sic iubeo*,[11] on the basis of the full power of the pope by which he can determine whether the gospel is to be called heresy or truth. For example, when Luther teaches the gospel and monks and nuns marry, then it is heresy; but if the pope gives the same permission to monks and nuns, then it is the true gospel. Or when someone misuses or prevents the use of church property, it is called snatching at the inheritance of Christ; but if they pilfer it from the poor and destroy it by means of whoredom and war, then it is called sanctifying the inheritance of Christ. The papacy is a mighty creator and god.

However, they should not suppose that I want to argue about words. For where everything else is in order, the words are not as important (although such an attitude is dangerous in regard to Scripture).[12] Very well, we are ready to concede and to permit not the sacrament itself but the reception or use of the sacrament, to be called a sacrifice, with this difference and understanding: First, that it is not called an interpretative sacrifice or sacrifice of works

[11] "As I wish, so I command."
[12] Cf. *WA* 38, 78, 15 ff.

but a sacrifice of thanksgiving; this means that whoever receives the sacrament is supposed to do it as a sign of thanksgiving by which he shows that he, as far as his own person is concerned, is thankful in his heart to Christ for his suffering and grace. Second, that the priests cannot make it into another sacrifice at the altar, but that they, too, receive it in no other way nor with any other significance than as a sign by which they indicate that they are in their own persons giving thanks to Christ in their hearts, in the same way that the other Christians to whom they offer it from the altar also give thanks. So there will be one and the same sacrament both of the priests and of the laity, and the priests will have nothing better or different or more in the sacrament than the laity, just as they do not have a better baptism or gospel than that which one receives from them. Third, that henceforth they do not sell to anyone the sacrament or mass as a sacrifice of works nor offer it as a sacrifice for others, either for the dead or for the living, in order to obtain grace. Rather, every priest should offer it for himself, like every other Christian, to demonstrate his thankfulness to God. Fourth (Dare I also touch on this?): If the use of the mass or sacrament has become a sacrifice of thanksgiving, they should repent and return all goods, seals, and letters, in addition to all cloisters and income from foundations, all of which they have received and possess through [their proclamation of] the mass as a sacrifice of works; for such possessions have been won with lies and deceptions, yes, with blasphemy of God and betrayal of Christ. If kings and princes had known that a priest could do no more with the sacrament on the altar than a layman who receives it, namely, that he solely gives thanks to God in his own person, do you think they would have been so senseless and would have given so many possessions to someone who does not offer a sacrifice for them nor reconciles them to God but gives thanks only for himself? Tut, tut, tut, how it sets my teeth on edge! I do not believe that I can get this point across to them; I am quite sure of that.

Further, I also want to concede that they may perform these sacrifices of thanksgiving for others, just as I can also thank God, apart from the mass, for Christ and all his saints, yes, for all creatures. Therefore, the priest may think thus in his heart: Behold, dear God, I am using and receiving this sacrament to your praise and thanks because you have made Christ and all his saints so glorious. For who does not know that we are in any case obligated to thank God for ourselves, for all people, for all creatures, as St. Paul teaches [I Tim. 4:4]? For this reason I am indeed able to tolerate the fact that the priests gave thanks to God in the mass for us all, if they do not do this as something special and regard it as being something other than the lay sacrament, as if the layman could not and should not also receive or use the sacrament by expressing the same thanks. I will not tolerate the "superpriest"[13] in this common and universal sacrament. Much less will I tolerate that they should give thanks for others, that is, on behalf of others, so that when the priest gives thanks it would be as if I gave thanks, and I could give him money so that he would give thanks for me and in my place. No, I do not want to have such commercialism nor do I tolerate such bartering and dealing.

If they do not want to accept these points, then we will also not tolerate their deceptive, false interpretation about the interpretative or memorial sacrifice, nor allow them to designate the sacrament thus. It is *abusus et katachresis;*[14] the misunderstanding is too gross and dangerous. For Christ completely separates the two matters, sacrament and remembrance, when he says: "Do this in remembrance of me." The sacrament is one matter, the remembrance is another matter. He says that we should use and practice the sacrament and, in addition, remember him, that is, teach, believe, and give thanks. The remembrance is indeed supposed to be a sacrifice of thanksgiving; but the sacrament itself should not be a sacrifice but a gift of God which he has given to us and which we should take and receive with thanks. For this reason I think that the ancients called this office *eucharistia* or *sacramentum eucharistie,*[15] that is, a thanksgiving. For in this sacrament we should thank God according to the command of Christ, and we should use and

---

[13] Luther uses the word *Sonderling* to denote the priest who believes that by virtue of his ordination he has a unique role to play in the celebration of the Eucharist.

[14] I.e., "an abuse and misuse."

[15] I.e., "the Eucharist or the sacrament of the Eucharist."

and receive the sacrament with thanks. In the course of time, however, through misunderstanding, this word [Eucharist] came to be applied only to the sacrament. Even that would not have been a bad way of saying it if people had said, when going to mass or to the service, "I want to go to the Eucharist," that is to say, I want to go to the thanksgiving, namely, to that office at which one thanks and praises God in his sacrament, as it appears the ancients intended that it should be done.

As a result of such an understanding I believe that many hymns were included and retained in the mass which deal with thanking and praising [God] in a wonderful and excellent way, as for example, the Gloria in Excelsis, the Alleluia, the Lord's Prayer, the Preface, the Sanctus, the Benedictus, and the Agnus Dei. In these various parts you find nothing about a sacrifice but only praise and thanks. Therefore, we have also kept them in our mass. Particularly the Agnus Dei, above all songs, serves well for the sacrament, for it clearly sings about and praises Christ for having borne our sins and in beautiful, brief words powerfully and sweetly teaches the remembrance of Christ. In short, God has wonderfully arranged it so that essentially the priest reads secretly the evil parts of the mass which deal with sacrifice and works, and this is called the secret mass;[16] but whatever is publicly sung by the choir or the multitude is essentially a good thing and a hymn of praise. It is as if God were actually saying in this way that he wants to preserve his Christians from the secret mass so that their ears might not hear such an abomination; and so let the clergymen torment themselves with their own abomination.

This is what I want to say about the first point or reason which should induce and motivate us to go to the sacrament with pleasure and love, namely, that we do this to the praise and thanks of God, out of love for and in the confession of Christ, as a good example and means of improvement for our neighbor, and, finally, for the

[16] The reference here is to the canon of the mass, which was regarded as so holy that the priest read it in a whisper. This part of the mass was designated by Luther as the *Stillmesse,* i.e., the silent or secret mass. Cf. his sharp attack on this practice in *The Abomination of the Secret Mass* (1525), *LW* 36, 311-328.

preservation of the sacrament, of the doctrine, of the faith, and of all Christendom. We should do this without worrying about whether we should or even could merit anything thereby. For in any case we are obligated to do all this; indeed, it is a universal command of God that we should praise and thank him, should love and honor Christ's suffering, benefit our neighbor, and help preserve the teaching, the faith, and Christianity. How much more should we do it in this instance, since he has established a particular ordinance for this purpose and also calls and attracts us to it. And even if we did not wish to or could not receive it, we should nevertheless gladly be present and watch others receive it, and hear them praise God and thank Christ. For this does not proceed from one's own devotion or human choice, but it is founded upon the word of Christ: "Do this in remembrance of me."

Part Two

Up till now we have said nothing about the benefit to ourselves which we can seek and obtain in the sacrament but only about the benefit which you can bestow upon God himself, Christ, the neighbor, the gospel and sacrament, and, in addition, upon all Christendom. Who can comprehend what a great benefit all this is, when you praise God, thank Christ, honor his suffering, benefit your neighbor, help promote and preserve the sacrament and gospel as well as Christendom, and in addition help check and prevent the opposite of all these benefits. Nevertheless, so that we might perceive what an extraordinarily ample, gracious institution of God it is, so that we might learn to hold it very dear and use it readily, we now want to see what benefit is offered and given in it particularly to us personally, and how Christ has not forgotten us in this sacrament. Although I have basically touched upon all this before in the Small Catechism,[17] so that a clergyman who wants to be diligent or needs this assistance can easily be helped by it, nevertheless, I want to deal with it again here.

---

[17] T. G. Tappert (ed.), *op. cit.*, pp. 351-352.

First, as I have admonished above, you should mark well the phrase "in remembrance of me," for with it Christ wants to induce and encourage you, out of love and gratitude to him and in praise and honor of his suffering, to participate in the sacrament gladly or at least gladly to be present for its observance. Also the words "for you" are to be diligently noted in this connection, when he says: "Which is given and shed for you." The two words "my" and "your" are indeed mighty words which should fairly impel you gladly to walk over a hundred thousand miles for this sacrament; for if you would consider who it is who speaks "my," and who says, "Do this in remembrance of me," you would discover that it is your dear Lord Christ Jesus, God's Son, who shed his blood and died for you. He desires no more of you with this word "my" than that you might recognize and believe the same, that you acknowledge it, and thank him that he went to such great pains to achieve it. Further, [he desires] that you do not so shamefully despise his sacrament and think so lightly of it and neglect it even though it is free and does not cost you anything.

Therefore, when you consider who they are of whom he says "for you," you will discover that it is for you and me, together with all human beings, that he died. But if we are the ones for whom he died, it must follow that we were subject to sins, death, hell, and the devil, even as the words clearly convey: "Shed for you for the forgiveness of sins." If sins are present, then certainly death is also present; if death is present, then certainly hell and the devil are present. Such consideration therefore helps you to thank him more diligently and to participate in the sacrament more readily in honor of his suffering, for what heart can comprehend with increasing adequacy what a benefit and grace it is that one is redeemed from death and the devil, from sins and all evil, and is righteous, alive, and blessed without one's merit and help, only through the blood and dying of the Son of God? Still, he desires nothing in return other than praise and thanks, and that we acknowledge and believe it and do not despise it so shamefully or disregard it.

Therefore, this is the primary benefit and fruit which accrues to you from the use of the sacrament that you are reminded of such favor and grace and that your faith and love are stimulated, renewed, and strengthened so that you might not reach the point of forgetting or despising your dear Savior and his bitter suffering and the great, manifold, eternal need and death out of which he has rescued you. Dear fellow, do not regard such benefit as trifling. Yes, even if there were no benefit in the use of the sacrament other than the remembrance of this blessing by Christ and of your need which would arouse you to faith in and love toward your dear Savior, it would nevertheless be exceedingly and sufficiently beneficial and fruitful, since such faith is very much needed by us so that we might remain with Christ in whom there is no abiding without such faith. In contrast, unbelief is a dangerous, daily, incessant devil who wants to tear us away from our dear Savior and his suffering by both force and deceit. It requires toil and trouble daily to practice, stimulate, and exercise such faith so that we do not forget Christ's suffering and benefit. What would happen, then, if we were to draw away from it, were rarely concerned with it, and despised or neglected his remembrance and sacrament?

The second benefit is this: Where such faith is thus continually refreshed and renewed, there the heart is also at the same time refreshed anew in its love of the neighbor and is made strong and equipped to do all good works and to resist sin and all temptations of the devil. Since faith cannot be idle, it must demonstrate the fruits of love by doing good and avoiding evil. The Holy Spirit is at hand; he does not let us rest but makes us willing and inclined to do all that is good and earnest and diligent in opposing all that is evil. Thus a Christian by such a right use of the sacrament continually, increasingly, day after day, renews himself and grows in Christ, as Paul also teaches us that we should always be renewed [Eph. 4:23] and increase [in holiness]. On the other hand, when a person abstains from the sacrament and does not use it, then harm has to follow and it cannot but happen that his faith daily becomes increasingly weak and cold; as a result, then, it must furthermore follow that he becomes lazy and cold in his love for the neighbor, sluggish and averse to doing good works, unfit and unwilling to resist evil. So with the passage of time he finds less delight in the sacrament until he becomes completely tired of thinking about his dear Savior; he despises him and deteriorates from day to day, inclining to and taking delight in all evil. For the devil is present and he does not rest until he brings about his fall into sin and shame.

In order that everyone may learn what a tricky knave the devil is, I want to give an example out of my own experience to all who are willing to let themselves be warned. It has happened to me several times that I resolved to go to the sacrament on this or that day. When the day arrived, my devotion disappeared or some hindrance came up, or I regarded myself unfit, saying: "Very well, I will go in a week." But the next week again found me as unfit and encumbered as on the former occasion: "Very well, I will go next week." Those weeks became so numerous that I almost got away from it entirely and hardly ever went to the sacrament. But when God granted me grace to become aware of the devil's knavery, I said: "Do you want to make a wager, Satan, that I don't know what you are up to? A plague upon your cleverness!"[18] So I broke out of the vicious circle and participated in the sacrament, even without making confession several times (which I do not ordinarily do) to spite the devil, particularly because I was not conscious of any gross sins.

And so I discovered this about myself: If a person has no longing or reverence for the sacrament and yet earnestly makes the effort to participate in it, then such thoughts and the action itself bring forth sufficient reverence and longing and do a good job of driving away the lazy and morose thoughts which hinder a person and make him unfit. For it is a gracious, efficacious sacrament; if one thinks about it only a little with earnestness and prepares oneself for it, then it kindles, arouses, and further attracts the heart to itself. Try it, and if you do not find it to be thus, you can accuse me of lying. I am willing to wager that you, too, will find that the devil has artfully fooled you and has cleverly kept you from the sacrament so that he might in time make you lose faith entirely and make you forget about your dear Savior and all your need.

If you had no other reason or need to participate in the sacra-

[18] An imprecation. Literally: "What do you say? Do you want to make a wager, Satan? Good luck to you with your cleverness and mine!" Cf. Thiele, *Luthers Sprichwörtersammlung*, No. 186.

ment, my dear fellow, would this not be a sufficient sin or need that you find yourself cold and indifferent toward the sacrament? What is this other than finding yourself cold and indifferent toward believing, thanking, and thinking about your dear Savior and all his benefits which he has shown you by his bitter suffering with which he redeemed you from sins, death, and the devil and made you righteous, alive, and blessed? How will you kindle your interest in the face of such coldness and disinclination? How will you awaken your faith? How will you be aroused to give thanks? Will you wait until the sacrament itself comes to you, or the devil gives you permission, or his mother[19] urges you to do so? Nothing will ever come of this. Here you must encourage yourself and hold fast to the sacrament; it is a fire which can kindle hearts. Here you must consider your need and poverty and listen to and believe in the benefits of your Savior. Thus your heart will change and you will get other ideas.

For this reason God acted rightly and properly when he has permitted us to remain in a state in which we must fight and wrestle with sins, death, the devil, the world, the flesh, and all sorts of temptations, so that we are obliged and compelled to seek and desire his grace, help, word, and sacrament. Otherwise, if this were not the case, no human would be at all likely to inquire either after his word or after his sacrament, or seek either grace or help. But now that such hounds, yes, devils, are after us and pursue us, we must indeed become more alert and, as a hunted deer longs for fresh water, we too should cry out for God, as Psalm 42 [:1] says. In this way our faith will become well exercised, experienced, and strong, and we shall abide and become established in Christ.

But if you say that you do not feel sin, death, the world, the devil, etc. and are not engaged in a fight or a struggle with them, and therefore no need compels you to partake of the sacrament, I answer: "I hope that you are not serious in believing that you alone among all the saints and people on earth should be without such a feeling." If I knew that you were really serious about it, I would truly arrange it so that on all streets on which you walk all the

[19] Luther often refers to reason as being the devil's mother. Cf. *LW* 40, 174 f. and *LW* 37, 210, n. 69.

bells would have to be rung and ahead of you they would cry out: "Here comes a new saint, exalted above all saints, who neither feels nor has sin." But I want to tell you without jesting: "If you do not feel any sin, you are assuredly completely dead in sins, yes, dead, and sin is reigning over you with might." I do not even have to mention coarse, external sins such as a desire for unchastity, adultery, anger, hatred, envy, revenge, pride, covetousness, lasciviousness, etc.; the fact that you have neither the need nor the desire to partake of the sacrament is in itself already a most serious and great sin. From this we perceive that you also have no faith, that you have no regard for God's word, have forgotten about Christ's suffering, and are full of unthankfulness and all kinds of spiritual abominations.

My counsel therefore is this: If you find that you are so utterly insensitive that you do not feel sin, death, etc., take hold of your mouth, nose, ears, hands and feel whether they are flesh or stone. If they are flesh, very well, then at least believe the Scripture, if you cannot trust your feelings. For Scripture says: "The desires of the flesh are against the Spirit" [Galatians 5:17], also, Romans 7 [:18]: "Nothing good dwells within me, that is, in my flesh," and so forth. In accordance with these sayings, speak thus: "Truly, I am aware of my bodily flesh. Surely there is nothing good in it. For that reason, so long as I have flesh, it is of course necessary for me to go to the sacrament to strengthen my faith and spirit against the flesh which is opposed to my spirit." Scripture is not lying to you, but your feeling and your lack of feelings are deceiving you: for, although sin is forgiven and also conquered by Christ so that it cannot condemn us or accuse the conscience, it nevertheless has remained to the extent that it can tempt us and thus can exercise us in our faith.

Consequently, if you do not feel the world, look around yourself and see whether you are not living among people where you see, hear, and encounter murder, adultery, robbery, error, heresy, persecution, and all kinds of vices. When you see this, then believe the Scripture which says: "Let him who stands take heed lest he fall" [I Cor. 10:12]. For under such circumstances you, too, can fall at any time, not only in your heart but also in deed, for you can indeed hate and injure your enemy, or hinder the good, etc. Accordingly, you must say: "Truly, I see that I am in the world, in the midst of all kinds of sins and vices into which I can fall. Therefore, as long as I am in the world, I need to go to the sacrament so that I might cling to my Savior and strengthen my faith, and in this way be enabled to resist this evil world and be protected against sins and vices. For, although Christ has indeed overcome the world so that it cannot force us to sin, it has nevertheless so far remained at hand to tempt, plague, and persecute us and thus exercise us in our faith."

Similarly, if you do not feel death, go to the charnel-house and the graves in the churchyard, or believe the Scripture which says: "It is appointed for men to die once" [Hebrews 9:27]. Then you will find that you are not yet bodily in heaven but that you face death and your grave awaits you amid the other graves, and you are not safe for one moment. When you see that, remember: "Truly, I am not yet over the hump, I still have to fight with death. As long as I am living, it is necessary for me to go to the sacrament in order to strengthen my faith so that death (in case it comes swiftly) may not scare me and cause me to despair. For it is a vicious foe, unbearable for the unbelieving, yes, even terrible for those who are weak in faith. Though Christ has indeed conquered it so that it cannot devour us nor hold us captive, it has nevertheless remained here to the extent that it can scare us, and tempt us to despair, and can thus exercise us in our faith."

Hence, if you do not feel the devil, how he can drive you to unbelief, despair, blasphemy and hatred of God, believe Scripture, which shows us how he has by such means plagued Job, David, St. Paul, and many others, and can also plague you. Accordingly, say this: "Truly, the devil is still a prince in the world, and I have not yet eluded him. As long as I am in his principality he is a threat to me. For this reason I must go to the sacrament and hold to my dear Helper and Savior so that my heart and faith may be strengthened daily and the devil may not impale me with his spear or kill me with his fiery, poisoned arrows. For although Christ has conquered the devil for us, he [the devil] has nevertheless still remained a lord in the world so that he can assail us with great spiritual temptations and thus exercise us in our faith."

I have had to say this so bluntly and simply on account of the coarse, lazy Christians who do not know how to reflect very deeply on matters, and therefore unconsciously become sluggish and secure as if they needed neither God nor his word. They amble along as if they were neither in danger nor in need and, in the process, they lose their faith and become incapable of doing good works. But God has permitted such enemies to remain for us so that we would have to fight and should not become lazy and secure, even as it is written in Judges 1 [:21 ff.] that he also permitted several kings and princes to remain here and there in the vicinity of his people Israel so that they might learn to wage war and remain accustomed to war. For God's word is almighty; therefore, faith and the Spirit are busy and never resting, and must always be active and engaged in combat. Consequently, the word of God must not have insignificant, but the most powerful, foes against whom it can gain honor according to its great might; these four companions—the flesh, the world, death and the devil—are such [powerful foes]. Therefore, Christ is called Lord Sabaoth, that is, a God of warfare or of hosts, who always makes war and is engaged in combat in us.

Consequently, we can confidently trust that we have a gracious God who can help us. And this is not all, but we must also be sure that he undoubtedly wants to be gracious toward us and help us. How can we become sure of this if he does not give us an indubitable sign of his grace and love for us? Otherwise, who could guess what his feeling toward us is? This he has shown us with the sacrament, erecting for us a sure sign of his love and grace. For the sacrament is indeed not a sign of his wrath, and he would never have given it to us, if he were angry with us. Rather, it is a sign of his sublimest love and fathomless mercy. How can he demonstrate sublimer love and deeper mercy than that he should therein truly give us his own body and blood as food? This is not only a gracious sign but is also supposed to be a food with which all of us who are in his army and are engaged in combat should be refreshed and strengthened. It is in reality the pay and provisions with which he remunerates and feeds his army and men of war until they finally conquer and carry the day along with him. Oh, it is good coinage, costly red gold and pure white silver, elegant, attractive bread and good, sweet wine! And all this is provided in abundance and richly so that it is very delightful to be a part of this military expedition.

But if you say: "Yes, but St. Paul describes it in such frightening terms in I Corinthians 11 [:27] when he says: 'Whoever, therefore eats the bread or drinks the cup of the Lord in an unworthy manner will be guilty of profaning the body and blood of the Lord.' With these words he makes us timid and reluctant about going to the sacrament, for who is there who could regard himself as worthy?" The answer is: My dear fellow, do you see whom St. Paul is criticizing? Namely, those who burst in like pigs and made of it physical gluttony and treated it no differently from mere daily bread and wine; besides, they despised one another and everyone had his own meal. But we are talking about those who believe that it is not at all something for a pig but the true body and blood of Christ and who know that Christ has instituted it for his remembrance and for our consolation. Further, they would like to be Christians, and praise, thank, and honor their Lord; also, they would like to possess his grace and love. But they are afraid because of their personal unworthiness and stay away from it, hindered and frightened away by such a false fear.

Dear fellow, you must not look at yourself, how worthy or unworthy you are, but at your need—your need of the grace of Christ. If you see and feel your need, you are worthy and sufficiently prepared, for he has not instituted the sacrament to act as a poison and to harm us, but to grant comfort and salvation. Above all, however, you must consider that, unworthy as you are, your Lord Christ is for all that most worthy, and you should praise, honor, and thank him and help to maintain his ordinance and institution, as indicated above, as you owe it to him and have promised to do so in baptism. Your heart should therefore reflect: "Very well, if I am unworthy to receive the sacrament, my Lord

Christ is so much worthier so that I thereby thank him and praise and honor his institution, just as I should do and have promised to do in my baptism." And again: "Though I am unworthy, I am also needy. Whoever must beg should not be ashamed to do so. Shamefacedness is an unnecessary domestic servant in a poor beggar's home. For that reason Christ himself praises an impudent rascal in Luke 11 [:8]."

See, thus you have two ways or reasons for receiving the sacrament. The first one is that you thereby thank and praise Christ. The other is that you are also obtaining comfort and grace for yourself. These two ways cannot be bad or constitute an abuse, but must be good and pleasing to God. For we cannot deal with God in more than two ways, namely, by giving thanks and by voicing our petitions. By thanking him we honor him on account of the blessings and gifts of grace we have already received; by praying we honor him on account of the blessings and gifts of grace we would henceforth like to have; for is not the person who goes to the sacrament with this attitude in reality saying: "Lord, I thank you for all your grace given to me, and I furthermore pray that you would help me still more in my need." This is *sacrificium laudis et sacrificium orationis.*[20] You cannot do more for God, nor render him greater honor.

Therefore, observe what a fine sacrament this is when you simultaneously give thanks for previous grace and pray for future gifts of grace. But who can keep on thanking and praying enough? Consequently, there is no reason for becoming sluggish and lazy; there is only ardent, fervent inducement so that we should readily receive the sacrament with delight and joy. Oh, if the dear prophets and patriarchs had only seen and heard of such a sacrament, how glad and desirous of it they would have been; how they would have been amazed that we should be such blessed people as compared with them! On the other hand, how it would have hurt them if they would have seen that we despise it so disgracefully. Yet it would have hurt them still more if they had seen the accursed,

[20] "The sacrifice of praise and the sacrifice of prayer."

abominable, commercial business which the papists and sophists have made of it with their private masses and similar things.[21]

Therefore, be careful that you do not use this sacrament in any way other than these two ways, namely, as a means of giving thanks and as a means of petition, *opinione laudis et precis*.[22] And beware of the papistical abomination! They make a sacrifice of it in which they do not give thanks for previous grace but seek to win and merit future grace as with a work. Moreover, they do this not only for themselves but also for others to whom they sell such a sacrificial mass, as we heard above.[23] But you should thank God in the sacrament and join in praising him for previous grace, especially for the grace shown you in Christ, and you should desire and petition for future grace in your need. Then you will not be able to make a commercial affair of it, nor a merit which you are able to share with or sell to others. Here every person must himself thank and pray to God along with all others.

This much I want to point out on this occasion to the preachers who do not know better, and I also want to request that they would help to impress this teaching upon the minds of the people and to spread it among them; for although some obdurate, unrepentant, uncouth persons will pay no attention to this, it will nevertheless bear fruit among many. As we say: "A good word finds a good lodging," and God himself says in Isaiah 55 [11]: "My word . . . shall not return to me empty, but it shall accomplish that . . . for which I sent it." But where some such scorners are found who pay no attention to this admonition and, moreover, make no use of the sacrament as long as their bodies are healthy and active, they should be left alone at the hour of their death and not be given the sacrament. If they have lived like dogs and swine, then let them also die like dogs and swine, unless they show very convincing signs of a penitent, believing heart; for we are not supposed to give what is holy to the dogs or throw pearls before swine, as Christ says [Matt. 7:6]. And God himself will also help bring consternation

[21] *Winkelmesse* was a mass said in private for the benefit of individual persons, usually for the souls of the dead. Cf. Luther's discussion of this practice in his *Exhortation to All Clergy Assembled at Augsburg* (1530), *LW* 34, 22 ff.
[22] "With the idea of praise and prayer."
[23] Cf. pp. 117-119.

among such scorners because they are not worthy of the Supper of Christ, nor should they partake of it. I want to illustrate this by telling of an incident which took place not long ago in the city of Torgau; both the clergyman and the chaplain[24] are still available to verify it.

There was a certain man, whose name I do not want to mention, who for a period of six or seven years did not go to the sacrament on the shameful pretense of Christian liberty. He put it off and waited until he became sick. Even then in his sickness he still procrastinated until his last hour came. Now when he began to feel that the end of his life had come, he called for the chaplain and asked for the sacrament. Just as the chaplain brought it to him and placed it in his mouth he died, and the sacrament remained on the tongue of his open mouth so that the chaplain had to take it back again. He was upset that he had to take it back, and when he asked me where he should put it, I told him to burn it. Dear fellow, let this be an example and a sign for you so that you do not live a dissolute life, even though you are now not compelled to partake of the sacrament. If you can despise God in his sacrament, he can in turn despise you in your needs, as he says in Proverbs 1 [:25 ff.]: "You have ignored all my counsel. . . . I also will laugh at your calamity; I will mock when panic strikes you." Moreover, it is right that the person who claims to be a Christian and yet disgraces that name by not desiring to partake of the sacrament, even if he has the opportunity, should also not be able to partake of it when he would like to have it.

Not that I would for this reason want to force or coerce a person to go to the sacrament, or to establish a law or a specific time, as the pope has done, for God does not want to have a coerced servant. Much less does he want to give something to someone against his will. However, I would like to give this admonition so that everyone, on the basis of his own devotion, might constrain and obligate himself to obtain such a valued, precious treasure for the soul. Besides, I should like to show how God rightly dislikes it very much that his proffered grace and goodness are being despised

---

[24] They were Gabriel Didymus and Laurentius Schröter. Cf. *WA* 30^{II}, p. 624, n. 1.

so disgracefully. Perhaps it will help people to learn to seek and receive God's grace without compulsion and laws. No doubt such great contempt and ingratitude deserve greater punishment than this, that a person has to do without the sacrament at the end of his life, and certainly there will be more dire consequences.

Consider yourself what ill-advised, desperate contempt and ingratitude this is: Previously under the papacy, when we were forced to participate in the sacrament, we went along with the crowd to take part in it. We even had to give plenty of money for it and to buy it all dearly, although not more than half of the sacrament, under one kind, was given to us. And what was still worse, we did not have to obtain it for our benefit or to God's glory, but simply to be obedient to the pope as though performing compulsory service. For he [the pope] does not care a great deal about what benefit we would receive or what honor God would derive from it. His followers also did not preach and teach it; but he was interested only in seeing how much obedience he could count on from us. We had to participate in the sacrament to the harm of both our body and our soul, for there was nothing taught about faith; rather, it had to be a work with which one benefited God, a work by means of which the right use, benefit, and fruit of the sacrament were hidden and stolen from us.

However, now that it is not only free, but the proper use of it is also taught, and it can be used for our benefit and to God's glory, we act so disgustingly and disgracefully as though we were not human beings (let alone Christians), but as though we were sticks and stones which do not need it and as though it did not concern us at all. It would certainly not be strange if God were to plague and punish us again! Indeed, because we claim to be Christians and act so despicably and blasphemously toward our Savior, it would be no wonder if God would plague us without ceasing with famine, pestilence, war, and all kinds of calamity. Why then have we been so graciously delivered from such an abominable prison of souls and from the snares of the pope and, in addition, are offered such rich grace? Yet not only do we not express thanks for such deliverance but also immediately scoff at the proffered grace as if it were an unnecessary, unprofitable thing.

For that reason I am being fair when I say on behalf of God: If you do not want to eat and drink of my Supper which I have prepared for you out of deep affection, I shall send you famine again so that you shall get neither supper nor breakfast. If you are filled to satiety so that you do not want my food, I shall make you hungry and you shall not even have your own food. If you do not want the bread of life which I am offering to you so plentifully, then help yourself to pestilence, fever, and all manner of sickness and die in continual subjection to the devil. If you do not want the sacrament of love, grace, and peace—which I bestow upon you through it—then engage in war, dissension, discord, and all kinds of trouble. What else should God do with us? How can he tolerate it that his grace is constantly being despised, with increasing intensity as time goes on, and ingratitude is always growing greater? For he purchased his grace very dearly and permitted his own Son to be crucified for the sake of it. He has to interfere and permit all kinds of trouble to afflict us, even as it has already begun to occur and will continue.[25] We are forcing him to anger, so that he has to suspend his grace and permit his displeasure to hold sway. He can do nothing else in the face of our incessant contempt and thanklessness.

At least I have tried to do my part and have faithfully tried to implore the preachers diligently to help me persevere in this matter so that at least we do not provoke God to wrath excessively. Without a doubt several pious hearts will accept this admonition and make amends. With regard to the others I want to be excused; let them take the consequences![26] Enough has been said to them. The same God of all grace and mercy grant us his Holy Spirit to arouse and admonish us to seek his glory with earnestness, and with complete devotion of the heart to give thanks for all his innumerable, unspeakable blessings and gifts, through Jesus Christ, our Lord and Savior, to whom be praise and thanks, honor and glory to eternity. Amen, amen.

---

[25] On August 24, 1530, Luther wrote to Melanchthon that the printer Hans Luft had reported to him that the plague had been brought by students from Leipzig to Wittenberg. *WA* 30^{II}, p. 626, n. 1.

[26] Literally the German reads: "Let their blood be on their heads!"

THE PRIVATE MASS AND THE CONSECRATION OF PRIESTS

1533

Translated by

Martin E. Lehmann

INTRODUCTION

The subject of private masses was one to which Luther was bound to give attention in his reform program. In the year 1521 he wrote a treatise on this theme under the title *The Abrogation of the Private Mass.*[1] In 1530 he again broached the subject of private masses in his *Exhortation to All Clergy Assembled at Augsburg.*[2] Though he did not deal with the matter at length in this writing, he made it clear that he looked upon the private mass as "a terrible innovation" which he believed could not be justified. For the time being, however, he was prepared to wait and see how the papal church would defend its practice of celebrating the private mass. Besides, there was a certain willingness on the part of the evangelical party at the Diet of Augsburg to accept the rule of the pope and the bishops, if it would not be compelled to accept unchristian articles of faith and could adhere to its understanding of the gospel.

After the Diet of Augsburg a number of occurrences influenced Luther to continue his literary attack against certain doctrines and practices of the Roman Catholic Church. First of all, Albrecht of Hohenzollern, the archbishop of Mainz, renewed his program of seeking forcibly to suppress evangelical teachings. This kind of action by Albrecht was deeply disturbing for Luther because during the Diet of Augsburg both Melanchthon and Justus Jonas had represented to him the archbishop's sincere desire to come to terms with the evangelicals. In response to this representation, Luther had written to the archbishop of Mainz on July 6, 1530, in which he asked this powerful prince in the Church of Rome to use his influence in seeking to bring about a peaceful settlement

---

[1] *De abroganda missa privata, WA* 8, 411-476. Cf. the references to Luther's rejection of the private mass in the introduction to *LW* 36, x, where Luther's words in a letter to Melanchthon on August 1, 1521, are quoted: "I will no more celebrate a private mass forever." In *The Babylonian Captivity of the Church* (1520) the private mass is also dealt with (*LW* 36, 54). His treatise of 1522, *Receiving Both Kinds in the Sacrament,* calls for the abolition of private masses (*LW* 36, 257 f.).

[2] *LW* 34, 22-23, and 30-31.

of the religious controversy.[3] Albrecht had in fact demonstrated an irenic spirit in the negotiations that took place at the diet. However, when in 1531 he proceeded to take stern repressive measures against members of the city council at Halle who refused to participate in the Easter mass under one kind, Luther became very indignant at the archbishop's conduct. In some preliminary notes on a planned *Open Letter to the Christians at Halle* the Reformer complained bitterly about Albrecht: "After the diet [at Augsburg] Satan entered into him, as he did into Judas [John 13:27]."[4]

Second, Duke George of Saxony, Luther's inveterate foe ever since the Leipzig Debate, came out with a literary counterattack on the writing *Against the Assassin at Dresden*,[5] which Luther had published in May, 1531. In addition to this, toward the end of 1532 and early in 1533, Duke George expelled a number of evangelically minded persons from Leipzig and Oschatz. Their expulsion elicited from Luther several letters of comfort.

Third, Luther was concerned about the princes of Anhalt—John, Joachim, and George—brothers, who were at the time inclined toward accepting the Reformation in their territories. Naturally, the surrounding Catholic rulers sought to keep them from embracing the evangelical cause. Luther, therefore, decided to send them his close friend Nicholas Hausmann as pastor in September, 1532, to frustrate the efforts of the Catholic rulers and to influence the three brothers in deciding for the Reformation.

Fourth, George Witzel, who had been at Wittenberg and had become an early adherent to the reform movement, serving for a time as a Lutheran pastor, became alienated from Lutheranism by several unfortunate incidents, and rejoined the Catholic Church.[6] In his inaugural sermon as a priest in Eisleben, Luther's birthplace, he strongly condemned the "Lutheran sect." Though Luther relinquished the task of replying to Witzel's attacks to his colleague Justus Jonas, the Reformer was nonetheless disappointed over Wit-

---

[3] *WA* 30^{II}, 397-412.

[4] *WA* 30^{III}, 402. The actual writing of an *Open Letter to the Christians at Halle* never materialized.

[5] *WA* 30^{III}, 446-471.

[6] Martin Lehmann, *Justus Jonas, Loyal Reformer* (Minneapolis: Augsburg Publishing House, 1963), pp. 95-102.

zel's apostasy from Lutheranism. In addition to Witzel, the humanist Crotus Rubeanus, Luther's one-time friend, who observed the early events of the Reformation movement with interest, gradually withdrew from the circle of its adherents and gave his support to the papal party. All these events that took place after 1530 undoubtedly played an important part in shaping Luther's polemic against the private mass.

Besides these historical developments which influenced the Reformer at that time, there was an internal development in his theological thinking which is worthy of note. Three different outlines, which Luther made successively in preparation for his book on private masses and priestly consecration, have been preserved. They are not the original outlines Luther himself made, but copies of them made by either Veit Dietrich or George Rörer, his two secretaries, or by both of them.

According to the first outline, made in the early part of 1533, Luther planned a polemical writing against the consecration of priests. The plan was conceived while he was ill. His sickness prevented him from doing further work on it. Moreover, the outline concerns itself only with the one theme, the consecration of priests, and does not deal with private masses.

After his illness Luther again addressed himself to the task of working on the outline he had begun. There were particularly two points which he continued to expand. One concern which agitated him was related to transubstantiation: "What if the papistical pastor receives only bread and wine?" His answer to the question was: "Here they themselves must reply."[7] The other concern had to do with the relationship of the consecration of priests to the private mass. While it was true that the early fathers had consecrated priests, they did not consider such consecration to be a sacrament or an article of faith. However, with the introduction of the private mass by Pope Gregory I (590-609), the consecration of priests came to be understood as a sacrament. In Luther's view it was both deplorable and wrong that the consecration of priests had become a sacrament under the papacy, particularly because the consecration

[7] *WA* 38, 185.

often took place for the specific purpose of having the priest say private masses, which eventually became a lucrative source of income for the church.

Luther's second outline is closely related to the first one and, like it, has as its starting point the consecration of priests. Again the question is raised as to whether the priests who celebrate the private mass are administering a genuine sacrament or not. By asserting that the consecration of priests for celebrating private masses is wrong, Luther is compelled to ask whether the sacrament might also be invalid.[8] In the face of this question he does not yet deny that such masses are a true sacrament; rather, because the priests always recited Jesus' words of institution, he believes that the true sacrament had in this way continued to be celebrated even under the papacy.

The third and final outline dealt with the theme *Against the Private Mass.*[9] The shift from the concern about the consecration of priests to one about the private mass meant that Luther's main area of investigation had now changed. In this last outline he also resolved his doubt about the presence of a valid sacrament, concluding that the priest had in fact no true sacrament when he said a private mass. In line with this focal change in the outline, the treatise was given the new heading *The Private Mass and the Consecration of Priests,* so that Luther's attack on the private mass became primary and his impugning of the consecration of priests secondary.

The idea of a disputation with the devil occurred to Luther while he was working on this third draft. This verbal exchange with the devil does not reflect his personal experience but is employed as an effective literary device in the first part of the book. The fact that Luther's plan for the book changed as he developed these three outlines in succession is reflected in the rather abrupt way in which he concluded his writing as well as the remark that the book had become longer than he had originally intended it to be.

---

[8] *WA* 38, 187.
[9] *WA* 38, 189.

The book appeared in print toward the end of 1533. Justus Jonas alludes to it in a letter to Spalatin under the date of October 26, 1533.[10] Nicholas Hausmann, in a letter of December 15, 1533, tells of his having taken a copy to Prince John of Anhalt two days earlier. Veit Dietrich mentions the book on January 1, 1534. Upon Luther's special request Justus Jonas translated the treatise into Latin. The work proved to be an important tool in carrying out the church visitation in Meissen in 1533.[11]

The translation of this treatise, *Von der Winckelmesse und Pfaffen Weyhe,* is based on *WA* 38, 195-256. The work appears also in *EA* 31, 307-377 and *St. L.* 19, 1220-1285, as well as in *Luthers Werke in Auswahl,* 4, 239-291, edited by Otto Clemen, *et al.*

---

[10] Gustav Kawerau (ed.), *Der Briefwechsel des Justus Jonas* (2 vols.; Halle, 1884, 1885), I, 201.

[11] Details about the historical circumstances, the three outlines, and the time of the appearance in print of this work are based on the material presented by O. Brenner in *WA* 38, 171-195.

THE PRIVATE MASS AND THE CONSECRATION OF PRIESTS

Dr. Martin Luther

We have at all times until now, and especially at the Diet of Augsburg,[1] most humbly declared to the pope and the bishops that we did not want to arrogate to ourselves their ecclesiastical rights and authority; rather, if they did not compel us to accept unchristian articles of faith, we would readily be consecrated and governed by them and would also assist in maintaining their rights and authority. However, we were not able to promote or to achieve this goal; instead, they want to turn or drive us away from the truth to their lies and abominations or want to see us dead. Now, if with their authority and consecration they (because they are such hardened Pharaohs) fare as they did with the indulgences, dear me, who will then be to blame? For when I offered to keep silent about indulgences, if my opponents would also keep silent about me, neither pope, nor cardinal, nor bishop wanted to listen to me. Rather, I was supposed to recant immediately and let my opponents shout. What did they gain thereby? Indulgences are lying there defeated, and letters and seals have been battered and scattered. And there is nothing more despised in the world than indulgences; in fact, at Augsburg they even petitioned the emperor himself to prevail upon the pope no longer to authorize indulgences in German territories in view of the fact that they had suffered decline and were regarded with contempt.

In Augsburg this petition caused much laughter, and indeed it is ludicrous, because now the papists themselves are petitioning against indulgences. But when I did this they charged me with being a heretic, condemned me, cursed me, burned [my writings],

[1] 1530.

persecuted me, and caused me all kinds of trouble. Is it not self-evident what they themselves think about indulgences? For if they regarded them as useful and good, they would not petition against them on the grounds that indulgences had suffered decline and were regarded with contempt. Otherwise, one would also have to petition against God's word and the sacraments which are despised daily. But they themselves regard indulgences as sheer deceit and lies, and yet I had to be called the worst kind of heretic and one who is deserving of death because I alone had doubts and engaged in disputes about indulgences, even though at the time I was not at all of the opinion that they were to be done away with entirely or dropped, but that one should preach about them and regard them in a moderate and sensible way. Now, I ask, what have they gained by making such a heretic out of me and by troubling me so on account of the precious indulgences?

First, they have thereby suffered the irretrievable, great loss that their indulgence business is in disrepute, despised by themselves, and no longer bringing in money and profit, as it had previously brought in an excessive amount of goods and money. They have incurred this loss on account of me, and yet they cannot blame me for it. Rather, they have to confess that their impenitent, stubborn defiance and boasting are to blame because they did not want to accept my offer to keep silent. So they got what was coming to them, and all the world is justifiably laughing at and deriding them in the face of such a loss. Second, they have met with everlasting disgrace because as the devil's apostles and impostors, they scandalously seduced the whole of Christendom and all poor souls by means of indulgences and cheated them out of such immense sums of money. If the pope and his papists had not perpetrated any other lies and deceits in Christendom than indulgences alone, for this they would nevertheless deserve to be scolded as the greatest heretics and robbers whom the earth has ever borne. For, tell me, what robber has ever robbed or stolen as much as has been robbed or stolen by indulgences? What heresy has seduced and deceived so many souls or has ever been so widely practiced as the indulgence sale? They wanted to have this honor. But why do they not make restitution for such robbery and thievery? Why do they not set these misguided Christians straight? Indeed, they do not even feel sorry about such things and would gladly indulge in such seduction and robbery forever, even while they remained pious, faithful shepherds who are feeding Christ's lambs.

What if in time the same thing would also happen to their church authority and consecration, so that as the indulgence letters were battered and scattered about, so too both chrism and tonsure would be strewn about and no one would know where a bishop or a cleric could be found? God is marvelous. He has abolished indulgences, quenched purgatory, suppressed pilgrimages and through his word destroyed a great deal of the worship of mammon and the idolatry of the papists. Did he not possess enough strength in his hands so that he could have swept away the rancid chrism[2] which, contrary to his will, was introduced by nothing but human imagination? Well then, if it should come to this, dear pope and bishops, you cannot blame me but your own impenitent, stubborn attitude, which did not concern itself with the matter at the right time but without hesitation pursued its own course in a violent way. You can no longer come to the rescue of indulgences. You have waited too long. Here [i.e., with church authority and consecration] you could still achieve something as long as we are alive; after our death you will discover how much your ranters with their reprimands and blasphemies can help you—just as much as they helped you with indulgences, purgatory, and similar things.

I want to begin with myself and make a short confession before you sainted fathers. Grant me a good absolution which will not be injurious to yourselves. Once I awakened at midnight and the devil began the following disputation with me in my heart (for he is able to make many a night bitter and troublesome for me): "Listen, you very learned fellow, do you know that you said private masses for fifteen years almost daily? Did you not in reality commit sheer idolatry with such a mass and did you not worship there simply bread and wine, rather than Christ's body and blood, and enjoin others to worship them?" I reply: "But I am a consecrated

[2] Luther uses "chrism," i.e., the oil used in consecrating a priest, as an alternative way of referring to consecration.

cleric; I have received chrism and consecration from the bishop, and, in addition, have done all this because of the command to do so and in obedience to it. Why haye I not performed the consecration validly, since I have spoken the words in earnest and said mass with all possible devotion? You certainly know this." "Yes," he said, "that is true; but the Turks and the heathen also perform everything in their churches because of the command to do so and in earnest obedience to it. The priests of Jeroboam at Dan and Beersheba performed everything perhaps with greater devotion than the true priests at Jerusalem [I Kings 13:33]. What if your consecration, chrism, and consecrating are also unchristian and false like those of the Turks and the Samaritans?"

At this point I truly broke into a sweat and my heart began to tremble and throb. The devil knows how to muster his arguments well and to make an impression with them, and he possesses a convincing, powerful way of speaking. Such disputations do not permit time for lengthy and numerous deliberations, but the answers come in quick succession. At such times I have seen it happen that one finds people dead in bed in the morning. He can kill the body. This is one thing; but he can also scare the soul with disputes so that it almost departs from the body, as he has quite often very nearly done to me. Now he had challenged me in this dispute, and I did not really want to be guilty of such a great number of abominations in the presence of God but wanted to defend my innocence. So I listened to him to hear the grounds on which he opposed my consecration and my consecrating.

First, he said, you know that you did not rightly believe in Christ and as far as your faith was concerned you were no better than a Turk; for the Turk and I myself, along with all devils, also believe everything which is written about Christ (James 3 [2:19]), that is, that he was born, died, and ascended into heaven. However, none of us takes comfort in him or has confidence in him as a Savior; but we fear him as a stern judge. This kind of faith and no other is the one you also had when you were consecrated a priest and said mass; and all the others, both the consecrating bishop and his ordinands, also believed this. For this reason, too, all of you turned away from Christ and depended on Mary and the saints, who had to be your consolation and helpers in need rather than Christ. This you cannot deny, nor can any pope. That is why you were consecrated and have celebrated mass like heathen and not like Christians. How then were you able to effect conversion?[3] For you were not the kind of persons who were to bring about this change.

Second, you have been consecrated and have effected conversion contrary to the ordinance and intention of Christ, for Christ's intention is that we should celebrate the sacrament or the mass in such a way that it might be distributed among his Christians and administered to others. For a cleric should be a servant of the church in order that he might distribute the sacrament and preach; all this is clearly demanded by the words of Christ concerning the Holy Supper in I Corinthians 11 [:23 ff.]. Therefore it is called *communio,* that is, a mutual participation, by the ancient fathers, to the end that not only the cleric should take it but others in the community should also receive it with him. Now you, contrary to the intention of Christ, have received the sacrament alone in every instance and administered to no one for fifteen years. Indeed, you were forbidden to do so; you did not have to administer it to others. What kind of consecration and conversion is that? What kind of a cleric have you been? One who was consecrated as servant of yourself alone and not of the church! Concerning such a consecration Christ knows nothing. That is certain.

Third, Christ's intention is that we should preach about him and his death in the sacrament and publicly confess him, as he says: "Do this in remembrance of me" [I Cor. 11:24]. That is, as St. Paul says, "Proclaim my death until I come." But you clerics who say private masses have never preached one word or confessed Christ in all your private masses. You partook of the sacrament by yourself. You have whispered it to yourself. Is this the way you uphold the intention of Christ? Is this what you call a true cleric? Is this the holy consecration? Have you received and used your clerical office and consecration in this way?

---

[3] The reference here is to transubstantiation, the changing of the bread and wine into the body and blood of Christ during the celebration of the mass.

Fourth, Christ's intention is that it should be a common sacrament to be imparted to other Christians, but you have been consecrated to sacrifice it to God. You have not been consecrated as a cleric for the sacrament but as a cleric for the sacrifice. For these were the words the consecrating bishop spoke when he placed the chalice into your anointed hand and said: "Receive the authority to consecrate and sacrifice for the living and the dead."[4] That is what I would call a perverted consecration. For you are making what ought to be a common meal, which God ordained should be administered to Christians through the clerical office, into a sacrifice to God for individual persons. O abomination upon abomination!

Fifth, if Christ's intention is (as we said) that the sacrament ought to be distributed to the community of Christ to strengthen its faith and to praise Christ publicly, but you have made of it a special work which is your own, and you have performed this work without the assistance of others, have given it to others and sold it for money, what can you disavow here? For what purpose were you consecrated, if you did not have a true faith, if you were consecrated contrary to every ordinance and intention of Christ—as a priest for your own sacrifice, as a priest for a special work, and not as a priest for the communal church—you who did not administer the sacrament to anyone, if you also did not preach anything, and if you did not do anything for which Christ instituted the priesthood but did the opposite? Then in fact you have been consecrated contrary to Christ's intention to do everything that opposes him. But if you have been consecrated in opposition to Christ's intention, then your consecration is certainly false, anti-Christian, and altogether meaningless. For that reason also you have surely not effected conversion, but you have sacrificed, received, and worshiped mere bread and wine and have charged others to worship them.

Here you see that in your mass, first of all, no one is present who should and can effect conversion, namely, a man who believes in Christ. Second, the persons are not present for whom you should effect conversion and to whom you should administer it, namely,

[4] *Accipi potestatem consecrandi et sacrificandi pro vivis et mortuis.*

the Christian community or people. Rather, you as a godless, unbelieving priest stand there alone and are of the opinion that Christ ordained the mass for your sake and should do as you say; he should permit his body and blood to be converted, though you are not a member of his but his enemy. Third, the proper intention and fruit or usage which Christ desires are not present; for the sacrament has been instituted to nourish and to strengthen the Christian community and to preach and praise Christ. But the Christian community knows nothing about your mass, hears nothing from you, receives nothing from you; rather, you are silent there in the corner and devour it alone, even though you are unbelieving and unworthy, and you nourish no one with it but sell it as your supererogatory good work. Because you are not the person who should do it, and the person who should have it is not there, and the proper intention, which Christ ordained and desired to have, has been perverted, and you have nevertheless been consecrated to be such a disgraceful, perverse priest, consequently, both your consecration and your conversion are simply blasphemy and temptation of God, and neither are you a priest nor is the bread the body of Christ in your mass.

Let me give you an illustration: If someone baptizes when there is no one present to let himself be baptized, or if a consecrating bishop baptizes a bell instead of the person who wanted to be baptized, tell me, my good man, would that truly be a baptism? Here you must say: "No, for who can baptize that which is nothing, or that which is not the person to be baptized?" What kind of a baptism would that be if I would say to the thin air: "I baptize you in the name of the Father, etc.," and would throw water toward it? Who receives the forgiveness of sins here and the Holy Spirit and other effects of baptism? The air or the bell? Therefore, you must understand that there can be no baptism here, even though the words of baptism are spoken and the water is poured, because there is no one present who is capable of receiving baptism. Is not this also what happens to you in your mass: You speak the words and receive the sacrament but, nevertheless, receive nothing but mere bread and wine. For the person, the church, is not present. So you as an unbeliever are as fit to partake of the sacrament as the bell or a stone is fit for baptism. In fact, you are a mere nothing with respect to the sacrament.

Here you might say: "Although I am not administering the sacrament to the church, I am at any rate giving or receiving it for myself. For many a person from among the multitude, who also does not have faith, receives the sacrament or is baptized, and yet the true sacrament and baptism are there. Why should then my mass not offer the true sacrament, etc.?" To be sure, my good fellow, that is not the same; for in baptism (even if it is an emergency baptism) there are always at least two persons present, the baptizer and the person to be baptized. Often there are many more persons present, and it is a ministry which of itself gives something to others just because they are members of the same community, not receiving something for itself and giving nothing to others, as you do in the mass. In any case, this work is carried out on the basis of the command of Christ, but your mass is not. Furthermore, why do you not also teach that one should or may baptize himself? Why is that no baptism? Why is that no confirmation when a person confirms himself? Why is that no consecration when a person consecrates himself? Why is that no absolution when a person absolves himself? Why is that no unction, when a person anoints himself? Why is that no marriage when a person wants to marry himself? Or can you cohabit with a maiden by force and say that it has to be a marriage, even against her will? I have enumerated your seven sacraments. If it is true that no sacrament can be performed by an individual alone, how is it possible that by yourself you are able to effect this unique and most sublime sacrament?

It is true (as has been said) that along with the disciples Christ also received himself in the sacrament. And a pastor along with the community itself also receives the sacrament. However, he does not administer and receive it for himself alone but receives it with the community or with others, and everything takes place according to the ordinance and command of Christ. But I am now talking about effecting conversion and constituting [the sacrament]: Can a person by himself effect conversion and constitute [the sacrament]? Certainly I know that where conversion has been effected, everyone by himself may take and eat along with the other persons, for it is a communal food. In the same way I ask whether a person can consecrate himself or issue a call to himself, though I certainly know that, if he has been called or consecrated, he may thereafter make use of such a call. Similarly, if he would sleep with a maiden who does not yet belong to him nor is engaged to him, it is doubtful whether it would be sufficient that he by himself alone would call it a marriage or consider it to be such. But I know very well that, if she consents to it and so belongs to him, after this, cohabiting with her is a marriage, etc.

In this fear and distress of mine I wanted to get rid of the devil. So I took hold of the old armor which I had learned to put on and use while under the papacy, namely, the intention and faith of the church [*scilicet intentionem et fidem ecclesie*]; that is, I had said mass according to the faith and intention of the church. For even though I did not have the right faith and intention, the church did have the right faith and intention. For that reason my mass and consecration had to be valid. In this matter he attacked me thus: "Dear fellow, tell me where is this written that a godless, unbelieving person can come forward and effect conversion on the basis of the church's faith and intention? Where has God taught or commanded this? How do you prove that the church offers and provides you with such an intention to perform your own illegal action? However, if people have said this apart from God's word, then it is altogether false. Indeed, you are then perpetrating a fraud in the name of the church, and accordingly your entire abomination should be called the intention of the church. Furthermore, do not try to teach me what the church's faith and intention are. The church does not believe and intend anything beyond Christ's intention and ordinance, much less anything contrary to his intention and ordinance of which I have spoken above. For Paul says in I Corinthians 3 [2:16]: 'We have the mind of Christ.'"

But how should one know what the intention of Christ and his church is except from his and the church's own words? How do you know that it is the intention of the church that adultery and murder are sin, that unbelief is condemned, and the like? Must we not learn it from the word of God? If, then, concerning works we must find out what the intention of the church is on the basis of the word of God, how much more concerning doctrine must we find out what the intention of the church is on the basis of the word of God? Why do you clearly act against the plain word and ordinance of Christ in your private mass and afterward lie in the name of the church, and why do you want to justify yourself with its intention as if its intention were contrary to Christ's word and ordinance? Who has commanded you to lie so shamefully in the name of the church? Because you have been consecrated for no other purpose than for the private mass, that is, to act contrary to the word and ordinance of Christ, contrary to the intention and faith of the church, you are more desecrated than consecrated, and your consecration is much more futile and worse than the baptism of a bell and the consecration of a stone. Therefore you will also certainly not have effected conversion; rather, you will have sacrificed mere bread and wine (like the heathen) and will have sold and given it to devout Christians as a good work, to nourish your belly. For you are a cleric of the belly and not a cleric of God. Who has ever heard of greater abomination, deceit, and damage in heaven or on earth, etc.? This was the gist of the disputation.

At this point the saintly papists will mock me and say: "Are you the great doctor and are unable to answer the devil? Do you not know that he is a liar?" Thank you, dear sirs, for your comforting absolution and answer, for I would not have known that the devil is a liar if you had not told it to me now. If I were a papist and the devil would let me alone, as he lets them live riotously and securely, then I, too, would know how to give him a good answer. For I, too, am one of those brave heroes who is not afraid of ten persons when I am not surrounded by them. However, if they should hear the devil debate they would not chatter with me very long about the church, about ancient custom and tradition. I am well aware of how David in the Psalter and the dear prophets plaintively cry out concerning such debate. And Christ himself (although for our sake) had to heave many bitter sighs and endure much anguish on account of the devil's oppression and harassment.

I believe that Emser and Oecolampadius[5] and others died so suddenly on account of such fiery darts and spears of the devil; for no human being can endure them without God's special help and strength. He gets his point across fast when he debates, for he makes short work of it and does not linger very long when he finds a man defenseless.

He is a liar; that is true. But he can lie better than any ordinary liar and more artfully than a man can perceive. For he takes for himself a piece of truth which one cannot deny and with it increases the cutting edge of his lies so that a person cannot defend himself. It was the pure truth when he brought home to Judas' heart that he had betrayed innocent blood; Judas could not deny that. It was the truth. But it was an invented lie when he told him to despair of God. Nevertheless, he increased this despair by means of the truth so mightily that as a result Judas felt obliged to go and hang himself. No, dear brother, the devil does not lie when he holds before us our manifest evil works and life. In this case he has two witnesses, whom no one can reprove, namely, God's commandment and our conscience. Here it is not possible for me to say, "No." If, however, I should say, "Yes," as I must do, then I am in the clutch of death and the devil. However, he is lying when he tries to force me to despair, as Cain did when he said: "My sin is greater than God's grace" [cf. Genesis 4:13].

At this point, then, the time is ripe for rescue and help from heaven above; either a brother will stand by you with a spoken word of God, or the Holy Spirit himself will be in your heart, reminding you of such a spoken word and saying: "You have confessed and not denied, for the devil has made you admit that you

---

[5] Jerome Emser, the Roman Catholic court chaplain at Dresden, died on November 8, 1527. Luther exchanged sharp polemical writings with Emser in the early 1520's. John Oecolampadius, leader of the Reformation in Basel, Switzerland, died at the age of forty-nine on November 24, 1531. He had sided with Zwingli in the sacramentarian controversy and was vigorously attacked by Luther for his views on the Lord's Supper. Cf. *This Is My Body* (1527) and *Confession Concerning Christ's Supper* (1528) in *LW* 37, and the exchanges between Luther and Oecolampadius in the Marburg Colloquy above, pp. 15-85.

have sinned and been justly condemned, like Judas. But now like St. Peter turn back to Christ, and look at what he has done for you. For Christ in turn has passed sentence on your answer of 'Yes' by his blood and nullified it and it shall not harm you. Apart from Christ, the devil would indeed be entitled to you. But because you are in Christ and call upon him, your answer of 'Yes' has in turn become a 'No,' and you can defy the devil and make your boast in opposition to him: 'If I am truly a sinner, I am nevertheless not a sinner. I am a sinner in and by myself apart from Christ. Apart from myself and in Christ I am not a sinner, for he has blotted out my sin with his holy blood; I do not doubt that. [As proof] of this I have baptism and absolution and the sacrament as sure seals and letters.' "

In short, we are rid of such private masses and chrism and shall let their masters, the papists, defend them. They are now writing many books filled with nothing but lies and blasphemies from cover to cover; they will indeed defend their chrism and mass. In this matter we want to instruct, warn, and console our followers and anyone else who wants to listen. We shall let the papists worry about whether or not there is simply bread and wine or the body and blood of Christ in their private mass. Are mere bread and wine present, as is quite uncertain and doubtful, then everyone must say and they themselves will have to confess that they are the greatest deceivers and seducers on earth. For they have offered mere bread and wine to Christians as Christ's body and blood; besides, they have given and sold this sacrifice and work of theirs as the sublimest divine service on earth by which to reconcile sinners to God, to redeem souls in purgatory, and to drive away all temporal and eternal misfortune, as if Christ were completely nothing and as if we could become holy and blessed and be redeemed from sin and death by mere bread and wine. Tell me, then, how could we regard and call such a cleric in his mass vestments, standing at the altar, anything but a loathsome devil coming out of the abyss of hell? Consequently, what would his consecration mean with which he is consecrated for such a mass? It would simply mean that after being consecrated a Christian in baptism, he would be desecrated by his bishop and chrism into being a devil.

Here it will do them no good to exclaim: "The church, the church and many fathers, St. Gregory, Bernard, etc., have said such a mass!" For we cannot trust or build on the lives and works of the fathers, but on God's word alone, because Christ himself has most assuredly admonished us in Matthew 24 [:22, 24] that such deception would occur and that even the elect might be led astray. He added: "If those days had not been shortened, no human being would be saved." There he shows clearly that among Christians word and sacrament and baptism, by which we must be saved and by nothing else, would be exposed to such danger that no one could be saved through them. Now we have experienced such a time under the papacy. For, although we did have baptism, sacrament, and the word, they were nevertheless so perverted and obscured by human doctrine and abuse (when we had grown up and become more mature) that we could no longer glory in them, but had to comfort ourselves with strange masses, our own works, monkery, pilgrimages, veneration of the saints, and similar matters in a manner no different from the way in which the Turks and the Jews console themselves with their works and worship. As a result of such a perversion and abomination of the papacy, all the world fared well. Even though the elect were seduced in this along with the others, God has indeed been able to rescue them at the end of their lives (as in the case of St. Bernard and many others), even as he rescued Lot from Sodom [II Peter 2:7] and the seven thousand in Elijah's day [I Kings 19:18]. For that reason one cannot rely on their deeds and words in such sublime, eternal matters apart from God's word.

If, however, the body and blood of Christ are present, then everybody must say and confess that they are the greatest thieves of God and robbers of the church who have ever appeared on earth; for the sacrament (as has been said above), according to Christ's intention, is ordained and instituted for this purpose, that one should administer or give it to other Christians as a communion and common meal to strengthen and comfort them in their faith. This our officiants at private masses do not do; rather, they take it and keep it for themselves alone and do not give anything to a single Christian. And after they have thus stolen it from Christendom, they give and sell in its place their *opus operatum*, their own sacrifice and work. In the same way they have also stolen baptism from us after we had grown up (for the children have according to them remained certain of salvation by God's action), for they said that baptism had been lost by sins that occurred after it. In lieu of this they teach us to do our own works, become monks, and serve the saints, etc.; as St. Peter says in II Peter 2 [:18-19]: "They have barely escaped (by baptism and God's word) from those who live in error. They promise them freedom, but they themselves are slaves of corruption."

What kind of peddling is this, yes, what thievery and robbery when I am robbed of the body and blood of Christ which by right ought to be given to me freely, and when in exchange for my money and goods I am offered the sacrifice and work of a godless, miserable man? I would call that robbing me of my nourishment and, moreover, selling refuse for money. Yes, it means robbing me of the kingdom of heaven and, in exchange for my money, selling me the fire of hell, which unfortunately I had previously earned without money and possessed because of my sin. Oh, what a terrible and great wrath of God was thus directed at the ungrateful world, as St. Paul prophesied: "Because they refuse to love the truth and so be saved, therefore God will send upon them a strong delusion, so that all may be condemned who did not believe the truth" [II Thess. 2:10-12].[6] How very appropriately in another passage he calls such times "abominable and dangerous times" [II Tim. 3:1]! Yes, indeed, the times were abominable and more than abominable during which this chief abomination gained the upper hand and seduced nearly the entire world and even took the world's money and goods as a reward for it.

How could we look upon and regard such a cleric at his altar in his priestly office as anything but a thief of God and a robber of the church, indeed, an unheard-of traitor and deceiver who for the sake of the world's goods sells his dirt and hell? Yes, [he is] an instrument of the dreadful wrath of God by which he sends a strong delusion on those who have not received his word with love

[6] Luther is quoting rather freely here.

and gratitude so that they might be saved. How could we interpret his consecration, by which he was consecrated for such a mass, to be anything but this, that his consecrating bishop had consecrated among Christians a public thief of God and a church robber who should execute God's wrath and punishment upon the ungrateful and the scorners? Thus one thief of God has sent out another, one church robber another, until they have filled the church with them and have destroyed everything that belongs to God and is called his own, as Daniel has proclaimed [cf. Dan. 11:36]. The papists should sweep before their own door when they write about the storming of the cloisters and the confiscating of the property of cloisters. Such cloisters are made of stone and wood, the property is a temporal possession (in fact, the pope, cardinals, bishops, and clerics more than the others also engage in confiscating the property of cloisters; furthermore, they previously took possession of them as thieves and robbers, as I shall point out more extensively some time). But here the Christian church is being robbed and plundered spiritually; sacrament and word are being destroyed. They even laugh about this and call it well done; but God has begun to laugh at them in return; this will have a more dire effect than their laughing. Amen.

At this point again it will do them no good to cry out: "Church and fathers"; for, as has been said, the conduct and talk of men without regard to God's word do not trouble us at all in such sublime matters, even if it were an angel from heaven; for we know that not only the prophets, like David and Nathan, have sinned and erred, but also the apostles, including St. Peter (Galatians 2 [:11 ff.]), have sinned and erred, and the holy church itself must daily pray: "Forgive us our sins." We must possess that man of whom alone it is written: "He committed no sin; no guile was found on his lips" [I Peter 2:22]. According to his Father's commandment (Matthew 17 [:5]) we listen to what this man does and says. In the light of these sayings we judge both apostles and churches and angels as well. Indeed, we obey the apostles and also the church insofar as they bear the mark of that man by which he speaks to them: "I send you; go and preach the gospel" [cf. Matt. 28:19]. And again: "Teach them what I have commanded you"

[Matt. 28:20]. If they do not bear this mark, then we do not listen to them any more than St. Paul listened to Peter, Galatians 2 [:11 ff.]. There is no use yelling about it; we cannot alter them [i.e., his words].

It is also useless when they plead that they are not robbing or stealing the sacrament from anyone because everyone may readily receive it in his parish, exclusively under one kind, etc. We want to deal with the parishes later. Now we are talking about private masses, which are supposed to offer the same sacrament as that which the parishes offer, and yet they do not distribute it to anyone. But it is not called a sacrament of the clerics but a sacrament of the church; and a cleric should be a servant of the church and not his own lord in opposition to the church. Now the church does not receive its sacrament in the private mass, as indeed it should, for the officiant at the private mass does not serve or administer the sacrament to it, as he is obligated to do; rather, he keeps it for himself and thus robs the church of its sacrament and in exchange gives it the husks, yes, the filthy scraps, of his own sacrifice and work for the sake of money and possessions.

Here a lay person, or whoever hears such a mass, might ask: "What should I do, for I have heard many such private masses and must yet hear them? What have our ancestors, who have endowed such masses and have contributed a great deal toward them, done?" Answer: We must commend our ancestors to God's judgment; he could indeed have spared some of them, as he spared the children of Korah when the earth swallowed up their fathers, and as was also said above concerning the times of Lot and Elijah. For St. Peter says in II Peter 2 [:9] that God "knows how to rescue the godly from trial, and to keep the unrighteous under punishment until the day of judgment." Because we have been tempted and burdened under the papacy with such abominations as private masses and many other things, and God by his word of truth is now calling on us to leave them and wants to redeem us, it is time for us to stop observing them, do as he says, and flee with Lot out of this Sodom. May God grant it, though brother-in-law, son-in-law, or even wife, and whatever else does not want to come along, remain behind, in order that we might save our souls and not perish with them; for we are now well able to extricate ourselves by means of God's word, just as Lot [was able to do] by means of the angels.

First, a priest or cleric of private masses has no difficulty here; for, since he is certain that such private masses, even if Christ's body and blood were present, have not been commanded by God but are completely the innovation of man, he can easily and with good conscience desist. Since there are many works and services of which you are sure that God has commanded them, do them and abandon the works that are not commanded and are uncertain. Who will compel you to do them as long as you know that God is not angry because you are abandoning them? Indeed, who will compel you or me to believe that the body and blood are present in the private mass? I know of no commandment of God concerning it. For that reason I am letting the cleric of private masses do what he does. His mass does not give me anything; nor does it take anything from me. If he produces the body and blood of Christ, he is robbing them from the church as an arch-thief of the church, and receives them alone and not I. If he produces nothing, this does not affect me; then his sacrificing and administering also have no meaning for me. It is useless, too, for them to drivel that we are eating and drinking the body and blood of Christ in the private mass spiritually by faith. Such spiritual partaking I shall find much more suitable in heaven where Christ's body and blood are sitting at the right hand of God; this is what I have surely been commanded to do and I shall not be disappointed. But I have not been commanded to perform the private mass and it is uncertain. In short, as St. Augustine says: *Tene certum, dimitte incertum*—"Rely on what is certain and abandon what is uncertain."

Yes, I even add, because it is uncertain whether the body and blood of Christ are present in the private mass and because it is certainly a purely human trifle, therefore you should never in your life believe that Christ's body and blood are present; for faith should be sure of its affairs and have a sure basis concerning which one must not and should not be in doubt. I personally cannot regard it as certain or make it so. For this reason I do not want to venture my faith upon it until I see the papists make it certain. Meanwhile, I am and remain sure[7] and abandon the private mass, letting it totter and hang fire, as indeed it totters and hangs fire. God has not commanded me to observe it, to be present for it, or to do, say, or remember anything there. Yet I shall be eager to hear how they want to make it certain. Indeed, they will come trudging along with the words "church, church, custom, custom," with which they also answered me when I attacked indulgences. Yet now they themselves find that neither church nor custom can preserve indulgences, the less so since others have perpetrated worse errors in the name of the church. But St. Peter says: Whoever speaks in the church should speak the word of God [cf. I Peter 4:11]. This they will be able to harmonize with the private mass when the devil ascends into heaven.[8] Now if they do not establish it as being certain, then tell me, what is the meaning of the chrism and consecration with which they have consecrated such private clerics for such private masses? It will be found to be the devil's dirt.

Second, a lay person or ordinary Christian, or whoever hears the private mass, has further reasons for not believing that Christ's body and blood are present in the private mass in addition to the reasons a private priest has. Specifically, he does not know whether the private priest consecrates or (as they call it) effects transubstantiation; moreover, he cannot know and does not even have to know it; for he is not permitted to hear the words which the priest is supposed to speak over the bread and the wine. Consequently, he cannot look into the heart of the cleric to see what kind of a faith is there, and so he must accept it unexamined.[9] Indeed, because it is a human trifle, he should not depend on it at all, as Christ says in Matthew 15 [:9]: "In vain do they worship me; teaching as doctrines the precepts of men." Even if the priest confesses or says that he believes and has spoken the words effecting

---

[7] I.e., of my belief based on the word of God.

[8] I.e., never. Cf. Ernst Thiele, *Luthers Sprichwörtersammlung* (Weimar, 1900), No. 128.

[9] *Im sack keuffen.* Luther says he has to buy it in the bag. Cf. Thiele, *Luthers Sprichwörtersammlung,* No. 464.

transubstantiation, one must not and dare not believe him. For God has commanded even in worldly affairs, when people are dealing with one another, that a decision should not be based on one person's witness, even as we say in a German proverb: One man is as good as no man.[10] How much less can or dare a Christian in such sublime divine matters that concern eternal life believe one person? For that reason he might well absent himself from such masses. Or if he has to be present on account of his official position, then he should let the cleric carry on and he can meanwhile remember his Lord Christ in heaven and recite the Creed or psalms, even as Naaman the Syrian, II Kings 5 [:17 f.], stood beside his king in church and let the priests sacrifice and worship their idol; but, meanwhile, he was in Jerusalem with his heart, worshiping the true God.

There is also no validity in objecting here that a private priest is a public person, publicly consecrated, etc., whom we should trust, as we trust a notary or public secretary; for, as has been said, this affair is spiritual and not worldly. In addition, in worldly matters we also do not trust a notary alone if he does not have witnesses for this purpose. In this way his affairs are also out in the open; they can be seen and heard. But here there are no witnesses; there is only a single person who whispers in the dark and performs his juggling, and afterward says that he has done thus and thus; we are supposed to believe that and wager our salvation on it. No, this is not valid, dear friend. We cannot believe it and we should also not believe it. Moreover, like the cuckoo they give themselves away[11] by calling it *missam privatam*, that is, the mass of a single person, indicating by this that the private cleric is not a public person, like a notary, but a private one. On the other hand, the ancient fathers called it *communionem*, a common mass, to which many in the community come, and not one person by himself receives the sacrament, while the others are permitted to go away empty-handed.

---

[10] *Ein man kein man.* Cf. Thiele, *Luthers Sprichwörtersammlung*, No. 37.

[11] *Da zu ruffen sie (wie der Kuckuk) jren eigen namen aus.* Literally this proverb says: "They call out their own name like the cuckoo." Cf. Thiele, *Luthers Sprichwörtersammlung*, No. 210.

Even if God had not commanded that we should not believe one person's word and work, experience and need would nonetheless compel us to take this position with regard to these secret or private masses. I was in Rome (for a short time), where I said so many masses and also saw so many masses said, that I shudder when I think of it. There I heard among other clever and coarse anecdotes at mealtime courtiers laugh and boast about how some said mass and in connection with the bread and the wine spoke these words: *"Panis es, panis manebis; vinum es, vinum manebis"*;[12] and with these words they elevated [the host and the wine for consecration]. Now I was a young and particularly earnest, devout monk who was offended by such words. What was I to think? What could occur to me other than the following ideas: Is this the way they talk in Rome so freely and publicly at mealtime? What if they all, pope and cardinals, including the courtiers, said mass in this way? How completely I would have been deceived, for I had heard so many masses said by them. Besides, it also disgusted me very much that they could say mass so confidently and efficiently and in such haste as if they were engaged in juggling. For before I got to the Gospel, the cleric next to me had concluded his mass, and they called aloud to me: *Passa, passa*[13]—"Get going, hurry up," etc.

Now we know that a great deal of the virtue and faith of the courtiers has been brought here from Rome and Italy, and both the religious foundations and the parishes have been defiled by it. For we have seen many unscrupulous canons, curates, and beneficed altar chaplains who day and night, without interruption, indulged in a wild, disorderly life of carousing and adultery, and nevertheless said mass in the morning. Who wants to be the guarantor for this and make us confident that they also have not said mass in such a Roman and courtierly manner and let us adore mere bread and wine? I shall be silent about what they believed, intended, and did, even if they had spoken the words effecting conversion. Should we not, rather, here too, comfort one another and say with the papists: We should hear and behold such a mass

---

[12] "Bread you are, bread you shall remain; wine you are, wine you shall remain."

[13] "It is finished."

with the intention and faith of the holy church. Yes, my friend, keep such a faith and intention. Don't give me that advice; I want a faith and intention which say: I have learned the hard way and have been warned by such deceit so that I shall never again be present at such a private mass, or if I have to be present, I shall nonetheless disregard it and consider it of no importance (indeed I am in duty bound before God to disregard it). Thus my faith remains undeceived; I am sure of that.

Furthermore, it is said that at present several papists are Zwinglian[14] and are of the opinion that in the sacrament there are merely bread and wine. They also boast that henceforth they would much rather celebrate mass, because the worry and danger with regard to handling the body and blood of Christ are gone. In addition, there are now very many Epicureans, skeptics, and satirical persons who for the sake of financial gain celebrate mass and flatter the pope and bishops. Yet they severely reprimand the Lutherans and also take an oath that they would let themselves be torn apart before they would believe otherwise than the church does. Because they do not believe in a God, they think such an oath does them no harm. At the same time they mock the entire Christian religion and regard us as great fools who believe such odd and whimsical articles of faith. Among them there are also bishops and very learned persons who are well versed in three languages. What did that poor fellow Thomas Münzer do when he was roaming around in the country and was looking for a place to perpetrate his evil deeds? While he was still in Allstedt he admitted to good people there, how he had been chaplain in a cloister at Halle and had to celebrate mass for the nuns early in the morning. At such times he was often reluctant and, omitting the words of transubstantiation, retained nothing but bread and wine. He even felt that he had acted quite decently and, boasting at Allstedt, said: "Yes, I devoured about two hundred of such unconsecrated honorable deities (that is what he called the wafers)."

Think of what other roving swindlers and tramps have done in

[14] Evidently a reference to George Witzel of whom Melanchthon wrote on October 22, 1533, that he embraced Zwingli's view of the Lord's Supper. Cf. *C. R.* 2, 679.

various places who did their begging at prime[15] mass, and yet were unconsecrated, evil scamps. Some of them celebrated mass with plates in their sleeves; when they covered the chalice again, they stole the paten and put a plate in its place. What a risk was taken by that poor fellow, the Jew, who was burned at Halle in front of the Moritz castle![16] How many more such abominations, of which we know nothing, occurred throughout many lands? For we can assume that we have not heard the half of it. Such examples should warn us sufficiently and cause us to regard with suspicion, yes even to regard as nothing, all private masses. But it served us right when, to please the devil, we wanted to be wiser than God and arrange the mass in a better way than God had ordained, putting in God's place our own self-conceit and opinion; as a result we had to fall into such a bottomless, infinite, most wicked abomination and "a blind man" had to "lead a blind man" [Matt. 15:14].

Furthermore, even if a lay person or an auditor were sure that his private cleric is speaking the words [of institution], how does he know with certainty that he is uttering them in faith? For a cleric is well able to speak the words and to think thus at the same time: "I want to speak these words on the basis of the command. I am not going to worry whether or not they produce the body and blood of Christ; let others worry about that." Who knows how many such clerics there have been and still are? In a similar way a lively fellow once asked whether it was sufficient for a Christian to believe and not to begrudge Christ his divinity, regardless of whether he was God or not. So, too, this cleric certainly does not object if by his word the bread and wine become the body and blood of Christ, except that he wants to avoid having to believe this strongly. What is the private mass here other than a disgraceful abomination which blasphemously seduces the hearers? But even if I assume that the cleric indeed believes that in the private mass the body and blood of Christ are produced, the layman cannot know it and must doubt and be troubled about whether he is adoring mere bread and wine. I am now speaking about the papal be-

---

[15] The first daylight canonical hour, beginning at 6 A.M. or sunrise.

[16] The reference is to the fate of the Jew, John Pfefferkorn, a convert to the Christian faith.

lief, that is, about the belief according to which they believe that it is the body and blood of Christ in the sacrament; godless and false Christians and all devils also have this belief, and it is nothing other than a human idea and delusion. For no papist has the true Christian faith; he cannot have it, because they do not believe that they have grace and life through Christ alone. Also, they do not use the sacrament in and for such a faith, but as a sacrifice and work which they also give and sell to others, dealing with it contrary to every ordinance of Christ.

Whoever has the true Christian faith cannot attend private masses, much less say them himself. For he cannot tolerate it that the mass is supposed to be a sacrifice and good work with which even a godless person can obtain reconciliation with God and win grace for both himself and others. Because he knows that in such a mass the cleric has no true faith nor can have it, he is not obligated to believe that anything but mere bread and wine are and remain in such a mass, as I have said above. For where there is no faith, there the Holy Spirit and his work are also not present. Consequently, in such a mass nothing is administered or communicated to Christians or to the church; therefore, one cannot say that although the body and blood of Christ are not present on account of the cleric, nevertheless they are there on account of those who receive the sacrament in true faith.

For example, there are some [clerics] with such a weak memory, whom I have indeed seen and heard, that they do not pay attention when they speak the words and often do not know whether they have spoken the words or not; still they are not allowed to repeat the words. Here fear and distress resulted. Here the theologians had to patch up and improve the matter with their "by virtue of the primary intention."[17] They console themselves by saying that it would be sufficient for a priest, when he wanted to begin celebrating mass, to have had the resolution and will to speak the words and to effect conversion. For that reason, whether he afterward forgets or perhaps does not speak the words, it was nevertheless his will and intention to do so, and that should be

[17] *Per virtutem intentionis prime.*

enough; therefore, the body and blood of Christ would be present on the strength of the original will and resolution. Oh, dear God, what diverse expedients these evil matters require, and one lie always needs seven more lies so that it might look like the truth.[18] What is the use of continually patching up and improving the fur if hide and hair are not in good condition?[19]

Who will make us certain here that it has been spoken correctly and that the strength of the primary will is that powerful? Where in this instance is God's word or the scriptural basis to strengthen and support the conscience? These are human words, and we are prohibited from basing our faith upon human words, as St. Paul teaches in I Corinthians 2 [:5]: "That your faith might not rest in the wisdom of men but in the power of God." Thus it is also the case when they console themselves that this does not harm their faith even if the cleric did not effect conversion and they would have adored mere bread and wine. Yes, dear fellow, this is what you say: Whoever has the seal and the letters has the guarantee of the truth.[20] Why is not something done so that we might be freed from such incorrect, dangerous, erring, unsure, injurious teaching and work? We can nonetheless readily abandon the private mass as something that we have not been commanded to do and that is a purely individual, fabricated, self-chosen, human doctrine and invention. Human doctrines tend finally to produce such fruits that one does not know what happens to the conscience, to faith, or to God. But they do not admit this; for if private masses would disappear, well then, dear children, the papacy would soon lie in ruins with its religious foundations and altars and all that they are and have, even as [the people of] Sodom perished along with all they were and had.

They have seized upon a saying on which they base their actions. It is called *intentio* and *fides ecclesie,* that is, whatever is done in agreement with the faith and intention of the church is correct. For this reason they claim that, together with the pope, they cannot err; for they designate whatever they do as being done

[18] A German proverb.
[19] Another German proverb.
[20] A reference to papal authority.

in agreement with the faith and intention of the church, and the church cannot err, as they say. For the present I am going to drop the question as to whether or not the church can err; for they do not differentiate between erring and remaining in error. To err does not harm the church, but to remain in error—this is intolerable. Christ himself says that even the elect would be made to err if this were possible [cf. Matt. 24:24]. For the church confesses in the Lord's Prayer that it sins and errs; but it is forgiven everything. That is why there is to be no relying on any of its activity or work, much less on its intention or faith (where it expresses an intention or faith apart from and without God's word). It remains a submissive sinner before God until the day of judgment and is holy alone in Christ its Savior by grace and the forgiveness of sins. This question, I say, I am now dropping. I have touched on it somewhat in other places and afterwards will speak further about it, if God wills.

But in this passage I want to try and see whether I can paint the devil and display him in his true colors. The faith or intention of the church is of two kinds. The one is called, and also is, the true, genuine intention of the church. It is manifest and known to everyone, and is found in and based upon Scripture; an example [is the belief] that baptism washes away sin. This the church considers and regards as certain, and therefore it administers baptism. In the same way the church also holds and intends that in the bread and wine the body and blood of Christ are offered if one proceeds according to the institution and command of Christ. In short, this intention of the church cannot err, for it adheres to the word of God and the intention of Christ himself in heaven. According to this procedure and understanding it is rightly said: Whatever is done according to the intention of the church, that is done rightly. For it is as much as saying: Whatever is done according to the word of God and the intention of Christ, that is done rightly. The ancient fathers and teachers used this to comfort the timid and weak Christians, as St. Paul teaches in the fourteenth and fifteenth chapters of Romans that we should welcome those who are weak in their faith, and that we who are strong should bear with the weak [cf. Rom. 14:1, 15:1]. It is the same as when I am supposed to baptize and my weak faith assails me with doubts as to whether I am truly administering the right baptism by which the candidate for baptism will be rid of and cleansed of his sins; for baptism is such a great affair and I am such an insignificant, poor, sinful human being. Here my brother should admonish me and say, or I should admonish myself and say: Even if I am unworthy and have difficulty in believing that by my baptizing such great things take place, nevertheless I know for certain that the church holds to all this about baptism and means it. For that reason I shall gladly baptize according to such an intention of the church.

To put it briefly, such an intention of the church is as significant as the example of the church by which a weak Christian is strengthened and made better. For even as a bad example weakens faith and causes confusion, so, on the other hand, a good example edifies and strengthens it. For example, if a number of Christians would let themselves be martyred at one and the same time for Christ's sake, then a person who by himself would be too timid and would deny Christ would readily gain courage also to suffer with them. In the same way a person who is weak in his faith can also receive baptism and the sacrament and all kinds of comfort when he sees, hears, or remembers how firmly and surely others believe this and act upon it and how the whole church does not doubt or waver in the matter. Here, however, it is well to note, as has been said, that such an intention of the church should be manifest and well known to the weak person who wants to be guided and strengthened by it. For it should be an example of faith which does not lie secretly hidden in the heart; rather, it should be shown and demonstrated outwardly. I say this on account of the other intention which follows, so that we do not go astray in the same darkness.

The other intention of the church is one which is produced by itself apart from the first intention, and although it is designated or called the intention of the church, this is not what it is; rather, it consists entirely of human ideas, contrived apart from Scripture, embellished with the name of the church, as, for example, when a pilgrim says: "I want to go to Rome or St. James[21] according to

[21] Cf. above, p. 110, n. 7.

the faith and intention of the church." Or another example would be when the pope and the bishops grant an indulgence and say that they are acting according to the church's intention; when they free souls from purgatory with masses, vigils, alms, and soul baths,[22] etc.; when they display relics; when they consecrate chapels, bells, stones; when they consecrate or become monks and nuns; when they establish private masses and consecrate private clerics; when they consecrate bunches of spices,[23] wine, salt, bacon, flatcakes, palms, and the like. These objects, of which there is an innumerable abundance, have all become articles of faith under the papacy because they have the maxim according to which someone can say: "I am doing it according to the faith and intention of the church." Whoever could say or think such words was in the right and could not err; for it is certain that the church cannot err. Here there was no need at all to inquire and ask what the church did or did not mean in such matters; rather, it is enough, even today, for a person to say these words: "I am doing it according to the church's intention." Then everything is right and well done in a Christian way, and it cannot go wrong or be in error.

Is this not a good and wonderful way to interpret and understand the intention of the church? The true intention of the church is an example, yes, the basis and pillar of truth [grounded] in the word of God, according to which every Christian, particularly the weak and the timid, should regulate and strengthen his life. However, the other intention is a subjective and arbitrary human notion, apart from God's word, according to which the church should regulate itself and to which it should hold. This would be the same as if the sow would teach Minerva;[24] here the egg instructs the chicken and the clay the potter. The church's intention is what it holds up to us and teaches us on the basis of God's word; we should follow that. But here we are told that the church should follow what you and I prescribe for it and teach apart from God's word. That is

---

[22] Soul baths (*seel bad*) were baths that were provided for the poor through bequests.

[23] Consecrated on the day of Mary's ascension as protection against lightning, sickness, demons.

[24] Luther has *Sus Minervam;* this is an abbreviated form of *Sus docet Minervam,* "the sow teaches Minerva." Minerva was the Roman goddess of wisdom. Cf. Thiele, *Luthers Sprichwörtersammlung,* No. 457.

putting the cart before the horse! How could such a vehicle go astray or miss the road to heaven? Do you now at last see the true color of the devil and his masquerade, and how, in the name of and according to the intention of the church, he has introduced and confirmed all his abominations as an excellent sophist and master in every kind of deception and lying? Continue to listen. We want to take a still better look at him.

By interpreting this phrase in such a way, they found the right loophole leading out of the church and arrived at a secure, open place which they liked. First, [they liked it] because they did not have to be concerned how they might believe, become godly, live, and act according to God's word in their individual lives; rather, they could say: "What need is there for me to believe and to act according to God's word or to become godly? It is sufficient and right if I act according to the church's intention. Then I cannot go wrong. I am freed, released, and delivered from worrying about how I can come to faith and become holy. At any rate they must accept everything from me as right and holy, if only I use the words 'the church's intention.'" Second (which is still worse), they not only freed themselves as individual persons in this way from the necessary obedience to the divine word, but they also arrogated to themselves the authority and right to oblige and compel all other Christians [to believe] that everything they wanted to devise, say, teach, and command had to be right and regarded by the church as articles of faith. For the authority of the church and its intention frightened everybody because no one wanted to do anything contrary to the church's intention. Here we became good companions and close friends. Then when the huge dam broke and God's word, the true intention of the church, was gone, it was inevitable that a veritable flood of all manner of human doctrines, that is, error, idolatry, and abomination, should prevail.

In this matter you rightly see the Antichrist sitting in the temple of God and "the sacrilege standing in the holy place" [Matthew 24:15]; by the working of the devil he destroys the word of God (as St. Paul says [II Thess. 2:4]), and in its stead has established his lies and abominations. That is, he has seated himself there in the place of God, has made himself God, and has manifested himself as if he were God. What else does this false, fabricated, blasphemous intention of the church afford other than the freedom to live securely without God's word, as they like, and in its place to teach and command in the church what they dream up or what seems good to them? They do not have to do any more than use the name of the church and say: "We are doing it all according to the church's intention." Thus the great robbery and extortion, which were called indulgences, gained ground for no other reason than that the holy fathers sold them and the people had to buy them according to the intention of the church. By name it was called a true, salutary, and great grace; and [because of it] at the very moment of death souls would even ascend into heaven. Meanwhile, the church still knew nothing of such an intention but believed and thought that it would not be saved through any work, whether it was done or bought from others (as the precious indulgences were), but through Jesus Christ, without merit and even without money. Such a coarse, abominable, great deception of countless souls, in addition to the overwhelming robbery and thievery of possessions, rests upon the souls of the papists. Because they know this and still do not humble themselves or repent, this one matter shows very clearly what kind of weeds they are; for in the face of such harm to Christendom they still laugh and are gay. But the Antichrist must behave in an anti-Christian way.

In the same way, in accordance with this intention, pilgrimages, purgatory, the veneration of the saints, monasteries and similar hellish dens of assassins without number arose and were endowed with indulgences; by these, souls were miserably seduced and the world's goods abominably devoured. They do not repent of any of these things but even murder those who tell them the truth. And to return again to our concern, according to this intention of the church, private masses also arose, were celebrated, sold for money and given to others as a human work and sacrifice. But how will they stand the test on that day when the holy church will openly say that it never knew anything about such an intention, but that it was a blasphemous lie of the Antichrist which was made efficacious through the operation of the devil for the purpose of misleading and punishing the unbelieving, ungrateful world. For, praise God, such a lie is beginning to become manifest already here on earth among the true Christians as a prelude of the final judgment, when it will be wholly uncovered and condemned in the sight of all, both the saints and the damned.

Here some will reproach me and say: "In this way you will not leave us a single preacher, pastor, or parish and you will even abolish the sacrament, which has until now been in use under the papacy, and make of it mere bread and wine." For no cleric has been consecrated by the bishops other than those consecrated for private masses. This is as plain as day. But if we have no true cleric or sacrament, then neither Christianity nor church has remained. This is clearly opposed to the article, "I believe in one holy, Christian church," and to the words of Christ, "I am with you always, to the close of the age," etc. [Matt. 28:18]. To this I reply thus: First, the church or Christianity has remained and must remain. This is a basic fact and is certainly true. Second, this too is true, that under the papacy no cleric was ever consecrated to be a pastor or a preacher but solely to be a private priest. No one can deny that. For the person who was supposed to become a pastor or a preacher, it was not enough that he had been consecrated and had received the chrism, but he had to be called or appointed anew and let himself be invested and inducted in order to receive and accept such a pastoral office, or he had to have this office previously as a claim before his consecration. For they also did not want to consecrate a private priest unless he had a claim, that is, a parish, a feudal tenure, or at least his board with a nobleman or burgher, to keep those same residences holy and pure against chastity, discipline, and honor, as the proverb says: "If you want to keep your house pure, then keep clerics and monks away from it."

Here now we want to be discerning as we look at the temple of God in which the Antichrist has seated himself, and the holy place in which the sacrilege is located. This much is certain (as has been said) that the bishop does not consecrate a pastor or a preacher but only private clerics for private masses. Yes, public preaching in the church and parish ministry is forbidden just as strictly after the consecration as before it, and he dare not undertake it without a special new order and call. Therefore, consecration or chrism is vastly different from ordination or a call to the public Christian office of preaching and the parish ministry, even though they have maintained that they have not called as pastor or preacher someone who was not consecrated but have only taken some of them from the consecrated company. Now this action and custom of theirs, according to which they consecrate clerics without a parish and yet do not ordain a pastor without consecration, do not constitute an article of faith for us so that it would have to be thus. We simply want to show at this point that their consecration does not lead to the ordination of a pastor or to a Christian office among the community of Christians but alone to the creation of a private cleric. Now what kind of consecration or priesthood is this, I ask, when the ordinary Christians receive from it neither baptism, sacrament, comfort, absolution, sermon, nor any kind of pastoral care or ministry? For whom are they consecrated and ordained? For the church? Indeed, they are consecrated for themselves and for their belly alone in order that they might be the sacrilege in the holy place. The church will never get to know any more whether they have been consecrated or how they are being consecrated, for it gets nothing from the consecration except a blasphemous swindler who wants to sell to the church his mass and work for salvation. This, however, it does not desire and should not desire.

The same holy church is now the holy place of the sacrilege. Yet, by means of his power and miracles, God has seen to it that under the pope there has nevertheless remained in the church: first, holy baptism; second, [the reading of] the text of the holy Gospel from the pulpit in everyone's native language; third, the holy forgiveness of sins and absolution, both in the confessional and publicly; fourth, the holy Sacrament of the Altar, which has been offered to Christians at Easter and also during the year, even though they have robbed it of one of its forms; fifth, the calling or ordaining to the parish ministry, the preaching office, or the care of souls, to bind and to loose, and to comfort at the time of death and at other times; for many have retained the custom of holding the crucifix before the dying and of reminding them of the sufferings of

Christ in which they should trust, etc.; finally, also prayer such as the Psalter, the Lord's Prayer, the Creed, and the Ten Commandments; also, many good hymns and canticles, both Latin and German. Now where such articles have remained, there surely the church and a number of saints have remained. For they are all the ordinances and fruits of Christ with the exception of the robbery of the one form [of the Lord's Supper]. For that reason Christ has surely been here among his own with his Holy Spirit and has preserved the Christian faith in them.

Nevertheless, everything proceeded feebly, just as it did at the time of Elijah when seven thousand were barely preserved in the faith, so that Elijah himself supposed that he alone was a Christian.[25] For as Christ had to preserve baptism so mightily against so many examples of works and sects, and the text of the gospel and the other articles of faith mentioned above against various false doctrines concerning the saints, indulgences, etc., so mightily did he have to preserve the hearts that they did not lose or forget about their baptism, the gospel, etc., in the face of so many vexatious conditions. He also had to forgive and overlook matters generously when his Christian people fell into sin or were deceived at times, as he had to forgive St. Peter and the apostles for denying him. Particularly, however, did he have to put up with the fact that his poor church, without its consent, had to suffer want when it was robbed by force of the one form of the sacrament. And even if his followers had been misled throughout their lives, he nevertheless at the last extricated them as out of a fire, as for example [he rescued] St. Bernard, Gregory, Bonaventure, and formerly also the kings of Israel and Judah who had led evil lives. He himself acknowledged that there would be "times of stress" [II Tim. 3:1], and the sacrilege would destroy everything, and his elect would be misled. But because they are the elect, they are the children of grace and no sin can harm them, no matter how great, excessive, or long-standing it might be. Their Savior Christ is

[25] Cf. Heinrich Bornkamm's interesting discussion on "Moses the Christian," *Luther and the Old Testament* (Philadelphia: Fortress Press, 1969), pp. 149-164.

greater and more powerful than anything; he remained holy for them when they became sinners.

In this holy place there now exists the sacrilege of the devil; it is so extensively and intimately blended with it that without the Holy Spirit it is not possible to distinguish it from the holy place. But the Spirit teaches us to recognize them by their fruits. Beginning with the lowest rank, there is in the holy place, first of all, the outrageous company of private clerics with their private mass, and those who adhere to them. These clerics do not practice any of the above-mentioned acts which Christ has commanded for the preservation of the church. They do not preach. They do not baptize. They do not administer the sacrament. They do not absolve. They do not pray (except to intone badly and hiss the words of the Psalter). They do not exercise the office of the care of souls, nor do they do anything with the dying; rather, they are a useless, lazy, idle crowd who alone, as they suppose, handle the sacrament and sell it as a sacrifice and good work. In exchange for this they devour the possessions of both Christians and non-Christians. Accordingly, every crowd has its own private bishop. These bishops also do not carry out any of the above-mentioned acts. They do not preach. They do not baptize. They do not administer the sacrament. They do not absolve. They do not pray. They do not care for men's souls and do not ordain pastors or preachers. All they do is consecrate their private clerics. When they have done this, they are thereafter solely worldly princes and lords, even though they called themselves bishops of the church. As much as they are greater and more exalted than the private clerics, so much the worse and more injurious are they in the holy place.

Accordingly, these private bishops (they are called *ordinarios loci*[26]) in each area have their own archbishop over them, the archbishops have a primate over them, the primates have a patriarch over them, and finally, at the top is the pope. There you have the king of parasites! This is the beautiful monarchy or (as they like to hear it called) the hierarchy, the holy Christian church. All these also do not perform any of the above-mentioned acts. They do not

[26] "Duly qualified bishops in residence."

preach. They do not baptize. They do not administer the sacrament. They do not absolve. They do not pray. They do not minister to men's souls. For such ordinary ministries, which God's Son himself and his highest angels have performed and over which the angels also rejoice, are too ordinary and too lowly for such great lords, even though they are called fathers and servants of all servants of God. It is characteristic of them that the greater part of them do not know what these acts and ministries are; some also do not know the Ten Commandments or the Creed from memory, even though children know them. It is a people living for themselves who occupy the holy place and nonetheless do not perform a single service for the church, as they, in conformity with their office and their name, are obligated to do. They might be called the "worthless shepherds who desert the flock," as Zechariah says in chapter 11 [:17].

But, O Lord God, how very wholeheartedly we poor Christians would be satisfied and most humbly give thanks that they have bestowed no benefit or service upon the church, if they would only remain lords and princes and lazy bellies, would live and do for themselves whatever they pleased, would celebrate private masses, consecrate private priests and remain private bishops according to their pleasure, if only they wou'd inflict no harm upon the church, would not destroy Christ's ordinance and word, and would permit others to teach and work for whatever is needful and beneficial for the church. But this is an impossibility. They have to live up to their name, as St. Paul calls them *antikeimenos* [II Thess. 2:4] and St. John *Antichristos* [I John 2:18], that is adversary and Antichrist; also Daniel had previously prophesied that the Antichrist would oppose everything. Therefore, they are not only a useless company in the church but they are also enemies and destroyers. We want to be convinced of this by a consideration of all the above-mentioned matters, beginning with their sublimest and best works, namely, their private mass and consecration, upon which they, as extra-special saints above all other Christians, take their stand and which they stubbornly defend.

First, they have opposed the Sacrament of the Altar, which Christ commanded his church to give to Christians to strengthen their faith and knowledge of him, in this way: The private mass (which to be sure is nothing but a human invention) was made to be much more precious than the reception of the sacrament in the community (which reception surely is in accordance with Christ's institution and ordinance). For whoever went to the sacrament was not able to make it a sacrifice or to perform or to sell it as a work for others like a private cleric; rather, he was only able to receive it for himself alone. Here the private mass received great esteem and high honor, whereas there remained only insignificant respect and almost no esteem at all for the sacrament and its reception, except for the esteem and honor which Christ marvelously preserved among his elect, as mentioned above. On account of the papists and private clerics the sacrament was destroyed. For aside from the fact that they made it more insignificant than their masses, they also did not instruct the people as to how they should receive it in faith for the comfort and strengthening of their conscience. Rather, they made them anxious and disheartened about how they were to receive it worthily, and as a result they also taught them to make of it a work by which they rendered obedience to the church; but [they said] that this work is in no way equal to the sacrifice and work of their private masses, so that they might be able to give and sell these private masses as a means of help to the poor people.

Thus the reception of the sacrament in the church (where Christ was not marvelously assisting his own) became a small work of obedience with which a layman offers satisfaction to the church (as they boast). Of course, this is completely contrary to Christ's ordinance and intention. However, they—the lords of the private mass—have become Christ. They are able to reconcile poor sinners to God with their sacrifice and work. This loathsome sacrilege of the devil is manifest, and no one can deny it. Religious foundations, churches, and every custom testify how magnificently and devotedly the private mass is respected, and, by contrast, how the poor work of receiving the sacrament is regarded as nothing at all. In this way the papists, that abominable company, have not only offered the sacrament to no one but have raged against offering and receiving it. They have impeded faith among the people and have perverted it into a despised, insignificant work of a layman, setting themselves with their sacrifice and work high above and against it. In this way they have taken from the sacrament all its strength and power (Christ has preserved his own). In order that it might become altogether a despised, obscure, insignificant work, they have robbed it of its one form so that their private sacrilege might soar to the very highest point of brightness and glory. Even if I assume that the reception of the one form is right (which it is not), how can they presume to say that the reception of both forms is wrong and to prohibit it as heresy, to drive away the people, and to burn and murder them besides? Yet it is clear and certain in the gospel and St. Paul's writings that it is Christ's word and ordinance. What kind of people are they who openly and unashamedly prohibit, condemn, reproach as heretical, and thus destroy and devastate Christ and his word together with the entire early Christian church which unanimously regarded both forms according to Christ's ordinance as being right and Christian? On the other hand, on their own authority they permit such a damnable, accursed, persecuted article of faith[27] to be foisted upon the Bohemians and upon whomsoever else they wish, as being right and Christian, and so among them Christ must at one and the same time be an angel and a devil and whatever else they wish. This matter alone testifies so clearly that even stone or wood could sense that the papists are the true arch-sacrilege in the holy place and the true church of the hellish Satan, seeking to devastate Christ and his church. What would they not do in other matters, since in this affair they rave and rage so unashamedly against Christ?

You see, this is the first fruit by which one can recognize the desolating sacrilege in the holy place, namely, that they make the sacrament a private mass and do not offer it to the rest of the members of the church. Second, they make a sacrifice and a work of it and sell it to Christians for money. Third, they rob the sacrament of one of its two forms and on that point condemn Christians

---

[27] This article prohibited the use of both forms in the Lord's Supper among the followers of John Huss in Bohemia. Cf. the decree of the Council of Constance (June 15, 1415) in H. Denzinger and A. Schönmetzer, *Enchiridion Symbolorum* (34th edition; Freiburg, 1967), Nos. 1198-1200.

as heretics and persecute them; on the other hand, they grant it to others in both forms as being right. Fourth, they also make the one form a work for the laity, an insignificant, despised work at that, in contrast with their mass, and thereby do not permit them to grow in their faith. I would call that devastating and destroying the holy sacrament! See, this is a little piece of work of the Antichrist who has elevated himself above and against Christ and his word and sits in the temple of God, wherever Christianity exists.

Second, they have raged and raved against baptism to the extent that they have also almost deprived it of all its strength and honor (I am going to be silent now about the fact that they do not baptize anyone in church), even though they do not yet understand to this day what baptism is, and also are not able to understand it. Now whoever has been baptized and has been able to remain faithful to baptism or to return to it, he is a miraculous work of Christ, as all his elect are. The others have had their baptism taken away from them and destroyed by the papal sacrilege. First, they have destroyed it not only by suppressing faith and the right use or understanding of baptism (since these leaders of the blind understood absolutely nothing about it), but in opposition to baptism they also taught various doctrines about works, penitence, confession, and satisfaction upon which their consciences had to rely, and so they had to forget about their baptism. They also taught private masses, monk's baptism,[28] pilgrimages, indulgences, veneration of the saints, and countless similar human fabrications by which to obtain forgiveness, to the great disgrace and neglect of baptism and of the blood of Christ. Besides, some of them are now beginning to preach shamelessly the blasphemous doctrine that Christ has made satisfaction only for original sin and sins prior to baptism; for sins that follow baptism we must ourselves make satisfaction.[29] This is simply to make Turks and heathen out of Christians. It does not take into account that John in the first chapter

---

[28] One of Luther's derogatory terms for the consecration of priests.

[29] In this statement Luther seems to have taken issue with the views expressed in a sermon by George Witzel who, after embracing the evangelical faith for a time, returned to the Roman Catholic fold and vigorously attacked Lutheran doctrines. Cf. *WA* 38, 226, n. 4.

of his First Epistle clearly says about all Christians and about himself: "But if we walk in the light, . . . the blood of Christ his Son cleanses us from all sin" [I John 1:7]. And in the second chapter of the First Epistle of John: "But if any one does sin, we have an advocate with the Father, Jesus Christ the righteous; and he is the expiation for our sins, and not for ours only, but also for the sins of the whole world" [I John 2:1-2]. The Epistle to the Hebrews gloriously portrays Christ's eternal priesthood, namely, how he intercedes for us before God [Hebrews 4:14], and Paul says to the Romans in the eighth chapter: Christ "intercedes for us" before the Father [Romans 8:34]. But what could such leaders of the blind and traducers of baptism understand about these matters?

The very best among them have taught and still teach that works or love give strength and form to faith, as they say: "*Fides formata,*" and "*Charitas est forma fidei.*"[30] And they adduce ever so grandly the statement of St. Paul to the Galatians, chapter 5 [:6]: "For in Christ Jesus neither circumcision nor uncircumcision is of any avail, but faith working through love." By this they understand that faith does not obtain grace and salvation prior to works but through works. Yet St. Paul does not speak here about what faith is or does by its own work (which he abundantly teaches earlier throughout the whole epistle), nor does he speak about what love is or does; rather, he briefly summarizes what an entire Christian life should be, namely, faith and love: faith in God, which apprehends Christ and receives forgiveness of sins apart from all works, and after that love toward the neighbor, which as the fruit of faith proves that faith is true and not lazy or false, but active and living. For that reason he does not say that love is active but, rather, that faith is active, that faith practices love and makes it active and not love faith, as the papists turn it around the wrong way and thus ascribe everything to love and nothing to faith. But St. Paul ascribes everything to faith which not only receives grace from God but also is active toward the neighbor and out of itself gives birth to and produces love or works. So, then, all doctrine

[30] "Faith informed by love" and "Love is the form of faith." Cf. Heiko A. Oberman, *The Harvest of Medieval Theology* (Cambridge, Mass.: Harvard University Press, 1963), p. 469.

that points us to works is opposed to baptism by which we, apart from works, receive grace and should keep it eternally, as St. Paul convincingly argues throughout his writings.

But what is most especially one of the real abominations opposing the dear and blessed baptism is that they boast that with their chrism and consecration they produce clerics in the holy church, that is, a far, far higher and holier estate than baptism bestows. To compare a cleric who is consecrated and anointed with chrism, with other baptized, ordinary Christians is like comparing the morning star with a glimmering wick. So baptism, in which we have been washed by Christ's own blood and anointed with his Holy Spirit for eternal life, as opposed to the rancid chrism, or oil, which was originated by human beings apart from God's word and command, is made to shine like dirt in a lantern when compared with the sun.[31] Yet they are not anointed with such chrism for eternal life but for private masses. For this purpose the tonsure and special dress, and the name "cleric"[32] come to their aid, as though they alone belonged to Christ. Likewise they have, as they imagine, the sign, the spiritual mark[33] in the soul, which no ordinary Christian is supposed to have except the consecrated priest alone. There was also the ostentatious ceremony when a priest was to be degraded; many bishops—at times probably seven—had to be present, even though he had been consecrated by one person alone. Still they were not able to deprive him of the mark by means of such a magnificent degradation.

These are the true, magnificent words and the powerful workings of the devil with which holy baptism has its glory and power weakened so that its spiritual God-chrism, which is the Holy Spirit himself, had to be as nothing at all compared with the natural and transient chrism of the papists, devised by man's religious zeal. Baptism has been unable to consecrate or produce a cleric by means of the blood of Christ and the anointing of the Holy Spirit; but a papal bishop has been able to consecrate and produce clerics with

[31] A German proverb.
[32] Luther uses the Latin *clericus*.
[33] Through ordination the priest is said to receive an indelible character.

his stinking, foul chrism. You godless, damned fools and leaders of the blind, how disgracefully you are here blaspheming the blood of Christ and the anointing of the Holy Spirit in our holy baptism and in exchange are foisting upon us your empty, disgraceful, abominable private consecration, directed toward saying private masses, by means of your earthly and temporal chrism which is nothing but a human trifle and possesses neither the commission nor the command of God!

I want to excuse the dear, holy fathers, and they should be excused, that they, too, consecrated or ordained with chrism and called those who had been consecrated clerics or priests. For they did not in this way consecrate private clerics nor anyone for private masses; rather, when they called someone to the true Christian office of the ministry or care of souls, they wanted to adorn and portray such a calling for the community with such pomp to distinguish them [i.e., the priests] from others who had not been called, in order that everyone might be sure and know who was supposed to exercise this office and who had the mandate to baptize, preach, etc. For basically consecration should not and cannot be anything other (if it is carried out rightly) than a call or a conferring of the office of the ministry or of the office of preaching. The apostles without chrism merely laid their hands on the heads and prayed over those whom they called to the office or sent out, as happened to St. Paul and Barnabas, Acts 19 [13:3] and as St. Paul instructs Timothy not to be hasty in laying hands upon someone [I Tim. 5:22]. The dear fathers augmented such ceremonies by the use of chrism and the like. They meant well. But man's religious zeal and good intention always turn out in such a way that afterward offense, error, and idolatry result if the spirit of the fathers does not accompany and remain with them, as has happened in many other instances. In this case, too, this good intention of the fathers and their consecration developed to the point where baptism and Christ were weakened and obscured by them, and there no longer remained a consecration to a calling or to the ministerial office, but it became a private consecration, ordaining private clerics for the private mass, and now at last it has resulted in a real division and distinction between true Christians and the devil's clerics. For they do not serve the church but are the sacrilege which destroys and devastates everything in the holy place.

In opposition to this you should again exalt and praise your baptism, and, on the other hand, as much as you are able, weaken and abolish the disgraceful abomination. For within Christendom producing and consecrating clerics is not important. I say that the chrism and the bishop will not make clerics out of us. We do not want them to make us clerics nor do we want to receive this [chrism] from them. I repeat, if we are not true clerics beforehand without a bishop and chrism, then the bishop and his chrism can never make clerics of us. He may well be able to make us into masqueraders and carnival clerics, even as he himself is a carnival bishop and masquerader and as boys in a play act as kings, maidens, and other persons. We want to be and to be called nonfabricated, born clerics and want to have our clericalism in a hereditary way by reason of our birth from Father and mother. For our Father is the true cleric and high priest, as is written in Psalm 110 [:4]: "The Lord has sworn and will not change his mind. 'You are a priest for ever after the order of Melchizedek.'" This he has proved and has sacrificed himself for us on the cross, etc. This same priest or bishop has a bride, a priestess or lady bishop, as is written in John 3 [:29]: "He who has the bride is the bridegroom."

We have been born of this bridegroom and bride through holy baptism and thus have become true clerics in Christendom in a hereditary manner, sanctified by his blood and consecrated by his Holy Spirit, as St. Peter calls us in I Peter 2 [:9]: "But you are . . . a royal priesthood" for offering spiritual sacrifices. St. Paul also extols us as priests in the Epistle to the Romans, chapter 12 [:1], for he calls upon us "to present your bodies as a living sacrifice, holy and acceptable to God . . . ." Now to make sacrifices to God is solely the office of the priests, as the pope himself and all the world must admit. Moreover, we are not only his children, but also his brothers, as he says in Psalm 22 [:22]: "I will tell of thy name to my brethren," and in the Gospel of Matthew: "Whoever does the will of my Father in heaven is my brother, and my sister, and my mother" [12:50]. So we are not only true clerics and priests according to our right as children but also according to our right as brothers. This, our hereditary priesthood with which we are born, we do not want to have taken away, impeded and obscured; rather, we want to have it brought out into the open, proclaimed and extolled with all its honors in order that it should beam and shine like the precious sun and blind the eyes of the devil and his hypocrisies and abominations, making his private mass and chrism in contrast with it an illusion and an evil odor, stinking worse than the devil's excrement. For this reason also the Holy Spirit in the New Testament diligently prevented the name *sacerdos,* priest or cleric, from being given to any apostle or to various other offices, but it is solely the name of the baptized or of Christians as a hereditary name with which one is born through baptism. For none of us is born as apostle, preacher, teacher, pastor through baptism, but we are all born simply as priests and clerics. Afterward, some are taken from the ranks of such born clerics and called or elected to these offices which they are to discharge on behalf of all of us.

With regard to this matter, this is the foundation which no one can overthrow. And if the papal consecration would want to do what is right, it ought to do nothing other than call such born clerics to the office of the ministry and not produce new, holier, and better clerics than baptized Christians are. See, this is the second means (as has been said) by which they have desecrated, obscured, and weakened our baptism besides suppressing and concealing from us, so disgracefully and blasphemously, our glorious, eternal, native, hereditary priestly honor. In exchange they have so loftily and gloriously represented to us their dead, obnoxious chrism that we have not feared and honored God himself so sublimely as these their empty masks and carnival play. However, that the fathers have called those who had been consecrated "priests"[34] and that the name thus became common usage—one should, I say, excuse them for that and for many other matters. If their consecration and ordination had been retained, then the name would have done no damage, for they consecrated pastors. But the abomination retained the name, because it was so glorious, and abandoned the fathers' consecration; in exchange for it, it set up its private consecration and therewith dis-

[34] Luther uses the Latin *sacerdotes.*

gracefully devastated and destroyed our true priesthood and baptism.

The third thing[35] [that they attacked], namely, the sermon, fared thus: First, they read aloud the text of the Gospel and of the passion of Christ in the pulpit. As a result there remained the name and knowledge of Christ among his elect, but they were preserved in the knowledge of Christ through the great might and the miracles of God, as we shall learn from the abominations which were perpetrated against this knowledge. And because the word of God is the greatest, most necessary, and most sublime part in Christendom (for the sacraments cannot exist without the word, but indeed the word can exist without the sacraments, and in an emergency one could be saved without the sacraments—as for example, those who die before receiving the desired baptism—but not without the word), Christ has also performed many more and greater miracles with respect to his word. Namely, they had to proclaim the text of the Gospel freely and publicly, not only in Latin but also in the languages of the individual countries so that it would be known among the elect in all the world and in all languages, since they administered the sacrament and baptism only in the Latin language that was not understood and so it was not necessary for anyone to hear it.

Against this [reading of the Gospel] they also protested with all their might, for after the reading of the text of the Gospel they strayed from the beaten path: One man preached from Aristotle and other heathen books; another from the decretals;[36] another brought up questions based on St. Thomas and the Scholastics; another preached about the saints; another about his sacred order; another about blue ducks; another about the milk of chickens.[37] Who can enumerate all this nonsense? In short, the art of preaching

---

[35] The first thing the papists had attacked was the Lord's Supper, cf. above, p. 180. The second object of their attack was baptism, cf. above, p. 180. Here preaching is the third thing impugned by them. Later in the treatise the office of the ministry, forgiveness, and prayer are given as the fourth, fifth, and sixth things opposed by the papal church. Cf. below, pp. 192 ff.

[36] Documents that purportedly safeguarded the power and patrimony of the pope. One of these documents, the Donation of Constantine, was exposed as a forgery by Lorenzo Valla *ca.* 1440.

[37] The reference to blue ducks and milk of chickens means that the sermon dealt with the most absurd and fantastic subjects.

consisted in wandering away from the text so that the people might not remember the Gospel or learn the Creed, the Ten Commandments, the Lord's Prayer, and the duties of their particular calling. All this had to be passed over in silence; rather, the people had to be directed to their own works and merits by means of such deceptive preaching, and Christ, whom they had insufficiently apprehended on the basis of the text of the Gospel, was thus suffocated in their hearts and buried. For this reason the whole world is filled with so many religious foundations, monasteries, churches, and chapels that now one could not erect half of them with the possessions and power of the whole world. False doctrine, however, erected them quite easily and gladly. So mighty and wealthy an empress is lying or false doctrine in the world. Beside it truth and the gospel have "nowhere to lay" their "head" [Matt. 8:20] and in their thirst and hunger have "to drink" vinegar "mingled with gall" [Matt. 27:34], finally receiving as their reward the cross and disgrace. All this the holy place derived from its disorderly sacrilege; for the pope, bishops, and clerics did not check such abuses, but saw them with pleasure and assisted in perpetrating and maintaining them. Tell me, who could have adhered to the gospel in this situation or rediscovered it without it having been a great miraculous work of Christ, as indeed all his elect are?

Now since such raging against the text of the Gospel did not suffice for the devil and could not completely annihilate the text of the Gospel, he proceeded to place his sacrilege not only in opposition to the gospel but above the gospel, as St. Paul and previously Daniel proclaimed, namely, that the Antichrist "opposes and exalts himself against every so-called god or object of worship, so that he takes his seat in the temple of God" [II Thess. 2:4; cf. Daniel 11:36]. It was done in this way: The devil emphasized more powerfully and extolled the command and doctrine of the pope (which do not preach faith in Christ, as the gospel does, but solely obedience to himself in temporal, unrestrained, and trifling matters such as eating meat, holy days, fasting, dressing, etc.) in opposition to all the words of God; and they[38] were also feared more and

[38] The reference is to the command and doctrine of the pope.

held in higher esteem, frightened the consciences more tellingly and held them captive, and made hell much hotter than both God's law and the gospel; for unbelief, blasphemy, adultery, murder, theft, and whatever else is opposed to Christ and his command they have regarded as being insignificant and these are quickly atoned for and forgiven. But when one of his [the pope's] commands was tampered with, then it had to thunder and lightning papal bulls; this they called damned disobedience and it meant [being put] under the papal ban. At these words heaven and earth had to fear and tremble; but concerning sins against God, in which they themselves were drowned, there was not even the quivering of aspen leaves. Rather, they mocked and laughed in their feeling of great security, even as they still do today; at the same time they persecute and murder in a gruesome manner all those who keep God's command in preference to the command of their abomination. He wants to make God and his word subservient and rule over them; this is the manner of his rule and activity without which he could not be the Antichrist.

They have indeed brought it to this point—these loathsome scandalmongers of the devil—that they are boasting, not in obscure language but outspokenly and publicly, that the pope and his church are above Holy Scripture and that he has the power to alter, abolish, prohibit, and interpret the same, as he wishes. This was his trade so to use Scripture, even as a potter might fashion a tile or pitcher or chamberpot, and however he [the pope] fashioned it, it was an article of the Christian faith. They still do this nowadays with Christ's words and his institution of both kinds in the sacrament. He rules over these very words of Christ like a potter over his clay; as he fashions it, so one must accept it, or be burned, murdered, or driven to flight without any mercy at all. For they call him an earthly god[39] who is not simply man but an admixture of God and man. Indeed, they would like to say that he, just like Christ himself, is true God and man. But, God be praised, in the

[39] Pope Julius II was in fact addressed as "a second god on earth" and Pope Leo X with the words "Your Divine Majesty." In respect to Leo X, his official on protocol wrote: "He is among us not as a man but as a demigod." Cf. *WA* 38, 233, n. 4.

face of such a horrible blasphemy the sun has begun to lose its light, the curtain of the temple is torn in two, the earth shakes, the graves are opened, and rocks split [Matt. 27:45, 50 ff.]. "Behold, I am doing a new thing; now it springs forth, etc." [Isaiah 43:19]. By this fruit, according to which the pope has placed himself in opposition to and above the text of the Gospel, one can indeed recognize the sacrilege in the holy place and distinguish between the gospel and his doctrine (I wanted to say blasphemy).

The fourth thing [that they attacked], namely, the ministry, the office of the word and its calling, or the call to the pastoral office or the care of souls (which they call consecration or ordination), this they certainly suppose that they alone possess; indeed, they would take an oath by their king of parasites[40] that no one could effect conversion in the sacrament without their consecration and chrism, or as they say, produce it,[41] no matter how holy or great he might be. For, as they boast, the angels in heaven, even Mary herself, do not possess such power as a consecrated priest has; in fact, not even a dead apostle, bishop, or martyr has it, nor do those in Christendom who are not priests. The power to produce it [i.e., the sacrament] or to effect conversion [belongs to the priest] even if he is not holy, yes, is the worst whoremonger, adulterer, murderer, thief, heretic, simoniac on earth; chrism has such great power. What do you suppose good, fresh butter in the month of May could do, if rancid chrism is able to do this? Because they regarded chrism as being so holy and glorious (even though the priest as a person was in both body and soul an infamous knave), whenever a child or a layman accidently touched the sacrament in his mouth or tried to loosen it from the roof of his mouth with a finger, they scraped and peeled the skin off the finger of the child (who in any case was baptized in body and soul and was holy) on account of the great sin incurred because a holy, Christian finger, anointed by the Holy Spirit, had touched the holy sacrament.

---

[40] Luther employs the term *Ratten Künig* to refer to the pope. Cf. above, p. 179.

[41] The expression Luther uses here is borrowed from the Latin *terminare*, meaning here "to establish" or "to produce." Cf. *WA* 18, 27, also n. 1, and *WA* 19, 97, n. 4.

And it is a wonder that they did not also forbid the entire sacrament to all of the laity because they are unconsecrated, or have not scraped and peeled off the skin of the tongue, the roof of the mouth, and the throat with which they must touch the holy sacrament or at least previously lined and protected them with their holy chrism so that the unconsecrated tongue, palate, and throat would not fall so deeply into sin by touching the sacrament, as the poor finger was obliged to sin against its scrapers and peelers. In this way the holy, stinking chrism had to be glorified with lies and a deceitful appearance to the disgrace and dishonor of holy baptism in order that the sacrilege alone might be glorious in the holy place and might receive the power to raise an evil, dissolute knave to great honors in a manner in which the salve of the Holy Spirit could not do for his true saints.

However, we have shown above how the chrism bishops with their consecration do not call a pastor or a preacher; rather, they produce nothing but performers of the private mass in order to destroy the institution and command of Christ in the holy sacrament, as indeed is fitting for the Antichrist and sacrilege to do in the holy place. From this it clearly follows: As far as the pope and his bishops are concerned, they have completely neglected the call or the office of the ministry or the office of preaching under the papacy and possessed none of them. In addition, they have abolished and destroyed the office; for no consecrated private priest has been allowed to administer the sacrament to the community or preach, as Christ's command and institution demand; rather, he had to stand there and by committing outrageous sins had to undertake the celebration of the sacrament contrary to Christ's command and ordinance —that is, if they actually received the sacrament and not mere bread and wine. For I have also indicated above that there is a danger that in the private masses there is no sacrament but simply bread and wine. I would also not know how to preserve it as a sacrament even if I would like to do so and would be a papist. If there would be nothing more in the private mass than abuse or sin, then I would surely know how to maintain that the body and blood of Christ are nevertheless present. *Quia abusus non tollit substantiam, sed substantia fert abusum* [that is], "Abuse does not abolish the essence, but the essence endures the abuse." For example, whoever receives the sacrament unworthily, although he indeed sins thereby and abuses the sacrament, he still receives the true body and blood of Christ.

In the private mass, however, there is not alone the abuse or sin that the priest is acting and receiving it unworthily. Even if the priest would be holy and worthy, *tamen ipsa substantia institutionis Christi sublata est* [that is], "they remove the essential ordinance and institution of Christ" and produce their own ordinance. For Christ's ordinance and intention are that one should administer the sacrament and preach about him in order to strengthen the faith. This ordinance they abolish and turn everything around. They retain the sacrament for themselves alone, and administer it to no one. Furthermore, they keep silent and preach to no one. Thus they do not strengthen the faith of any Christian but lead him away from faith to the sacrifice and work of their masses which they give to them or sell for money. You see, this is not only sinning or abusing the ordinance of Christ but changing and perverting the ordinance of Christ itself. On that account no one can or should believe that Christ's body and blood are there because his ordinance is not there. It is just as if you would baptize someone without water or with ashes; even though you might speak the right words, such a baptism would not forgive sin but would simply be a mark of good fellowship! You see, this is not only sinning against baptism but changing baptism itself and perverting Christ's intention. That is why there is no baptism. Likewise in the private masses there is also no sacrament in which to believe, because the ordinance and intention of Christ are not there, but a completely new and self-made human ordinance.

In short, just as the furious sacrilege of the papacy has destroyed baptism, sacrament, the preaching of the gospel, so it has also destroyed *ministerium* and *vocatio,* the call and the true consecration to the office of preaching or the office of the ministry with its disgraceful private chrism. But here Christ was present with his miraculous power and has, nonetheless, in the face of the accursed sacrilege, continually preserved the office and the call to the office of preaching among his saints. For the parishes or preaching offices have at all time been bestowed outside of and beyond the chrism by princes, lords, cities, also by bishops themselves, abbots, abbesses, and other estates, and by such bestowal the call and the true consecration to the ministry or office have remained. In addition, these called pastors, who had received such a feudal tenure and office, were also presented, that is, they were directed to the private bishops to be invested or inducted, although this did not constitute the call or feudal tenure but was a confirmation of such a call and was not necessary. For the called pastor would also have been able to perform the office of his ministry without such a confirmation, even as the Maccabees, although apart from this they were native and called priests, nevertheless humbled themselves for the sake of peace and permitted themselves to be confirmed in their calling by the followers of Antiochus and Demetrius, kings in Syria, who were nothing but heathen and their enemies [II Maccabees 13:23 ff.; 14:23, 26].

Such humility we have also tendered until now to our present-day Antiochuses and Demetriuses, namely, that they should have the power to confirm our pastors in their calling, even though they may be our enemies, in order that they might not be able to complain that we were proud and would do or permit nothing for the sake of peace and unity. However, because such humility does not count among them, and they simply want to have us bound by an oath and compelled to submit to their chrism and other abominations, and beyond that want to kill and torture us, from now on it is not going to be as easy for them. Let them keep their abomination and chrism; we shall see to it that we get pastors and preachers on the basis of baptism and God's word without their chrism, ordained and confirmed by our election and call. And although up till now we have tolerated the private chrism, from now on we shall labor in defiance of and in opposition to the papal, obstinate, impenitent, murderous, bloodthirsty abomination; so a pastor from among us, to show the difference between his former private consecration and our call, will have to rub his anointed fingers with lye, salt, and soap, and wash away the imprint or sign of the Antichrist and let his tonsure grow. If the private consecrators or bishops do not want to regard our called pastors as consecrated, that is indeed up to them; we are no longer going to beg them to do so; let them heed this warning.

Even the pope himself has ordered in his spiritual statutes (though they were taken from the ancient fathers), that one should regard the consecration or ordination performed by heretics as a true consecration and not reconsecrate those who had been consecrated by heretics. Now we Lutherans are not heretics; this the papists themselves must admit. For that reason they should regard our consecrating and ordaining as valid (even according to their own papal statute and command); they do not deserve any special thanks for it. For we have, God be praised, the word of God in its purity and certainty, as the pope does not have it. However, where God's word is pure and certain, there everything else must be: God's kingdom, Christ's kingdom, the Holy Spirit, baptism, the sacrament [of the Lord's Supper], the office of the ministry, the office of preaching, faith, love, the cross, life and salvation, and everything the church should have, as Christ says: "We will come to him and make our home with him" [John 14:23]; "And lo, I am with you always, to the close of the age" [Matt. 28:20]. But if the papal abomination does not want to regard our word as the true word, this does not concern us. They indeed know otherwise in their conscience. We are nevertheless sure that we have the word of God.

If they claim that the heretics who consecrated in this way were bishops and that is why the pope and the fathers have allowed their consecration to be valid, this is true. They were bishops, not princes or lords; but as St. Jerome and St. Paul prove, bishop and pastor were one and the same thing.[42] Such heretics and other bishops, too, often did not have as large a parish or, as one now calls it, bishopric, as at the present a pastor has at Torgau, Leipzig, or Grimma. For every separate city had a bishop, even as they now have pastors. St. Augustine, who was consecrated or ordained a preacher by his pastor or bishop, Valerius, and after his death be-

[42] Jerome, *Commentary on the Epistle to Titus* (*Commentariorum in epistolam ad Titum*), Titus 1:7 (*MPL* 26, 562): "The presbyter is the same as the bishop . . . . the bishops should have known that they were greater according to custom rather than according to the truth of the Lord's ordinance."

came bishop in his stead, did not have a larger parish than our parish at Wittenberg, if indeed it was as large. Yet this same small bishop or pastor at Hippo, St. Augustine, is greater within Christendom than any pope, cardinal, or archbishop ever was or will be. And the same little pastor or bishop, St. Augustine, consecrated and ordained many pastors or bishops in his little parish (since they were not yet consecrating bishops or bishops of princely ranks but nothing but pastors), who were sought and called by other cities, as we ordain and send them out of our parish at Wittenberg to other cities which want them and do not have any pastors among them. For ordaining should consist of, and be understood as, calling to and entrusting with the office of the ministry; Christ and his church, wherever it is in the world, have and must have this power, without chrism and tonsure, just as they must have the word, baptism, the sacrament [of the Lord's Supper], the Spirit, and faith.

At this point it is again necessary to note the difference between the sacrilege and the holy place. For the private lords go too far with their consecration and chrism; they claim to be the persons who produce the sacrament or effect conversion *quasi ex opere operato,* that is, they boast of possessing such power, by virtue of their chrism or consecration, that by speaking over the bread and wine, forthwith the body and blood of Christ must be present (although by the working of God). Therefore, they also boast that neither an angel nor the Mother of God, nor a single saint on earth could effect conversion[43] because they have not been consecrated with chrism and have no tonsure. However, if one demands from them an argument which could prove that God has tied his power in this manner to their chrism (of which God knows nothing) and to their *opus operatum,*[44] they direct us far from the beaten path, saying: "It is the intention of the church." This suffices; they need no further proof.

For this reason you should note and know that such a doctrine is the doctrine of the abomination, that is, that a priest on the strength of chrism or consecration changes bread into the body of

[43] For documentation of such a view, see *WA* 38, 238, n. 2, where relevant medieval sources are quoted.
[44] "The efficacy of the action."

Christ, *ex opere operato,* by means of his speaking or action. It is all such an ugly lie and odor as the chrism itself is. The holy place or church teaches that neither priests nor Christians produce a single sacrament; even the holy Christian church itself does not do so. Our office is called and ought to be not one of producing or effecting conversion but solely one of offering and bestowing. For example, a pastor or preacher does not produce the gospel and by means of his preaching or office his word does not become the gospel; otherwise, everything he would say would have to be the gospel. He only offers and bestows the gospel through his preaching. The gospel is there beforehand and must be there beforehand; this gospel our Lord Christ has produced, brought about, and left behind as a legacy. First he imprinted it upon the apostles' hearts and then, through the apostles' successors he continued to imprint it upon more and more Christian hearts, besides also letting it be preserved visibly in books and pictures. Thus there remains nothing for the office of the ministry or the office of preaching other than this single work, namely, to bestow or to present the gospel which Christ commanded to be preached. The pope and his abominations have indeed produced many doctrines out of their head, but they are not called God's word or gospel.

Thus the baptizer produces no baptism, but Christ has produced it beforehand. The baptizer solely offers and bestows it: For there we have Christ's ordinance, which is, as St. Augustine says: "The word is added to the element, and it becomes a sacrament."[45] When one takes water and adds his word to it, then it is a baptism, as he commands in Matthew, the last chapter: "Go therefore and make disciples of all nations, baptizing them in the name of the Father and of the Son and of the Holy Spirit" [Matt. 28:19]. This command and institution do it; they cause the water and the word to be a baptism. Our work or action *ex opere operato* does nothing; for it is not therefore called a baptism because I am baptizing or doing the work, even if I were holier than St. John or an angel; but my baptizing is called a baptism because Christ's word,

[45] Augustine, *On the Gospel of St. John* (*In Ioannis evangelium*), Tractate 80, 3 (*MPL* 35, 1840).

command, and institution have ordained that water and his word should be a baptism. This ordinance of his, I say, and not our action or *opus operatum* constitutes baptism. Our action only offers and bestows such baptism, ordained and constituted by Christ's command and institution. For this reason he alone is and remains the one true, eternal baptizer who administers his baptism daily through our action or service until the day of judgment. So our baptizing should properly be called a presenting or bestowing of the baptism of Christ, just as our sermon is a presenting of the word of God. It could, however, be called our sermon or baptism, yet with the understanding that it does not become a baptism or God's word by our actions but that we have received it from Christ and give or administer it to others. Similarly, a servant may call the bread which he distributes his bread; yet he must understand it to be his lord's bread and must let this be known to be the case.

So, too, it is not by our doing, speaking, or work that bread and wine become Christ's body and blood, much less is it by the chrism or consecration; rather, it is caused by Christ's ordinance, command, and institution. For Christ commanded (as St. Paul says in I Corinthians 11 [:22 ff.]) that when we meet together and speak his words with reference to bread and wine, then it is to be his body and blood. Here, too, we do nothing more than administer and bestow bread and wine along with his words according to his command and institution. This command and institution of his have the power to accomplish this, that we do not present and receive simply bread and wine but his body and blood, as his words indicate: "This is my body, this is my blood." So it is not our work or speaking but the command and ordinance of Christ which make the bread the body and the wine the blood, beginning with the first Lord's Supper and continuing to the end of the world, and it is administered daily through our ministry or office. We hear these words, "This is my body," not as spoken concerning the person of the pastor or the minister but as coming from Christ's own mouth who is present and says to us: "Take, eat, this is my body." We do not hear and understand them otherwise and know indeed that the pastor's or the minister's body is not in the bread nor is it being administered. Consequently, we also do not hear the command

and ordinance according to which he says, "Do this in remembrance of me," as words spoken concerning the pastor's person; but we hear Christ himself through the pastor's mouth speaking to us and commanding that we should take bread and wine at his word, "This is my body," etc., and in them according to his command eat his body and drink his blood.

For we must believe and be sure of this, that baptism does not belong to us but to Christ, that the gospel does not belong to us but to Christ, that the office of preaching does not belong to us but to Christ, that the sacrament [of the Lord's Supper] does not belong to us but to Christ, that the keys, or forgiveness and retention of sins, do not belong to us but to Christ. In summary, the offices and sacraments do not belong to us but to Christ, for he has ordained all this and left it behind as a legacy in the church to be exercised and used to the end of the world; and he does not lie or deceive us. Therefore, we cannot make anything else out of it but must act according to his command and hold to it. However, if we alter it or improve on it, then it is invalid and Christ is no longer present, nor is his ordinance. I do not want to say, as the papists do, that neither an angel nor Mary could effect conversion, etc.; but I do say that even if the devil himself came (if he would be so pious that he wanted to or could do so), and let us suppose that I found out afterward that the devil had inveigled his way into the office by stealth or, having assumed the form of a man, let himself be called to the office of the ministry, and publicly preached the gospel in the church, baptized, celebrated mass, absolved, and exercised and administered such offices and sacraments, as a pastor would, according to the command of Christ—then we would for all that have to admit that the sacraments were valid, that we had received a valid baptism, had heard the true gospel, obtained true absolution, and had participated in the true sacrament of the body and blood of Christ.

For our faith and the sacrament must not be based on the person, whether he is godly or evil, consecrated or unconsecrated, called or an impostor, whether he is the devil or his mother, but upon Christ, upon his word, upon his office, upon his command and ordinance; where these are in force, there everything will be carried out properly, no matter who or what the person might happen to be. If we would consider the person, then the preaching, baptism, and Lord's Supper which Judas and all his descendants have performed and administered and would still be performing and administering according to Christ's command, would be nothing but the devil's preaching, baptism, and Lord's Supper, for it would then be administered and given to us by the devil's members. But because the office, word, and sacrament are the ordinance of Christ and not of Judas or the devil, we permit Judas and the devil to remain Judas and the devil, and yet accept through them the blessings of Christ. For when Judas went to the devil he did not take his apostolic office along with him but left it behind, and Matthias received it in his stead. Offices and sacraments always remain in the church; persons are daily subject to change. As long as we call and induct into the offices persons who can administer them, then the offices will surely continue to be exercised. The horse has been bridled and saddled; if you place on it even a naked lad who can ride, the horse will proceed as well as if the emperor or the pope were riding it.

In my youth I heard a story of how at one time the preacher suddenly took ill just when he was supposed to preach. At that moment a person came to him and offered to preach for him, and hastily paged through a book and sketched a sermon. Still, he preached so excellently and earnestly that the entire congregation wept. At the close of the service he said: "Do you want to know who I am? I am the devil and have preached so earnestly to you in order that I might be able to accuse you all the more justly and severely on the day of judgment to your greater condemnation, if you have not lived according to it." Whether this story is true or not, I do not care to investigate; but I know full well that it is not far from the truth and deals with the principal point in the right way, namely, that the devil can indeed possess and bestow the word, the offices, and the sacraments of Christ; for he can disguise "himself as an angel of light" [II Cor. 11:14] and as the majestic God himself, Matthew 4 [:8-10]. I would not want to vouch for the fact that the devil has never been a pastor or a preacher. Indeed, very horrible things have taken place at the hands of some pastors and clerics by means of magic and trickery and similar transactions of the devil.

The same rule, that our activity or work does not accomplish anything but solely God's command and ordinance, applies also in the realm of nature. For example, when we plow, sow, and plant, we are doing the work we have been commanded to do in Genesis 3 [:17 ff.]. However, our particular work does not produce one little grain; rather, it is the command and ordinance of God. He says to the earth, Genesis 1 [:11]: "Let the earth put forth vegetation, plants yielding seed, and fruit trees bearing fruit in which is their seed. . . ." It is as St. Paul says in I Corinthians 3 [:7]: "So neither he who plants nor he who waters is anything, but only God who gives the growth." Whether now the devil or man, a knave or a godly person, does such a work and plants, sows, or waters, God's ordinance and command nevertheless are in force in and of themselves, and the earth brings forth its fruit. For instance, man and woman in a natural way become one body, as God has commanded and created us. However, as a result of this same work there never will be fruit or a child but it will be as a result of the command and ordinance of God who says: "Be fruitful and multiply" [Genesis 1:28]. Now even if the devil brings man and woman together, as happens in adultery or whoredom, nevertheless, God's ordinance is in force and fruit or a child results. When a knave, a bastard, or a thief falls heir to the ancestral estate of other people, all the property has as much value as if the rightful heir would possess it. The same rule also applies here as far as the sacraments are concerned: We join the water to the word, as he commands us to do; however, not this action of ours, but Christ's command and ordinance make it a baptism. According to his command we join bread and wine to the word of Christ; however, not this action of ours, but Christ's word and ordinance effect the change. Now if in this instance the devil or his follower would observe the ordinance of Christ and act according to it, it would nonetheless be the true baptism and sacrament; for Christ does not become a liar or deceiver of his church on account of the devil or of evil people, but baptizes persons and gives them his body and blood, no matter whose hand it is or what kind of a hand it is by which he does it.

The papists themselves admit that baptism, administered as a joke or playfully, is a true baptism, as is written in the *Ecclesiastical History* of St. Athanasius. According to this account he was playing with his companions and children on the seashore and baptized them, as he had seen it done in the church by the bishop. Bishop Alexander regarded it as a true baptism, and did not baptize the same children again. One can read about similar matters in the legends according to which several real buffoons wanted to please the heathen in a play and mock the Christians' baptism, as if it were a foolish, ludicrous belief to want to become holy through water, etc. However, in the middle of the play there appeared to one of them a writing which consisted of these words of St. Paul to the Ephesians, chapter 4 [:5 ff.]: "One Lord, one faith, one baptism, one God and Father of us all," etc. On the basis of these words he became a believer and accepted the mock baptism as a true baptism, took it seriously, and freely confessed Christ. However, when the heathen seized them all, supposing that these buffoons had produced the play in honor of the Christians and to spite the heathen, the rest reviled this one companion of theirs and said he had gone mad. However, he adhered to his baptism and faith, letting himself be martyred for it. Thus he went to heaven after the play was over.

However, the papists are blind and leaders of the blind. They consider only their own person and work, just as if the sacrament had to take place simply because they are such persons and perform such works. They do not inquire about the ordinance or institution of Christ. Yet our person and our work cannot add to it; the ordinance of Christ alone must do it. Chrism, tonsure, chasuble, and similar pomp are of no help. For this reason they themselves do not know and also cannot know what they are doing in their masses. Let me once and for all answer the question I raised above, how one should regard the pastor in the papacy because they have all been consecrated in no other way than by private bishops for private masses. This is what you should do: You should esteem and look upon his chrism and private consecration as nothing, for it certainly is nothing, and does not help or serve the church and you. You should, rather, consider the fact that he possesses the office of the ministry which is not his but Christ's office. Also do not let yourself be led astray as to whether he has been properly called or whether he has bought or forced himself into his office, how he obtained it, whether standing on his head or on his feet, whether he is Judas or St. Peter; do not concern yourself with that at all. Distinguish between the office and the person, and between the holy place and the sacrilege.

Very well then, he is a pastor, and Christ has thus preserved his holy, beloved office of the ministry in the papacy with its sacrilege. When he preaches the text of the gospel purely, then say: "This is the holy place of Christ." When, besides this, he preaches a different doctrine contrary to the gospel, then say: "This is the sacrilege of the devil who destroys the word." When he baptizes and in this adheres to the ordinance of Christ (even if he does not understand baptism correctly), then say: "The baptism is valid on account of Christ's ordinance, not on account of the pastor or his work." When he absolves you in private or public confession or forgives your sins, even though there is not a papist in the world who might rightly understand what the forgiveness of sins means, for they do not know (as all their books show) whether they forgive guilt or punishment, do not be concerned about this; if he adheres to the words and form and absolves you in the name of Christ, then say: "This holy, comforting absolution is granted to me by my Lord Christ himself through his keys which he has given to the church." If, in addition to this, he imposes upon you penitence according to which you should make satisfaction for your sins, then think of it in this way: "You see, this is the sacrilege which desires to destroy for me the absolution of Christ, as if Christ were to sell me his grace on account of my merit. I want to make amends to my neighbor before the world wherever I have injured him, but before God my satisfaction is founded on Christ himself with his precious blood. I shall abide by this and rely upon it."

When the pastor celebrates mass diligently, note this difference: Insofar as he observes the ordinance and institution of Christ and also administers the sacrament to others, be assured that Christ's body and blood are certainly there on account of Christ's ordinance and not on account of the pastor's work or holiness. Insofar, however, as he does not observe the ordinance and intention of Christ but changes and perverts them, it is not necessary for you to believe that it is Christ's body and blood. In fact, you are not to believe it,[46] even as has been said above concerning other private masses. For whether it be high mass or early mass, or whatever they may be called, they are private masses because nothing of the sacrament is given to the church. For here you clearly have Christ's ordinance and institution: "Do this in remembrance of me." What are we to do? And what does "this" mean? It means that he is to do it and shows what he is doing with words and actions, in this way: He "took bread, and gave thanks, and broke it, and gave it to his disciples and said: 'Take, eat; this is my body given for you. Do this in remembrance of me.' In the same way also he took the cup, and gave thanks, and gave it to them, saying: 'Drink of it, all of you. This is the cup of the New Testament in my blood, which is poured out for you for the forgiveness of sins. Do this, as often as you drink it, in remembrance of me.' "[47] If Christ's ordinance is to be kept (as he says, "Do this"), then we must not alone take the bread and wine with the words of Christ but also give and administer them to others.

Therefore, when a pastor at Easter time, or at any other time during the year, has administered the one kind to the people from the altar, this is truly the sacrament, even though it has been only half of it; the other kind, which he has not administered but has drunk by himself alone, I do not consider to be the sacrament (until they prove it), but simply wine. Thus they have not only robbed the laity of half of the sacrament and even while they were committing such a robbery, have nevertheless celebrated mass, as if it were no sin, but they also have robbed themselves along with others, and have even disgracefully fooled and deceived themselves

[46] By making this statement Luther seemingly invited the suspicion of embracing a Zwinglian view of the Lord's Supper.

[47] A conflation of texts from I Cor. 11:23-25; Matt. 26:26-28; Mark 14:22-24; Luke 22:19-20.

by taking the wine as a sacrament. How can their bad excuse pass muster, according to which they say that Christ has given both kinds in the Lord's Supper to the priests alone, and after that the church, apart from Christ's command and by virtue of its own mercy, communicated the one kind to the laity? At this point it seems to be apparent that they also gave to the priests and to themselves no more than half of the sacrament. Even when the priests during Passion Week or otherwise during the year received the sacrament and did not themselves celebrate mass, they, just like the laity, had to do without the other kind, without regard and consideration for the fact that they themselves say that Christ has commanded the priests to take both kinds. This is how well their own words and deeds agree with one another! In short, they may make of the private mass whatever they want; we do not want to and should not regard it as a sacrament but as an abomination and destruction of the sacrament because it alters Christ's ordinance and offers nothing to both priests and laity, or offers only half of it once a year.

The church or ordinary Christians who have been unable to receive both kinds are indeed to be excused as the ones who have been betrayed and led astray by the Antichrist who has allowed only one kind to be given them. In the church the faith has nevertheless remained firm and pure that in the sacrament Christ has instituted and commanded that all Christians should receive his body and blood; all this is proved by many hymns and poems, particularly by the congregational hymn, "God be praised and blessed, who himself has nourished us with his flesh and blood," and later, "Lord, by your holy body, which came from your mother Mary, and your holy blood, help us, Lord, in every need."[48] With this and similar hymns which were sung during [the administration of] the sacrament, in fact, during the procession and in churches, the church has in public, loudly and urgently, deplored the Antichrist and the rapacious private clerics. In this way it confessed its faith publicly that Christ has ordained and given to it both his body and his blood as food, and that it is entitled according to Christ's

[48] Cf. *LW* 53, 253, where this hymn appears in translation.

command to receive them, as it believes, confesses, and sincerely desires in this hymn. Indeed, by means of such true faith, desire, and free confession in opposition to the church's thieves and robbers in the papacy, Christ has preserved his elect, and through the forgiveness of sin has not imputed to them their ignorance that they had to make use of the one kind only, as he pardoned many shortcomings of the apostles.

And what must the Christians do who are held captive in Turkey? They cannot receive the sacrament and have to be content with their faith and desire which they have for the sacrament and the ordinance of Christ, just as those who die before baptism are nevertheless saved by their faith and desire for baptism. What did the children of Israel do in Babylon when they were unable to have public worship at Jerusalem except in faith and in sincere desire and longing? Therefore, even if the church would have been robbed completely of the sacrament by the pope, still, because the ordinance of Christ remained in their hearts with faith and desire, it would nevertheless have been preserved thereby, as indeed now in our time there are many who outwardly do without the sacrament for they are not willing to honor and strengthen the pope's abomination under one kind. For Christ's ordinance and faith are two works of God which are capable of doing anything.

However, look at the hymn which was mentioned. Is it not a Christian, pure, and excellent confession fashioned by a right spirit? It bears witness to the fact that at the time when it was written the laity received both kinds. It says: "Who himself has nourished us with his flesh and with his blood." Who are those who say "us"? They are laymen who have sung it in German and still sing it and surely confess that they have been nourished not only with one kind, with his flesh (which they indeed knew, as the clever papists today propose to us, cannot be without blood), but also with the other kind, with his blood. It is especially sound and Christian when they say that Christ himself has nourished them; not the pastor or priest but Christ himself is the one who gives nourishment, who through his ordinance and not through the priest's work gives us his body and blood; similarly, they do not boast of it as a sacrifice or good work, as the sacrilege maintains and sells it to others, but as food for their souls, etc. But I must cease praising this hymn. Otherwise, the abominable, impenitent blasphemers, if they found out about my praising it, would perhaps henceforth also prohibit the hymn which they themselves and all their forebears have sung, certainly many years before Luther came on the scene, even as they otherwise prohibit many hymns in which nothing but God's word and our faith are sung about, so that they may palpably prove themselves to be the true sacrilege in the holy place. Or they will (according to their new art) interpret flesh and blood as one kind, just as, contrariwise, in the Lord's Supper they interpret one kind as being both. For however they alter it and do it, it is right; but however God himself does it and ordains, it is wrong. Let them alone. We are singing it in our church with joy and with a simple, certain meaning about both kinds, flesh and blood, as the words clearly say and declare.

For, God be praised, in our churches we can show a Christian a true Christian mass according to the ordinance and institution of Christ, as well as according to the true intention of Christ and the church. There our pastor, bishop, or minister in the pastoral office, rightly and honorably and publicly called, having been previously consecrated, anointed, and born in baptism as a priest of Christ, without regard to the private chrism, goes before the altar. Publicly and plainly he sings what Christ has ordained and instituted in the Lord's Supper. He takes the bread and wine, gives thanks, distributes and gives them to the rest of us who are there and want to receive them, on the strength of the words of Christ: "This is my body, this is my blood. Do this," etc. Particularly we who want to receive the sacrament kneel beside, behind, and around him, man, woman, young, old, master, servant, wife, maid, parents, and children, even as God brings us together there, all of us true, holy priests, sanctified by Christ's blood, anointed by the Holy Spirit, and consecrated in baptism. On the basis of this our inborn, hereditary priestly honor and attire we are present, have, as Revelation 4 [:4] pictures it, our golden crowns on our heads, harps and golden censers in our hands; and we let our pastor say what Christ has ordained, not for himself as though it were for his person, but he is the mouth for all of us and we all speak the words with him from the heart and in faith, directed to the Lamb of God who is present for us and among us, and who according to his ordinance nourishes us with his body and blood. This is our mass, and it is the true mass which is not lacking among us.

Here everything is done, first of all, according to the ordinance and command of Christ, so that it is offered and given to the church under both kinds on the basis of the words of Christ: "Take, eat, this is my body," etc., and "Do this in remembrance of me." The pastor does not receive it only for himself, as the pope's sacrilege does. He also does not sacrifice it to God for our sins and all kinds of needs, as the pope's sacrilege does. He does not give it to us and he also does not sell it to us as a good work to reconcile God, as the pope's sacrilege does, having made such a blasphemous commercial affair of it; rather, he administers it to us for the comfort and strengthening of our faith. In this way Christ is made known and preached. Here there can be no avarice or idolatry. Here we surely have the intention of Christ and of the church. Here we do not have to be concerned whether the pastor is speaking the words secretly or whether he also is effecting conversion or whether he, too, believes, for we hear the words of institution publicly and say them along with him in our hearts. And the institution of Christ (not our action or the chrism) effects a change or gives us the body and blood of Christ. If the pastor does not believe or doubts, we do believe. If he blunders in speaking the words or becomes confused and forgets whether he has spoken the words, we indeed are there, listen to them, cling to them, and are sure that they have been spoken. For this reason we cannot be deceived, and because the ordinance and true faith are present, it must be certain that we are receiving the true body and blood of Christ. God be praised and thanked, that I have lived to see the true Christian mass and the pure Christian usage of the holy sacrament. I behold it with delight and joy in my heart, after seeing the abominable, horrible abuse which unfortunately I helped to carry on so many years under the pope's sacrilege.

For I am often frightened at this when I think about how I and others at that time celebrated the private mass so very reverently; but we did it out of ignorance. That is why the dear man

Jesus Christ overlooked it and forgave us; for we never want to do it again. However, now the papists know it, but do not want to know it, persist petulantly in their sacrilege, proceed insolently and in a self-willed way, and pervert Christ's ordinance; they create a new, different ordinance, celebrate mass not only in disobedience to God but also by blaspheming his ordinance and command, do not administer the sacrament to anybody, retain it for themselves alone and, besides, cannot be certain whether they are taking mere bread and wine or the body and blood of Christ, because they do not enact it according to Christ's ordinance but according to their own ordinance contrary to Christ's ordinance. Also, no one can be sure whether they speak the words [of institution] or not. Therefore no one can be obliged to believe their secret whispering. Consequently, they also do not preach anything to anyone, as Christ nevertheless commanded. It is also impossible that they should believe rightly; for to believe rightly, and knowingly to rage against God's word[49] cannot exist side by side in a heart. Consequently, they also cannot pray or give thanks so as to please God. And finally, beyond such abominations and desecrations, it is their sublimest worship that they sacrifice this sacrament to God (if indeed it is a sacrament), desecrated and blasphemed by so many abominations, and give and sell it to other Christians for money. There is neither steel nor iron, neither rock nor stone, that can compare with the hardness of such hearts that knowingly continue in such an abomination.

This book, however, in the course of my writing it, has become longer than I had planned, and I must condense it a little until I or someone on our side writes more about the subject some other time. Because the papists, desperate and obdurate in their abominations, do not want to cease both lying against the acknowledged truth and murdering the innocent, devout Christians, we must

[49] Cochlaeus' reply to Luther's argument was as follows: "We firmly hold to the church . . . and believe surely and without doubt that when a true priest speaks these words that produce transubstantiation over the bread and the wine, transubstantiation assuredly takes place, even though it is nowhere written in the entire Bible. . . . [Christ and the apostles] taught it as well as many other mysteries to the church orally, and these should not be cast before the dogs and swine in public writings." Cf. *WA* 38, 250, n. 1.

henceforth deal with this subject often and diligently in order that our own people might see a clear and certain distinction between the true, holy church and the papacy, between the temple of God and the Antichrist who dwells in it (II Thessalonians 2 [:4]), between the holy place and the sacrilege in it. For, according to Matthew 24 [:15], Christ himself bids us to distinguish between the two: "So when you see the desolating sacrilege spoken of by the prophet Daniel, standing in the holy place (let the reader understand)." We do not permit the papacy to be the holy church, nor a part of it, and we also cannot do so; rather, it is the desolating sacrilege and Antichrist, the enemy and opponent who destroys the church, God's word and ordinance, and places himself against and above them as a god above all gods, as Daniel and St. Paul have prophesied. However, it is not possible for us or for the holy church to divorce or separate ourselves bodily from the sacrilege, the papacy, or the Antichrist until the day of judgment. (For as Christ teaches, the sacrilege should and must not be outside of but in the holy place, the Antichrist must dwell not outside of but in the temple, and the papacy must be not outside of but in the church.) Nevertheless, we must know how to separate ourselves from him spiritually and with true understanding, and to beware of and to protect ourselves against his destruction in order that we might remain pure in the true faith of Christ and resist and defend ourselves against his dirt and vermin.

Therefore, I shall now omit the fifth and sixth things [that they attacked], namely, the keys or forgiveness, and prayer. They have made light of them and have destroyed true forgiveness and prayer. Yet Christ has preserved them both marvelously and mightily, and now he has begun again to destroy their chrism and private mass, to assist in removing such offense from the kingdom of God, and to assure and make available to the church once again the call or true consecration and ordination to the office of the ministry, as it possessed it from the beginning, but which the great bishops arrogated to themselves alone and took away from the small bishops or pastors. This is and must be our foundation and sure rock: Where the gospel is rightly and purely preached, there a holy, Christian church must be. And whoever doubts this may as well also doubt whether the gospel is God's word. But where there is a holy, Christian church, there all the sacraments, Christ himself, and the Holy Spirit must be. Now if we are to be a holy Christian church and to possess the most important and necessary parts such as God's word, Christ, the Spirit, faith, prayer, baptism, the sacrament, the keys, the office of the ministry, etc., and should not also possess the humblest part, namely, the power and right to call some persons to the office of the ministry who administer to us the word, baptism, the sacrament, forgiveness, which in any case are available, and serve us through these, what kind of a church, I ask, would this be? What would happen to Christ's word when he says: "Where two or three are gathered in my name, there am I in the midst of them" [Matt. 18:20]? And again: "If two of you agree on earth about anything they ask, it will be done for them by my Father in heaven" [Matt. 18:19]? If two or three possess such power, how much more an entire church?

However, listen how simply St. Paul speaks about ordination in II Timothy 2 [:2]: "What you have heard from me before many witnesses entrust to faithful men who will be able to teach others also." Here there is neither chrism nor butter; it is solely the command to teach God's word. Whoever has received the command, him St. Paul regards as a pastor, bishop, and pope, for everything depends on the word of God as the highest office, which Christ himself regarded as his own and as the highest office. Indeed, all sacraments must become such through the word, which is the most essential part in all sacraments; the papists themselves call it "the form of the sacrament" [*formam sacramenti*].[50] Christ, too, has disgracefully forgotten about the chrism in the last chapter of Matthew when he says: "Go therefore and teach all the heathen to observe all that I have commanded you" [cf. Matt. 28:19 f.]. But what did he command them? Publicly to preach the gospel, to baptize, to administer the sacrament, forgive sins, etc. If now all heathen are to observe this, they must naturally possess the power and right to preach, baptize, administer the sacrament, forgive sins, etc. In fact, they are hereby commanded to do so, as St. Paul also writes to the

---

[50] The form of the sacrament refers to Christ's words of institution.

Corinthians that he had received it [the sacrament] from the Lord and delivered it to the Corinthians [I Cor. 11:23]. He is not thinking of any chrism but solely of the office and command.

At the close I entreat and exhort the factious spirits,[51] as well as some impious papists who themselves do not trust their idol, to leave this book of mine alone. Just because I have excused the holy church for sinning out of ignorance by the use of one kind (although all Christendom did not sin in this respect), this does not mean that I allow or confirm the sacrilege of those who now knowingly condemn both kinds. I have also not served any factious spirit by speaking about the bread and wine of the private masses; but my intention was to serve our own people, to attack the private consecration and the private mass and to show a difference between the church and the papacy. I would like to assist in destroying the private consecration and private mass, just as they destroyed our Christian consecration and mass. This matter is of no concern to the factious spirits and ferocious papists. They also do not understand it at all. Therefore, they should not embellish their cause with it.

When I again deal with the subject at a later date, I shall further attack the entire consecration in the papacy, for they have seven consecrations before they consecrate a person as a private priest, namely, doorkeeper, lector, exorcist, acolyte, subdeacon, deacon, priest,[52] and after that there is the high consecration of bishops and the pope. They call the doorkeeper that person who has been consecrated for the rope, that is, who is supposed to lock the church and ring the bell. This consecration has long ago been dropped, and yet this office, without any consecration, the sacristan, his wife, servant girl, and servant perform both in the villages and in the cities. The lector was the person who had to read the lessons in the church during the masses and vigils and had to sing the psalms. This office students now perform without any consecration, and thus the consecration has been dropped and the office has re-

[51] The term *Rotten geister* is used here by Luther to refer particularly to the Zwinglians. He wanted to make it explicit that he was in no sense embracing a Zwinglian interpretation of the Lord's Supper.

[52] *Hostiarium, lectorem, exorcistam, acolytum, subdiaconum, diaconum, presbyterum.*

mained. The exorcist was the person who exorcised the devil before baptism; now the person baptizing does this himself, so both the consecration and the person who was called thus are gone; the office alone has remained. The acolyte was called *admissus* or *licentiatus* and was admitted to the altar to serve the priest. They are the ones who prepare the altar, light the lamp and candles, and assist at the mass. For this reason they called them candle-bearers [*ceroferarios*] because they did not know what acolyte meant. This consecration also disappeared, and this office is now performed by the sacristan, the student, the sacristan's wife, daughter, maidservant, without any consecration, both in cities and in villages. All these belonged to the spiritual estate and had to be called *clerici*.

Likewise, the epistolers, or gospelers, were those persons who read the Epistle and Gospel during the mass, and prepared the corporal and chalice. These offices the priests themselves now execute (except in several monasteries which during high festivals and high masses utilized such separate offices), so that this kind of consecration and the persons themselves also have disappeared and the offices have remained. Therefore, we also want to have the seventh consecration abolished, which the papists have separated from the office of the ministry and have destroyed with their private consecrations, and we want to have the office of the ministry confirmed so that in this way all seven consecrations with their dissembling should not lead us astray with regard to the offices of Christ and the church. Our consecration shall be called ordination, or a call to the office. And if the fingers of a person are not smeared with chrism, they shall be anointed sufficiently when they shall have touched the sacrament, just as the papists regarded the chalices and corporals as consecrated when mass was celebrated with them—even as some among them dared to do apart from the bishop's consecration. Without the bishop's consecration (according to their strict canons), one was not allowed to celebrate mass with an unconsecrated corporal or chalice. But a consecrated corporal even a nun was not allowed to wash, no matter how holy the dear bride of Christ might be! However, there is too much to be said now about the innumerable evils of consecration. God willing, I hope to write more about this some other time. Amen.

A LETTER OF DR. MARTIN LUTHER CONCERNING HIS BOOK ON THE PRIVATE MASS

1534

Translated by

Martin E. Lehmann

INTRODUCTION

Ostensibly Luther wrote this letter to a good friend of his in order to dispel any suspicions about his adherence to a Zwinglian view of the Lord's Supper. According to the opening statements in the letter, the Reformer's book *The Private Mass and the Consecration of Priests* had aroused the suspicion in "several good people" that Luther was siding with "the enthusiasts or enemies of the sacrament." However, the assumption that the letter in question was actually addressed to a good friend whose identity cannot be established does not seem to be tenable. It is much more likely that Luther employed the fictitious address, "To the Honorable and Steadfast N., My Most Gracious Lord and Good Friend," as a literary form in order to clarify and confirm his doctrine of the real presence of the body and blood of Christ in the sacrament.

The above conclusion is warranted because there is no evidence that any followers of Luther actually misunderstood the argument he developed in his book on private masses. In fact, in Halle and Leipzig those who adhered to the evangelical principles of Luther defended their participation in the Roman Catholic mass during Easter on the basis of Luther's contention in his treatise of 1533 that Christ's body was present under one kind in such a celebration of the mass. Nor is there any evidence that certain Lutherans were led to believe that some statements in this work could be regarded as Zwinglian in connection with Luther's discussion of the meaning of the Lord's Supper.

The suspicion that a Zwinglian view of the sacrament lay behind the Reformer's polemic against private masses was in reality raised by his Roman Catholic opponents. Prince John of Anhalt, brother of the princes Joachim and George,[1] was not yet convinced that Luther was right in his reform measures; but he did not openly take issue with Luther's teachings because his two brothers were

[1] See the introduction to *The Private Mass and the Consecration of Priests*, above, pp. 142, 145.

inclined to embrace the Reformation. On December 13, 1533, the evangelical pastor and close friend of Luther in the principality of Anhalt, Nicholas Hausmann, took a copy of Luther's *The Private Mass and the Consecration of Priests* to Prince John. Early on the next day, a Sunday, prior to the public worship, the prince came to see Hausmann in order to tell him that in his reading of Luther's book he was unable to agree with his contention that the private mass was an utterly impious practice. It seemed to him that in this matter Luther was upholding a Zwinglian view of the sacrament. At that time Hausmann did not discuss the subject in detail with the prince, but tactfully deferred dealing with it at length until his brother, Prince George, would arrive.

Luther, who, in a letter from Hausmann, was made aware of this reaction of Prince John to his book, instead of dealing with the prince as an opponent and thus perhaps alienating him altogether from the Reformation, conceived the idea of writing a letter to a "good friend" who did not exist in order to clarify and underline certain basic views and convictions which he had expressed in his book.[2]

In the resulting letter Luther makes special mention of the fact that his book on private masses was somewhat lengthy and that only a few people would therefore read it entirely. Evidently this was a cryptic allusion to Hausmann's report that Prince John had read the book rather hastily. Moreover, the explicit mention in the letter by Luther that his opponents were in the habit of extracting certain sentences from the book and interpreting them apart from the context in which they were written seems to apply to Prince John's superficial reading of Luther's polemical writing. In other words, the letter was designed to be an indirect response to the prince's criticism of the book. Luther had the letter published in order to make it crystal clear that he held to the doctrine of the real presence of Christ's body and blood in the sacrament, even while he categorically rejected the private mass on the ground that it was a sacrifice and good work offered to God. The tone of the letter is not irenic or compromising; rather, it sets forth the Re-

---

[2] *WA* 38, 180, 257-260.

former's specific teaching on the Lord's Supper in a forceful manner, and fearlessly denounces false papal doctrines associated with the celebration of the private mass.

The letter was published prior to May 4, 1534, under the title *Ein brieff D. Mart. Luth. Von seinem Buch der Winckelmessen, an einen guten freund.* The translation of it is based on the printed text in *WA* 38, 262-272. The letter is also reproduced in *EA* 31, 377-391, and *St. L.* 19, 1286-1299.

A LETTER OF DR. MARTIN LUTHER CONCERNING HIS BOOK ON THE PRIVATE MASS

To the Honorable and Steadfast N.,
My Most Gracious Lord and Good Friend

Grace and peace in Christ our Lord! I have taken note of your writing along with the oral representation of your emissary about my book on private masses. You say that several good people fear that it will be understood to mean that I am siding with, or will in time side with, the enthusiasts or enemies of the sacrament. And even though I had indeed protested in the aforementioned book against them and had testified that I did not side with the enthusiasts at all, nor had written this to confirm their error, still the book was too long and only a few people read it entirely. So it is now the supreme art of the opponents to extract several points from my books which they turn and twist to discredit me so that they might obscure and hide from the people the other things I have written which would vindicate my integrity. Therefore, you consider it desirable that, in order to quiet such false tongues, I should issue a brief letter in which I testify that I am not at all siding with the enemies of the sacrament, or (to express myself quite clearly) with the erroneous teaching of Karlstadt, Zwingli, and their associates, nor shall I ever side with them.

Here (I hope you will forgive me) I must again point out to you this distinction: If it is papists who are requiring this of you and are thus tempting you, then you should tell them that as far as I am concerned I am not going to write a single letter [of the alphabet] on account of them, but I am going to let them read this same book. If it causes offense, I shall praise God. "Let the filthy still be filthy" [Rev. 22:11]. Even if every word in it would become pure ammonia or the poison of vipers in their ears and hearts, I would just as soon laugh as cry; for that is the way they want it. The Jews have made their Messiah into nothing but an infernal and eternal poison for themselves. Should Christ therefore be eternally troubled about it? The papists have arbitrarily made my gospel, which they know and which they must acknowledge to be the precious truth, into sheer heresy of the devil in their hearts and ears, and there are no bounds, nor is there an end to it. And should I be eternally concerned about them so that they might not take offense at my writing? This would be according to their liking. In that case would I not also have to be concerned about the loathsome devil himself so that he might indeed not take offense at the word of God? Let them alone, says God and my Lord Christ, and just let them be offended that a blind man "falls into a pit" [Matt. 15:14] with a blind man. They ought to be annoyed and take offense at me. That is what I want and that is why I have also written with the intention that I might indeed irritate and embitter the snakes and evil worms (although that was not my primary intention in this book); but the main purpose was to instruct our people and to confess the truth.

If, however, it is not papists but simply good people who perhaps do not read my book and yet hear others say that I want to become an enemy of the sacrament, even though this letter might also not help them if they do not read it, still in this way I would like once more as a service to you to set forth my intention and confession publicly. Certainly many of my books are available, particularly my *Confession* against the enthusiasts,[1] which presents my testimony before God and the world forcefully enough. And in a superabundant way I desire herewith in this letter once again to make, repeat, and confirm the same confession word for word as it has been written, printed, and issued. With God's help I also want to die and go to my Lord on the basis of it, even as I am now living and doing and enduring everything—and there is a great deal—in accordance with such a confession and faith. And (if God wills)

[1] Luther is referring to his *Confession Concerning Christ's Supper* (1528), *LW* 37, 153-372.

even the gates of hell are not going to tear me away from it; for I am in earnest, that I know full well and am even more convinced of it with the passage of time.

Besides, my book concerning private masses quite frequently acknowledges that also among the papists (if they adhere to Christ's ordinance), the true body of Christ is nevertheless present and is received—even though it is under one kind only. If I wanted to be an enemy of the sacrament, I would surely have good grounds for undertaking such an attack on the papists, because they are my devils and would like to have me utterly annihilated. They fortify themselves against the enthusiasts by means of my confession and writing and have to bestow on me the honor that I have defended the holy sacrament of the body and blood of our Lord better than they themselves. I know, too, that all of them put together could not defend it so vigorously and powerfully, since they are quite superficially instructed in the Holy Scripture (may God have mercy on them) and do not care sincerely about such matters either. How could I bring about the fall of their majesty and pride more quickly and powerfully than by teaching that there was no sacrament among them? Just because all their concern is based upon commercial gain and on the abuse of the most worthy sacrament, even as the greatest strength of all heretics, including the devil himself, is based on the abuse of the divine name and word, should I for that reason deny God's name and word?

Therefore, I most cordially request that (in addition to this letter) you tell these good people not to be anxious. Unless God should want to vex me in particular and let me be possessed by the devil, I shall, God willing, abide by my confession. And although I am a human being and can fall, as we are all human and can fall, nevertheless, I hope in dependence on my dear Lord Jesus Christ, who has brought me into many a difficult situation[2] for his name's sake and yet has never forsaken me, that he will not have granted me such a serious concern about the holy sacrament in vain. If he should want to put me to the test and let me go astray

[2] Literally, Luther says that he has been brought "into many a steambath." This was a German proverb. Cf. Ernst Thiele, *Luthers Sprichwörtersammlung* (Weimar, 1900), No. 3.

in this or other articles of the faith, he will, nonetheless, not permit me to fall deeper than St. Peter, who indeed denied him with his mouth out of fear and terror and yet remained true to him in his heart, weeping soon after his fall and confessing with sorrow his true love for his Lord.

Thus I again confess here before God and all the world that I believe and do not doubt, and shall also with the help and grace of my dear Lord Jesus Christ adhere to this confession until the last day, that where mass is celebrated according to Christ's ordinance, be it among us Lutherans or under the papacy or in Greece or in India, even if it is also only under one kind—which is nonetheless wrong and an abuse—as is the case under the papacy at Easter and otherwise during the year when they provide the sacrament for the people, nevertheless, under the form of bread, the true body of Christ, given for us on the cross, under the form of wine, the true blood of Christ, shed for us, are present; furthermore, it is not a spiritual or imagined body and blood but the genuine natural body and blood derived from the holy, virginal, true, human body of Mary, conceived without a human body by the Holy Spirit alone. This body and blood of Christ are even now sitting at the right hand of God in majesty, in the divine person called Jesus Christ, who is a genuine, true, eternal God with the Father of whom he was born from eternity, etc. This body and this blood of the Son of God, Jesus Christ, not only the holy and worthy but also sinners and the unworthy truly administer and receive bodily, although invisibly, with their hands, their mouths, the chalice, paten, corporal, and whatever they use for this purpose when it is administered and received in the mass.

This is my faith; this I know, and no one shall wrest it from me. I am confessing it not only because I, for my own part, have many a time derived great consolation from such a belief in the sacrament in the midst of my profound and great fears and needs—which experience has been enough for me personally to confirm my faith—but also because I want to stand by the clear, public, and certain text of the gospel with my testimony (as much as I am able) against all errors and heresies, both old and new; and in the service and for the betterment of my dear brothers and sisters in

Christ in accordance with the duty of Christian love, I want to resist the devil's malice and purposes.

Just as neither I nor any true Christian can deny that it is the genuine, true, natural name of God when a false knave takes an oath or swears by it and it does not, on account of such a knave or devil, become another name of God, so, on the other hand, when a holy St. Paul or Isaiah uses God's name, takes an oath or swears by it, it does not therefore become a still better name of God for it is just the same name which the knave used abusively. God and his name and all that he is, says, and does, remain and continue forever, no matter who it may be who abuses them, be he a human being or a devil.

I have provided a drastic example in my book concerning the private mass, by stating that God's word and work cannot be hindered or altered at all by our abuse or sin, if only his ordinance is kept. But where his ordinance is altered, that is of course a different matter. That would be the same as if I desired to plow water and sow grain in it, or catch fish in the air, or if a woman wanted to procreate children by means of a stone or a man by means of a tree. Certainly nothing would come of it, for God has not ordained it thus and does not want to have it that way. However, if I, out of mischief, wou'd sow seed in another person's field or would fish in another man's pond, even though such sowing or fishing would be wrong, nevertheless grain would grow in the field and I would nonetheless catch fish in the pond.

Therefore, I stated in that book that the papists, if they adhere to the ordinance of Christ, undoubtedly have in the sacrament the true and real body and blood of Christ. If it is under one kind, then it is the body of Christ. If it is under both kinds, then it is both body and blood according to the utterance and ordinance of the words of Christ. Now if they (without impairing the ordinance of Christ) sell, present, abuse, or administer or receive it unworthily, this neither adds nor takes away anything from the sacrament. God remains God even in hell. Christ remains godly even among those who crucified him. A gulden remains a gulden even in the hand of a thief and robber, if only it is itself a true gulden struck according to the king's or prince's mint regulations. But if it is a counterfeit gulden, struck contrary to the king's mint regulations, it will never become a genuine gulden, even if the king himself or the angel Gabriel wanted to buy something with it.

Consequently, in my book I did not attack the sin against the sacrament or its abuse, but the perverted ordinance of the mass which is opposed to the ordinance of Christ. I put the papists to the test to see how they would defend their private mass, not for our sake (for we have been rid of the private masses now for more than ten years), but in order that their own people might see on what kind of rotten, vicious lies and knavery their idol, that is, their mass business, is founded. Indeed, I wish and would very much like to see and hear that the two words, "mass" and "sacrament," would be understood as being as different as darkness and light, yes, as different as devil and God. For the mass, as the performance of it and all their doctrines and books prove, is still nothing other than a transgression of the ordinance and a commercial use of the holy sacrament, even if it is most reverently celebrated. They themselves have to confess that "mass" does not mean the reception of the sacrament as Christ instituted it; rather, they call and, whether they like it or not, must call, the reception of the sacrament *synaxis* in Greek, *communio* in Latin, and *berichten* in German.[3] "Mass," however, refers to what the priest does alone at the altar, to which no ordinary Christian or layman adds anything. For they indeed know that no layman or ordinary Christian can celebrate mass and they will not allow it. Nor do they allow it to be or to be called a mass when a layman receives the sacrament; but they (masters of all gods and of the sacrament) alone celebrate mass; all other Christians simply receive the sacrament and do not celebrate mass.

From this you can readily observe that I am not contending against the sacrament but against the mass, and would like to separate the sacrament from the mass so that the mass might perish

[3] *Synaxis* in its Greek derivation means "assembly"; the Latin *communio*, "fellowship" or "community"; and the German *berichten*, "to provide" or "to administer." Actually the three words have different meanings, but all presuppose the presence of more than one person for the celebration of the sacrament.

and the sacrament alone, without the mass, might be preserved in its honor and according to the ordinance of our dear Lord Jesus Christ. May God grant to all devout Christians such hearts that when they hear the word "mass," they might be frightened and make the sign of the cross as though it were the devil's abomination; on the other hand, when they hear the word "sacrament" or "Lord's Supper," they might dance for pure joy, indeed, in accordance with genuine spiritual joy, cry sweetly. For I am very fond of the precious, blessed Supper of my Lord Jesus Christ in which he gives me his body and blood to eat and to drink even bodily with my own mouth along with these exceedingly sweet and kind words: "Given for you, shed for you," etc.

I am the more hostile and angry about the mass, because the papists have thereby arrogated the holy sacrament to themselves alone, have taken it from and robbed Christians of it, and have made a business of it and yet have woven both into one another so inseparably when they provide it for Christians at Easter time, that the common man is unable to distinguish between the mass and the sacrament. They themselves have also not been able to differentiate between the two; nor was I myself able to make the distinction; I, who was an archpapist and a more zealous reader of masses than they all are now, said mass for over fifteen years and do not know yet whether I received the sacrament in the mass or not. So completely did the devil rule. For me mass and sacrament at the altar were one and the same thing, as they were at that time for all of us. Yet they are not one and the same thing. It is the mass when I sacrifice the sacrament to God for my sins and the sins of others as a work performed by human beings (whether they be evil or godly). This they have to acknowledge. It is the sacrament when I receive from the priest the body and blood of our Lord Jesus Christ under the bread and wine. Such sacrificing and reception of the sacrament the devil has mingled together so inseparably in the mass, even as dishonest innkeepers mix water and wine with one another and as deceitful minters mix silver and brass. There is need here of an acute tester and of a hot fire (which is the word of God, Psalm 17 [3 ff.]) so that they might again be separated from one another.

Now when I am talking about the sacrament, I am truly in earnest about meaning the genuine natural body and blood of Christ in the bread and wine, regardless of who the persons are who give or receive it. For Christ, my Lord, will not lie to me; I shall venture my life on that, if God wills. This is clear, unadulterated, pure wine into which no host pours water. However, when I am talking about the mass, I am truly in earnest about meaning the loathsome business and abominable abuse of the holy sacrament, according to which they sell their sacrifice of the body and blood of Christ (as they teach) to other Christians as a satisfaction for sin. Yet the ordinance of Christ clearly declares that his sacrament should be there and should be used, not for satisfaction through our sacrificing, but for the forgiveness of sin through his blood. Let them tell [us] whether in this instance the intention of Christ is adhered to in the mass when it is performed as a work by human beings and also sold to others as satisfaction for sin; and (I say) let them defend [the contention] that according to Christ's ordinance his body and blood are there, since it is not a sacrament but a mass. I do not want to defend it, but want to attack it and probe into their superficially profound skill.

I, too, am a doctor in their theology and neither as unlearned nor inexperienced in it as their ranters (who do not understand their own theology) believe. Still, I did not know a good argument to defend the mass. I could also say, "Church, church, fathers, fathers," as they do, and with that vindicate everything. However, I do not possess that kind of strange faith (God who once saved me from it will also guard me against it) so that I could call those the church of Christ who are factions of the godless and the church of the devil, who embellish themselves with the name of the church of Christ and glory in it and yet the fruits cogently convict the tree of being evil. Just as little am I able to place the church above Christ and allow it to change and pervert what he teaches and ordains. For he should and must be the head, and the church (as St. Paul states) is subject and obedient to him out of fear and reverence. Otherwise, by what means could one make the distinction between the true church of Christ and the church of the devil except by its obedience or disobedience to Christ, especially when disobedience, publicly known and understood, excuses itself wickedly and shamelessly and claims to be in the right? For the holy church sins and stumbles or can even err, as the Lord's Prayer teaches. However, it does not defend or excuse itself, but humbly asks for forgiveness and improves itself as it is able. Thus it is forgiven so that henceforth its sin is no longer reckoned as sin.

Now if I do not know or distinguish the true church from the false one on the basis of obedience and obdurate disobedience, then I am unable to speak of a church any longer. Then one might accordingly also with due deference call all heretics, all factions and sects that are wantonly disobedient to Christ, the holy church; for they are in no way worse than the pope's church, if indeed wanton disobedience against God does no harm. On the other hand, the papal church is no better because it is just as stubbornly disobedient to God and wickedly perverts his word and, besides, it is more insistent on being right than any other faction and heretic. This would finally be the upshot that there would no longer be either a church or heretics on earth, for by what criterion would we prove that this or that faction consists of heretics? If we say "By the criterion that they are wickedly disobedient to God and pervert his word shamelessly," then they can answer, "The papal church is doing it too, more than we are and still it claims to be in the right and to be the holy church. If this is permissible for it, it is also permissible for us."

Indeed, what is still worse: How shall a prince or lord constrain his subjects, a father and a mother their children? If we say, "God has commanded that lords and parents should be obeyed," then they have the papal church as an excellent example and can say, "Even the papal church does not keep God's command; rather, it forbids keeping it and strangles and persecutes all those who want to keep God's word." Thus, according to the praiseworthy example of the papal church, all servants would like to strangle and drive away their lords and all children their parents when one wants to constrain them to be obedient in accordance with God's commandments. If God himself did not look after things mightily, it would truly have to turn out in this way.

The result of the superlative skill of the papists is twofold:

God's kingdom is being destroyed by sheer heresy, and the worldly authorities are set at variance by constant revolts, and homes are filled with lost children.[4] Nevertheless, it has to be regarded as justly done, and whoever wants to reprove it finds himself condemned and reproved as a heretic, rebel, and lost child. They should be thanked, these excellent teachers. But enough of that now; for I am indeed ready, if God so wills, to write something that deals particularly with the church.[5] In such a writing I should like to show who indeed they are who most assiduously teach people to be disobedient to God and man, who destroy both God's and the world's kingdom (as much as they are able) and make themselves free of them, and who alone possess the rule in heaven and on earth and yet do as they please.

Finally, this is what I want you to consider: If the mass would produce and bestow as little of temporal honor, riches, and power as the precious gospel and the truth, how many ardent celebrants of the mass, do you think, one would find today? In truth, for the past six hundred years (I do not want to calculate backward too far) we would have seen neither pope, cardinal, bishop, nor other servants of the mass, but they all would have become evangelical or Lutheran, and we would at the present time truly wonder what these names, pope, cardinal, bishop, mass, clerics, etc., meant, and what kind of creatures they would have been, whether elf, dwarf, water nymphs, or malicious demons. However, because the mass brought in money, honor, and power, such great goods were gained as a result of this commercial activity and business that they have now subjected the world's kingdom to themselves and have also undertaken to subject heaven and God's kingdom and majesty to themselves, and would like to have his word be subject to themselves. However, at this point, Lucifer becomes too ambitious, desiring to establish his throne as being equal to God's, yes, above God's. As a result he knocks his head against the vault [of heaven] and falls down into the abyss below.

There is no doubt about it: If God would give me enough

[4] Analogous to the predicament of the lost son in Luke 15:11-32.

[5] The reference is to Luther's treatise *On the Councils and the Church* (1539). Cf. *LW* 41, 3-178; *WA* 50, 509-653; *PE* 5, 125-300.

[power] so that I would be able to make the pope and his papacy as rich and as mighty as they have been till now, and they would be certain that it would remain that way, ah, I would within a month's time make better Lutherans out of the pope, cardinals, bishops, clerics, monks, and all the worms and avaricious vermin than I myself am. These highly learned, thoughtful, thievish, and rapacious lords still think that no one, not even the Holy Spirit himself, should perceive that they are contending so fiercely for their mass solely on account of their avarice, their belly, their rule, and their power. They claim that it is the church's and the ancient fathers' teaching, even though their own conscience bears witness to them that it is something else. Truly, how others feel about this matter I do not know, but I feel this way about it: If I know that a person is fighting with and going against his conscience, then I do not have to be afraid of him, even if he at first puts on a bold front and looks cross or perhaps strikes a blow; for if the opposition [of his conscience] continues to plague him, the evildoer has to give way to his bad conscience, despair, and flee. For thus says my book: "The Lord will give you a trembling heart" [Deut. 28:65], and "One chases a thousand" [Deut. 32:30]. In this way, by God's help, I have been able to avoid fearing the papacy until now; in the past they have been very much afraid of me, a miserable human being, and they still have to be afraid of me. Their conscience is on my side against them; they feel that the truth is contending against them and that they are protecting themselves solely with lies and brute force. They cannot continue like this indefinitely. Yet I have truly not wished them any evil or done them any evil, but I only wanted to point them to Christ, the truth.

However, they do not want to be reformed (as they say) by this former mendicant monk. Yet this same mendicant monk (I must brag a little, but secretly, so that they do not hear about it) has reformed them considerably. I have, God be praised, reformed more with my gospel than they perhaps might have done with five councils. So far they have done nothing more in the councils than play around with unprofitable matters that do not concern the Christian church. However, now our gospel comes along, takes away indulgences, abolishes pilgrimages, puts a stop to bulls, checks covetousness, and achieves marvelous results, which they themselves accept and utilize and would not have attained by any councils. I am not even mentioning the chief articles of the faith. However, they indeed perceive that the Reformation is about to become too powerful now that the chief article and the true cornerstone of the papal church, the holy mass, is also being attacked. This is going to be too much for them. At this point—and it is time—they really have to shout, lie, murder and resort to all kinds of insults and abuses in order that their one rock of consolation and chief fortress might not fall. However, it must fall, nothing can be done about that; for Daniel has appeared on the scene and will do what the angel Gabriel has shown him.

For this prophet writes that he will make his appearance at the end of the world. This he is doing now and he says that the Antichrist will take his stand on two points: the idol and a womanless being [Daniel 11:37 ff.]. He calls the idol *Maosim*, using the letters which form the word "mass"; he would have liked to call it plainly the mass, if he would not have had to use a cryptic word (as commanded him by the angel). Nevertheless, he portrays the idol in such a way that one perceives that he means the loathsome mass; for he says that it is going to honor its God with silver, gold, and jewels, and those who assist it in establishing such a God it will entrust with the distribution of the riches of all lands. Who does not perceive that this portrays the mass excellently? For where on earth are there greater possessions and money, embellishment and edifices, worship and devotion, employed than for the mass? Who has also distributed the lands? The mass has brought in most [of the wealth] for the pope, bishops, foundations, and monasteries, and they [foundations and monasteries] are all founded upon the precious idol, the mass. Yet it is a God (says Daniel) about whom his [the Antichrist's] forebears knew nothing, for in the writings of the apostles and the fathers something far different is found from that which the papacy teaches and believes about the mass. The apostles and fathers regarded it as a sacrament, instituted by Christ; at that time it did not bring forth money but spiritual profit for eternal life. After that the Antichrist made it into the mass which produces profit and dominion and the pope with three crowns as a lord over heaven, earth, and hell.

The womanless being, or celibate life, has confirmed all this and has duped the whole world with false holiness. These are the two pillars on which the papacy rests, like the house of the Philistines in Samson's time [Judg. 16:23 ff.]. Now what if God had made Luther a Samson over them, a Samson who would take hold of and tear down both pillars so that the house would collapse and they would all perish? Who could hold this against him? He is God and, therefore, beyond our comprehension. They gouged out both of Luther's eyes because according to them I hold that both the worldly and the spiritual authorities are opposed to each other.[6] And the whore Delilah, to whom I made love, is the holy, beautiful monkery which shaved off the hair that had grown for me as a Nazirite from my baptism. But I am elaborating too much. Some other time I shall write more about it and do better. Meanwhile, I pray, as I did above, that you tell the good people the best about me, and let the papists lie and say the very worst about me; they do not deserve any better. With this I commend you to God. Amen.

---

[6] Cf. Heinrich Bornkamm, *Luther's Doctrine of the Two Kingdoms*, trans. Franklin Sherman (Philadelphia: Fortress Press, 1966).

THE DISPUTATION CONCERNING THE PASSAGE: "THE WORD WAS MADE FLESH"

(John 1:14)

1539

Translated by

Martin E. Lehmann

INTRODUCTION

The new statutes for the University of Wittenberg in 1533, written by Melanchthon, called for the reintroduction of the festive, public quarterly disputations. The statutes of 1508 had also made provision for these quarterly disputations but they had evidently been discontinued, for as dean of the theological faculty Luther made the following entry into the dean's register in 1521: "There are two kinds of disputations. The one kind takes place every week. The other kind involves presiding over those who are respondents for the sake of attaining degrees, and it follows a particular course."[1] Here Luther seems to recognize only the weekly circular disputation, which was held on Friday afternoons for the benefit of the students and which the professors took turns at conducting, and the disputation in which candidates for degrees participated as respondents.

In conformity with the provisions of the new statutes, Elector John Frederick's endowment charter of 1536 expressly required the holding of quarterly disputations at the university.[2] In 1538 a committee of twelve professors, representing the various faculties, studied the implementation of the new statutes; in the formal Opinion which they issued we hear that Luther offered to lecture and engage in disputations whenever he would be able to do so. Thus he stood ready to conduct the public quarterly disputation also. The purpose of this last-named kind of disputation, according to the committee's report, was to help those who engaged in them to acquire greater intellectual skill in dealing with opponents in theological controversies.[3]

Luther's enthusiastic endorsement of the quarterly disputation and the leading role he played in its revival at Wittenberg reveal his conscientious concern for excellence in educating future theological leaders and pastors for the Lutheran Church. The theme for this particular quarterly disputation as well as the theses he

[1] Paul Drews, *Die Disputationen Dr. Martin Luthers* (Göttingen, 1895), p. xvii.
[2] Drews, *op. cit.*, p. xviii.
[3] *WA* 39^{II}, 1.

prepared for it clearly indicate his own theological stance. As chairman and only respondent to the arguments brought forward in this instance, he articulated the objective of this disputation as one of setting forth the new theology taught at Wittenberg in opposition to the tenets of the famous center of the old theology, the University of Paris, which he called "the mother of errors."

It is not possible to determine when and under what circumstances the University of Paris advanced the proposition that truth is "the same in philosophy and theology."[4] Yet it is known that the Fifth Lateran Council (1512-1517) condemned the doctrines of Peter Pomponazzi about a dual truth and ordered theological teachers at universities to uphold the one truth of the Christian religion in philosophical statements also.[5] Luther, opposing the assertion that whatever is true in theology had to be true in philosophy as well, pointed to the philosophical absurdity of the Johannine dictum: "The Word was made flesh." He maintained that theological concepts often have a different meaning in philosophy. The road to understanding the incarnation was blocked for philosophy because it taught the way of the law and the meritorious character of works. In its own sphere, however, Luther conceded that philosophy had its independent meaning and was qualified to set forth the truth in the realm of nature. In the realm of grace, however, theology was to hold sway.

The theses for this disputation appear in Latin in *EA* Var. Arg. 4, 458-461, and in German in *St. L.* 10, 1168-1173. The theses and the disputation are printed in Latin in Paul Drews, *Die Disputationen Dr. Martin Luthers* (Göttingen, 1895), pp. 485-531, and in *WA* 39^{II}, 3-33. Our translation is based on the text in the Weimar Edition. The theses were published under the title *Disputatio theologica XI. Ianuarii anno XXXIX, an haec propositio sit vera in Philosophia. Verbum caro factum est.* The body of the disputation on these theses has been preserved in three different reports, identified as A, B, and C. All three reports are presented successively in translation, and while they often repeat the same arguments almost verbatim, they represent accounts of the disputation given by three different individuals, and thus at times supplement one another.

---

[4] *WA* 39^{II}, 3.
[5] *WA* 39^{II}, 2.

THE DISPUTATION CONCERNING THE PASSAGE: "THE WORD WAS MADE FLESH"

(John 1:14)

January 11, 1539

The Theses

1. Although the saying, "Every truth is in agreement with every other truth," is to be upheld, nevertheless, what is true in one field of learning is not always true in other fields of learning.

2. In theology it is true that the Word was made flesh; in philosophy the statement is simply impossible and absurd.

3. The declaration, "God is man," is not less but even more contradictory than if you would say, "Man is an ass."

4. The Sorbonne,[1] the mother of errors, has very incorrectly defined that truth is the same in philosophy and theology.

5. And has impiously condemned those who have argued to the contrary.

6. For by making this abominable statement, it was taught that articles of faith are subject to the judgment of human reason.

7. This is nothing other than attempting to enclose heaven and earth in their own center or in a grain of millet.

8. Paul, on the contrary, teaches that all thought (no doubt this also includes philosophy) is to be taken captive to the obedience of Christ [II Cor. 10:5].

9. St. Ambrose has rightly said that the dialecticians have to give way where the apostolic fishermen are to be trusted.[2]

---

[1] The University of Paris.

[2] Cf. Ambrose, *On Faith* (*De fide*), I, 13-14 (*MPL* 16, 548).

10. On the basis of the doctrine of the categories[3] it would follow excellently that God is man and, therefore, he is a rational, living being, capable of feeling, alive, having a body, actually a created substance.

11. But because Christians are to speak soberly and (as Augustine teaches) according to what has been prescribed, such conclusions are simply to be rejected.

12. Neither are the subtle inventions of mediate and immediate suppositions to be used nor to be taken advantage of in matters of faith.[4]

13. For disputations about words and empty discussions in the church are dangerous and full of offenses.

14. But wherever either the syllogistic form or philosophical reason encroaches [upon theology], this saying of Paul, "Let the woman be silent in church" [I Cor. 14:34], and that other passage, "Listen to him" [Matt. 17:5], must be applied to it.

15. To be sure, theology encroaches upon the rules of philosophy, but, contrariwise, philosophy itself encroaches more often upon the rules of theology.

16. This expository syllogism is good: The Father generates in divine things; the Father is the divine essence; therefore, the divine essence generates.

17. And although the premises are true, the conclusion is false; so what is false follows from what is true; this is contrary to philosophy.

18. This common syllogism is good: The Father is the entire divine essence; the Son is the divine essence; therefore, the Son is the Father.

19. But again the premises are true and the conclusion is false; and this is not a case of truth agreeing with truth.

20. This is indeed not because of the defect of the syllogistic

---

[3] Aristotle enumerates the categories in his ontology: substance, magnitude, quality, relation, the where, the when, position, possession, action, and passion. Cf. A. Schwegler, *A History of Philosophy*, trans. by Julius H. Seelye (New York and London: D. Appleton & Co., 1913), p. 132.

[4] Cf. E. Gilson, *History of Christian Philosophy in the Middle Ages* (New York: Random House, 1955), pp. 492-494, for a helpful discussion of "Supposition" and "Signification" in medieval philosophy.

form but because of the lofty character and majesty of the matter which cannot be enclosed in the narrow confines of reason or syllogisms.

21. So it [the matter] is not indeed something contrary to, but is outside, within, above, below, before, and beyond all logical truth.

22. This syllogism is good in philosophy: Whatever was made flesh became a creature; the Son of God was made flesh: therefore, the Son of God became a creature.

23. Even if it [the above syllogism] could be defended by means of the subtle, empty discussions of the sophists,[5] nevertheless, it ought not to be allowed in the church of God.

24. How much less is this syllogism to be considered: All flesh is a creature. The Word is flesh. Therefore, the Word is a creature.

25. Or this one: All flesh is a creature. The Word is not a creature. Therefore, the Word is not flesh.

26. In these and similar statements the syllogism is a most excellent form, but it is useless with regard to the matter itself.

27. Therefore, in articles of faith one must have recourse to another dialectic and philosophy, which is called the word of God and faith.

28. Here we must take a stand, and the arguments of philosophy drawing the opposite conclusions must be regarded as the vain croaking of frogs.

29. Nevertheless, we are also compelled to affirm with regard to other arts and sciences that the same thing is not true in all of them.

30. For it is false and an error in the area of weights to say that weights can be attached to a mathematical point or line.

31. It is false and an error in the area of measurement to measure a pint with the measure of a foot or of an ell.

32. It is false and an error in the area of linear measurements to compare them with an ounce or a pound.

33. Yes, it is false and an error to say that a straight line and a curved one are proportionate to one another.

---

[5] Cf. above, p. 32, n. 38.

34. This applies also to those who square the circle, although they are not speaking wrongly when they call a straight and a curved line both a line.

35. Nevertheless, it is false if they want to make the straight line proportionate to the curved line.

36. Finally, something is true in one area of philosophy which is, nonetheless, false in another area of philosophy.

37. Liquid moistens—this is true when speaking of the atmosphere, but it is manifest heresy when speaking of fire.

38. Thus, in particular liberal arts, or rather crafts, if you look them over, you will never discover that the same thing is true in all of them.

39. How much less is it possible for the same thing to be true in philosophy and theology, for the difference between them is infinitely greater than that between liberal arts and crafts.

40. We would act more correctly if we left dialectic and philosophy in their own area and learned to speak in a new language in the realm of faith apart from every sphere.

41. Otherwise, it will turn out that, if we put the new wine in old wineskins, both of them will perish; this is what the Sorbonne did.

42. In articles of faith, the disposition of faith is to be exercised, not the philosophical intellect. Only then will we truly know what this means: "The Word was made flesh."

The Disputation

A The Disputation of the Reverend Father Doctor Martin Luther: Whether the proposition is true in philosophy: "And the Word was made flesh"

Preface

You know that at the command of the most illustrious prince, the elector, each field of learning has been ordered diligently to treat its own pursuits by lecturing, exchanging views, reflecting, and disputing. This is what the theologians, the jurists, the physicians are doing, in order that they may search out and set forth for their followers those matters which can most effectively be applied in life; and, by learning, they practice their art lest they turn out to be completely inept in the management of their affairs. Although this order of the most illustrious prince, the elector, is a human one, nevertheless, since we theologians are, besides this, all debtors, we ought to discharge our office before others with the greatest fidelity, and labor in the vineyard of the Lord, as Paul also gives the command to show concern, so that the word of God may abound among us. It is therefore fair that we obey this ordinance of the most illustrious prince, the elector, sincerely and gladly. There are also other reasons which ought to encourage us theologians to engage in disputations of this kind. For since we have become a spectacle throughout the whole world [I Cor. 4:9], and are accused of heresy and of being the authors of a new doctrine, we ought to burn the more with zeal for the word of God so that we ourselves may be certain about our doctrine and faith and that we may be prepared to respond. We ought not only to be opposed to our reason but also to the devil and the gates of hell, and, contradicting them, to expose them and to offer conclusive proofs. Peter also commands that we should be prepared to give an answer to all who seek it from us concerning the hope which is in us, and to do this with gentleness and reverence [I Peter 3:15]. This is something no one can do unless he is practiced in this arena and has defended himself against these monsters from his youth. Therefore, if the strength of my body should prove adequate, I, too, would debate on all the principal articles of our doctrine in order every week, and make you more alert in opposing the adversaries and arm you against future heresies, of which there will be many after our death. However, I shall do only as much as I am able. But now we shall argue against the Sorbonne of Paris; for the Parisian theologians have concluded that the same thing is true in theology as in philosophy, and vice versa. They have not been able to prove this impious doctrine, just as we do not prove it either, as we point out in these propositions. Nor is it this matter alone, but they have entangled themselves and many good men in other innumerable disputes. Therefore let us—you and I—dispel these errors of theirs. We shall debate, so that we may see what is to be said in answer to those men and so that we might not seem to be ignorant of their skills of which they brag so pompously. Thus Daniel learned the wisdom of the Chaldeans and Egyptians. Thus we elders should discuss the opinions of our opponents so that we might prepare you, the younger men, lest by their actions they might at some time deceive you because you were not warned, and subdue you because of your carelessness. Even though we may have departed this life, possibly this ability will not abandon others. For it is not granted to all to expose errors and objections aptly and appropriately, as Ovid says: "It is not the same thing to recognize and to cure illness; everyone can sense what is wrong; it takes skill to remove the trouble."[6]

So here we shall debate against the Parisians that things which may be true in theology are true in philosophy, and vice versa. Neither can all the same things be true in the various fields of learning. For you know that it is one thing to believe and something quite different to understand, as Paul says, "I do not see, I hope" [cf. Rom. 8:24 f.]; the one is indeed invisible, the other is visible. Here theology and philosophy differ. No one would hold them to be one, since each has a different starting point and goal which it pursues. This is an essential teaching of theology and of philosophy. Therefore, we shall here condemn the Parisians and others who likewise establish conflicting principles. This, therefore, is the reason for this disputation and the cardinal point, namely, that God is not subject to reason and syllogisms but to the word of God and faith. For as God has established distinct spheres in heaven, so also he rules on earth so that every single work and skill may retain its place and form and may not move outside its own center in which it has been placed.

Argument 1

If philosophy attributes to God infinite power, we seem to attribute to him also that the Word can be made flesh. However, philosophy does attribute to God the highest power. Therefore,

---

[6] Ovid, *Pontic Epistles* (*Epistulae ex Ponto*), III, 9, 15.

it also attributes to him the fact that the Word was made flesh.

Response: All philosophers, even Aristotle, do not discuss this matter concerning creation in this way, neither does Plato, who indeed says that God is the Founder of heaven,[7] but he does not attribute to him infinite power. Therefore, Pliny says that God cannot do all things; that is, he cannot make increate what has been created, and from this he infers other things. Then, too, other more distinguished philosophers admit that God is of infinite power, that is, that the world is infinite; but they say no more. Therefore, the minor premise is simply to be denied. For although the power of God is infinite, still, according to philosophy God cannot be spoken of as both Creator and creature, as God and man. It is true that philosophy acknowledges that God exists and that he is omnipotent; nevertheless, it is in no way possible to acknowledge on the basis of philosophy that he can become man, because God himself is infinite. For if he is of infinite power, he cannot become finite man because man is a part of the finite.

Argument 2

That which has been created cannot become increate. But the Word was made flesh. Therefore, he cannot become increate.

Response: This argument is in no way against us and we acknowledge it altogether because that matter already stands firm and it is impossible for a thing now to come into being after it has once come into being. But it is another question whether God can reverse the process and, after he has assumed human nature, can also lay it aside again. Why would it not be possible, since he is omnipotent? In fact, your argument is irrelevant to this matter. Whatever has been made—this is an argument about the fact of things, not about the Creator. But when God begins to create, then it is accomplished. But philosophy thinks of God as being himself an invisible and uncreatable reality.

Argument 3

If sin is in the matter itself and not in the form, then we ought to teach that matter is sinful either according to the major or the

[7] Plato, *Sophista* 265, C. Cf. *Phileb.* 28, C 29.

minor premise. However, in this syllogism sin is not there either according to the major or the minor premise. Therefore, neither is matter sin.

Argument 4

Every man is a creature. Christ is a man. Therefore, Christ is a creature.

Response: This is a sophistical argument. You admit the form, and yet beneath the form you attack the matter, something which the syllogism itself will not admit because where there is neither a major nor a minor premise, there is no syllogism. But in matter there is neither a major nor a minor premise; therefore, form without matter can be rejected. *Response:* When I abolish the form, I am abolishing either the major premise or the minor premise, and I am referring to the matter itself, which is completely without a major premise and is quite different; especially it is to be considered simply and straightforwardly among the articles of faith.

Response: I deny the minor premise because "man" is an equivocal term and so four syllogistic terms result. It is mentioned in one way in the major premise, in another way in the minor one. In the major premise it designates physical man, in the minor premise another, both the divine and the incarnate God. Therefore, they themselves concede that the major premise is false. And they devised the distinction between equivocal and univocal so that philosophy might be in harmony with theology. So we say that the Parisians have erred in this, that they here treat the major premise equivocally, to use their terminology. For unless you assert the minor premise, there is an error in theology. But right here the matter immediately becomes doubtful. The demonstration of proof has no validity at all because they are not to place ambiguous matters in a syllogism, even as the rhetoricians say that speech should be straightforward. It is therefore remarkable that they have concluded that a word is identical in theology and philosophy. You are right to distinguish a word which you deny, but still we call this a distinction of the Scholastics. If the word is the same, then the middle term should be the same, without the addition of another meaning. But they themselves disunite by uniting, as they do by means of their "immediate suppositions." And I simply say: If a distinction is made, the meaning of the word is not the same. We ought to rely upon the word alone. Oecolampadius says beautifully that "man" has another meaning here than in the [genealogical] tree of Porphyry.[8] He should rather have said that it is a communication of properties.[9] The philosopher does not say that God is man or that man is God and the son of God. But we say that man is God, and we witness to this by the word of God without a syllogism, apart from philosophy; philosophy has nothing to do with our grammar. You should note this because "man" is and should mean something beyond what it means in the [genealogical] tree of Porphyry, even if it is truly said that God was made man, as they and I say. For here it means something greater and more comprehensive.

Argument 5

Whatever is predicated of the subject of the major and the minor premises can also be predicated of the subject of the conclusion. On that account the conclusion is valid and not false, as you say in proposition nineteen. I prove the inference on the basis of principles of logic: If the premises are true, a true conclusion follows, etc.

Response: We deny that the principles of logic are valid in this matter, and we say that truth is not identical in theology and in philosophy. You must prove that because the inference is true in theology, the same thing is true in both theology and philosophy.

Argument 6

The wisdom of God does not contradict itself. Philosophy is the wisdom of God. Therefore, philosophy does not contradict itself.

---

[8] Reference is here made to Porphyry's *Introduction to Aristotle's Categories*, trans. by Boëthius. This translation became the accepted textbook of medieval Scholastic logic. In it we find the reference to the genealogical tree of concepts, beginning with universal essence and concluding with concrete man.

[9] The communication of properties (*communicatio idiomatum*) refers to an interchange of certain characteristics between the divine nature and the human nature in the one person of Christ. Thus, on the one hand, certain properties of the divine nature are communicated to the human nature of the Son of God, and, on the other hand, certain properties of the human nature are communicated to the divine nature of the same person even while each nature retains its distinctive and separate characteristics.

Response: This is the chief argument on this theme and the major premise needs to be further elaborated. Wisdom does not contradict itself; this we also say. Therefore, our argument does not contradict you. For this reason we have spoken of it below in the second proposition and admit that there is that legal wisdom concerning which Paul speaks, and we admit many other things, such as, that there is the entire Decalogue which natural laws and other teachings and theories of philosophy explain somewhat, particularly that which pertains to the second table of the Decalogue. But here we especially oppose the men at the Sorbonne who allow such things as the forgiveness of sins and the mystery of the incarnation and eternal life to be deduced by logic. They have asserted that they are there and can be obtained by living according to the law and through philosophy. This we deny. For they speak thus and allege that whoever has done what he was able to do is justified and merits grace according to his fitness, and afterward even in strict justice.[10] This we deny. What use would there be here for Christ? He would be set aside and buried completely. For when they want to be justified altogether without Christ, what else are they doing than consigning Christ to oblivion so that Christ might be completely useless for us and have died in vain? We admit that philosophy teaches and all men know by nature that theft is unlawful, as are many other things. But we cannot and ought not tolerate the fact that these chief theological articles—for whose sake alone Scripture was given—namely, those concerning justification, the forgiveness of sins, liberation from eternal death, are actually attributed to philosophy and human powers. For that reason Paul says concerning philosophical knowledge: "For although they knew God they did not honor him as God or give thanks to him" [Romans 1:21]. Thus this argument is destroyed. We say that theology does not contradict philosophy because the latter speaks only about matrimony, obedience, chastity, liberality, and other virtues. But

[10] Cf. Heiko A. Oberman, *The Harvest of Medieval Theology* (Cambridge, Mass.: Harvard University Press, 1963), pp. 471-472. *Meritum de congruo* is "an act performed in a state of sin, in accordance with natural or divine law, and therefore accepted by God as satisfying the requirement for the infusion of first grace." *Meritum de condigno* is "an act performed in a state of grace and therefore worthy of divine acceptation."

it is one thing to believe in the Son of God, to possess and to expect eternal life, and something else again to be chaste, to marry, to live honestly in the world, to be liberal, meek, obedient, kind, and peaceable.

Argument 7

Philosophy attributes to God incomprehensible matters. Therefore, it also attributes to him the power to become man.

I prove this from Romans 1 [:20]: "His power is eternal."

Response: If it attributes infinite qualities to God, then it is not philosophy. For Paul in Romans 1 [:19] says that "God has shown it to them." Besides, no philosopher, neither Plato nor Cicero, admits that the incarnation is a possibility and neither does he tell how this world began. But they have said that the world has its own course and is carried along in its own way and that there is an Intelligence which governs the entire mechanism of the world. Another philosopher has said: There is no first human being, nor last one, nor does anyone return to life afterward. But Cicero and Plato argue impressively about the immortality of the soul. These are very good thoughts. Nevertheless, although these matters are admitted and acknowledged, it does not follow that philosophy believes in the incarnation or that eternity can become temporality which is taken into the infinite. These matters can be reflected on by man, but they can in no way be believed, just as I am able to think about many other things which are beyond my capacity to understand. Anyone can reflect on the word and on all the articles of the faith, on eternal life, and many other things; but it is not possible by oneself to conclude that they are true, nor that that which is infinite can be made finite like man. For if they could have understood it, they would have believed. In short, I said it thus above: Philosophy deals with visible matters, but theology deals with invisible ones.

Argument 8

Whatever harmonizes with the truth of the faith proves the truth of the faith. The truth of philosophy and of reason is of this kind. Therefore, philosophy proves the truth. Or to put it otherwise:

Whatever is on our side is not against us, as Christ says: "He who is not with me is against me" [Matt. 12:30]. However, philosophy is not against us but for us. Therefore, philosophy is on the side of theology and not against it.

Response: But Christ spoke in that passage about the Spirit and true theology. "Whoever is with us" means "in the same faith." Now we also admit that philosophy is not against us but for Christ, as our sixth proposition proves; for all created things such as sun and moon, are for Christ and are not against him, because all things work together for good with the godly, even the devil, death, and hell. But you cannot conclude from that, that truth is the same in theology and philosophy, for they will continue to be different in kind and in matter.

Argument 9 Against the Solution Offered

The same thing is true in theology and false in philosophy, and vice versa. Therefore, philosophy and theology are opposed to one another and are not for us as you stated in the first proposition.

Response: Contrariety should be shown, and contradictories also. However, white and black are contraries in the same person, not in different persons. God and man are representations; they do not have the same meaning among the heathen. In philosophy the representation means one thing and in theology something else. For that reason contrariety must be established in the same genus and in the same proposition. God is man. In philosophy it is false to say that he is God and man. For this reason we separate these spheres in creation to the furthest extent, as the philosopher says. If someone has been continent and aspires to live honestly before men, he is not against Christ. Nevertheless, a tree must be good before it can bring forth good fruits. So a person is pleasing to God on account of Christ's merit and obedience before he does godly, good, and honest works. Therefore, the barbarians[11] are to be resisted who make everything equivocal if a matter of faith seems to be in question. But we ought to adhere to and speak of

[11] The non-Roman authors of the medieval period; e.g., Averroës, Porphyry, Maimonides, etc.

the word. I understand "man" here in a twofold way, in one way as a corporeal substance subsisting by itself, in another way as a divine person upholding the humanity. Is this, I ask, harmonizing theology and philosophy when you distinguish like this, when in fact you even distinguish univocal terms?

Argument 10

Where the premises are true, there the conclusion is also true. But in your syllogism the explanations [of the major and the minor premises] are not true. Therefore, the conclusion is not true either. For that reason it follows that the conclusion is false. If the conclusion is true, then the syllogism is true according to the rule: Things equal to one and the same thing are equal to one another. For example, the Father generates in divine things. The Father is the divine essence. Therefore, the divine essence generates.

Prove that the conclusion is true.

Opposing Argument: Thus I prove it: God of God, Light of Light.

[*Response:*] The Master of the *Sentences*[12] treats the manner in which this generation takes place. The Abbot Joachim[13] wrote against him; he argued that the Master of the *Sentences* was setting forth [the doctrine of generation] contrary to the doctrine of the eternity and Trinity of God. At this point the pope, through an investigation by the monks, decided against the abbot and the statement by which he had condemned the Master. That affair was

[12] Peter Lombard (died 1160), famous medieval Scholastic, whose *Four Books of the Sentences* (*Sententiarum libri quattuor*) was a standard textbook for instruction in theology until the Reformation.

[13] Joachim of Fiore or Flora (1130-1202), abbot of a monastery in southern Italy, developed an interpretation of history which exerted a deep influence upon the Middle Ages as well as upon modern thought. In his doctrine of God he opposed Peter Lombard who, in accordance with Augustine's teaching, emphasized the essential oneness of God and then proceeded to deal with the trinitarian nature of God. Joachim, influenced by the theologians of the Eastern Church, made the three persons of the Godhead his point of departure and affirmed that these three persons were "one substance" or "one God." In other words, he stressed the three persons before speaking of the unity of the Godhead. At the Fourth Lateran Council in 1215 the Western Church sided with Augustine and Peter Lombard in its understanding of the doctrine of the Trinity.

treated in great debates by the Parisians, and the pope came to the conclusion that the divine essence does not generate. However, at length, when many teachers had come together, they decided that Scripture indeed conceded that the divine essence generates, but that the essence does not prove the fact of generation, and I do not know what matters besides this they inferred apart from Scripture.[14] But our theology ought to be dependent neither on the pope nor on those teachers; and even if the Sorbonne investigates this, it still does not know today who is to be especially defended. But we say by way of conclusion that essence designates the total Trinity and majesty of God. If, therefore, we wou'd say that, it would also follow that there are two Gods, as if one Trinity would generate a third Trinity. Therefore, it is more appropriate, for the sake of both a surer and a better theological confession, to say that the Father generates rather than that the essence or the Trinity generates, so that you do not understand a somewhat personal essence but one that is common to the three persons of the Godhead and that God is one in essence and a Trinity in persons. We do not condemn confessions of faith; we are speaking of what follows excellently, not from the imperfection of a syllogism but from the greatness of the subject matter.

Argument 11

Your fourteenth proposition, "Let the woman be silent in church" [I Cor. 14:34; I Tim. 2:12], is contrary to Scripture. Therefore, it is not to be tolerated.

The premise is proved from Genesis 21 [:10], where Sarah admonishes and instructs Abraham that he should cast out his son, and he does it.

Response: A special command does not abolish a universal one, even apart from the fact that Sarah was in the private church [the home] and that the same thing is said of Rebekah with the approval of the Holy Spirit in Genesis 27 [:6]. The woman should speak about domestic things and in the home.

But let us go on to other matters.

[14] Fourth Lateran Council of 1215. Cf. H. Denzinger and A. Schönmetzer, *Enchiridion symbolorum* (34th edition; Freiburg, 1967), Nos. 803-807.

Argument 12

Propriety must be observed in interpreting Scripture. But propriety requires that it be understood that the Logos is the thought of the Father, that is, a representation or person. That is, it designates only the ideas in the mind of God. Therefore, this propriety is to be retained. The argument is whether or not propriety is to be defended.

Response: It is not, because a philosophical word becomes new in theology so that man according to philosophy is an existing person, but in theology he is a certain divinity in Christ. Therefore, this is the propriety required in speaking of the Word. So it is with regard to the blessed Virgin Mother. "Mother" is something other in philosophy than in reference to the Virgin Mary. Many passages in Scripture, which attribute to the Logos divinity, sufficiently prove that the Logos is a person.

Argument 13

In God nothing is transitory or accidental. Those who say that God is Father and Son attribute to God an accidental quality. Therefore, you are ascribing accidental qualities to God.

Response: Augustine says: "Everything that is in God is substance, even that which is accidental for us; speaking, hoping, and the knowledge of God are all substances."[15] Thus what is an accident for philosophers is substance in God.

Argument 14

Whatever existed before creation was not born. Christ existed prior to creation. Therefore, Christ was not born a man.

Response: The form is valid, but the conclusion is false. The premises are true; nevertheless, the major premise must be differentiated. It is true in philosophy, not in theology.

Argument 15

If the Son were of the same substance and power with God, Scripture would not say that all things were made subject to him

---

[15] Augustine, *On the Trinity* (*De trinitate*), V, 4-5 (*MPL* 42, 913 f.).

by the Father [I Cor. 15:27 f.; Eph. 1:22]. However, all things were made subject to Christ by the Father. Therefore, Christ is not of the same substance and power with the Father.

Response: You have often pointed to and spoken about the communication of properties, and that fact is to be diligently noted. For by this fact the proper attributes of each nature are attributed to the person of Christ. For even if he is identical with the Father, nevertheless, because he became incarnate, suffered, and was crucified for us, all things were made subject to him by the Father. For the person [of Christ] is God and man; inasmuch as he is God, he did not suffer, because God is not capable of suffering; but inasmuch as he is man, he suffers. Nevertheless, because God and man in the one person cannot be separated, we are compelled to say that Christ as true God and true man suffered for us, and the whole person is said to have died for us. For thus it is said in the Creed: "He ascended into heaven." Thus, too, Paul says: He "made him sit at his right hand" [Eph. 1:20]. The Son of God himself was born of the Father from eternity, and it was necessary for him who is the Son with the Father, and who descended, to ascend again. These two natures in Christ ought not to be separated but unified as much as possible because the Son of God is God who suffered, was crucified, was dead, and rose again. So Paul says: "They would never have crucified the Lord of glory" [I Cor. 2:8]. But these are not philosophical matters. We say: "I believe in God," not "I understand God."

[XV[a]]

I ask whether "word" always signifies a person.

Response: The word has this meaning. But it has also at times referred to events, as in: "Let us see the word, that is, the event."[16] However, where circumstances are not such that you can understand "word" as a thing or an event as in this case, that it is the Word and is truly God, then it is not a thing or an event. It is a question of a Word spoken out, not retained in thought, the Word which he spoke from the beginning, which was identical with the

[16] Luke 2:15 according to the Vulgate.

Father and of the same substance. Paul of Samosata[17] does not speak of the word expressed, but unexpressed, which is false. We do not speak thus, but [say] that he was with the Father from the beginning and at the appropriate time was fashioned as flesh. The Arians said that he was certainly brought forth, but that he had not remained the same substance with the Father and truly and naturally God. They themselves spoke solely about the Word as about a man, which also is not true.

Argument 16

There is a distinction between unity and threeness in theology. But there is also such a distinction in philosophy. Therefore, a certain amount of mathematical philosophy is necessary in theology.

Response: Mathematics is completely hostile to theology and there is no part of philosophy which so contends against theology. Take an example: The mathematician says that one cannot be two and three cannot be one, as in the article of the Trinity. Likewise, in the Sacrament of the Altar, the mathematician does not believe that the bread is the body and the wine the blood of Christ. Therefore, we say that mathematics ought to remain in its own sphere and place. To argue about oneness and numbers does not concern us at all, because mathematics itself is unable to concede that the Trinity is a unity. Nonetheless, it is true that the Trinity and unity in God are something entirely different. Even if it is not true in nature, nevertheless, in God it can be true, and it is.

Argument 17

James says that with God "there is no variation" [James 1:17]. Christ was changed, that is, was made man. Therefore, Christ is not by nature God.

Response: As was said above: In God there is nothing acci-

[17] Paul of Samosata, bishop of Antioch (ca. 260-272), taught dynamic Monarchianism. Accordingly, Jesus, born of the Virgin Mary, was a man upon whom God bestowed his Logos. By the indwelling of the Logos, or wisdom from above, he was progressively raised to the status of the Son of God. Thus he attained a permanent oneness with God. Cf. Reinhold Seeberg, *Lehrbuch der Dogmengeschichte,* 4 vols. (5th edition; Basel/Stuttgart, 1960), I, 566-570.

dental. To be, to live, to hope, to know are substantial matters, not accidents, as they are in man.

Argument 18

God is not at all visible. Christ is visible. Therefore, Christ is not God.

Response: These are syllogisms which are valid in logic, but not in theology. For Christ is visible and invisible in accordance with the properties of his natures. But in the concrete person of Christ there is unity. Therefore, Christ is visible and invisible. The man Christ is one person because the Virgin is the mother of the Son of God who suffered and was crucified. How? Because the two natures in him are inseparable.

Argument 19

Is that Word which is rightly said to be consubstantial with the Father consubstantial with us? The Greeks have spoken of *homoousias.*[18] The Latins speak of one and the same person. Therefore, I am of the opinion: He is of divine *homoousias*; he is of the same divine essence which would be of the same kind as was also with us in his humanity.

Response: That does not necessarily follow. As all other things are similar and the same in their highest nature, so we are sons of the Father in Christ, not as he would be one with the Father, but we are sons by adoption because of Christ. One and the same deity, which is only in Christ, is of such a *homoousia* in the divinity, because they are of the same substance, that is, as Christ is true God in the genus of the divinity, so the Father is also true God in the genus of the divinity. So also Christ is true man, like us, and partaker of our nature. We insist upon this point, lest we make a fictitious God out of Christ; but by nature he is really true God and truly natural man like you and us. Otherwise, he is of no help to us, as we have often said.

If it is *homoousia* of persons, in what way, therefore, does the Father generate the Son?

---

[18] The word means "of the same essence."

In summary this is the way: The Father, generating, transfers his substance in the divinity to the Son. Thus the Father and the Son and Holy Spirit are three distinct persons, and yet in truth one essence. These things can be believed but they will never be capable of being understood by human reason. However, I say that the Father, remaining the same God, transfers his divinity to the Son in such a way that the Son is the complete and perfect image and stamp of the Father. We cannot thus transfer ourselves to another person so that that same image itself or person is the same as we are. Images can reflect our outward appearances, as we see in statues, but they cannot be the very same thing that we are. Nevertheless, that is true of God. However, these things have to be believed.

Argument 20

The art of logic is a means divinely given for the sake of searching for the truth. Therefore, it is to be used also in theology.

I prove the inference, because logic is the art of arts, the science of all sciences in all the fields of learning.

Response: It is not as mistress but as maidservant and bondwoman and most beautiful helper that it teaches a person to define and to classify. But even for theology [logic has this function]. There [i.e., in theology], if logic falls short, this maidservant also lies dead.

Argument 21

Everything that is begotten is a creature. Christ was begotten. Therefore, he is a creature. I prove the minor premise from Psalm 2 [:7]: "Today I have begotten you."

Response: Christ has a twofold nature, and according to one of the two he was born outside of time, in opposition to time, and before the circumstances of time. The Psalm speaks of an eternal generation, that he was born of the Father from eternity.

Argument 22

The Son of God is called the wisdom and power of God [I Cor. 1:24]. Yet the Word that was made flesh is not called the wisdom or power of God. Therefore, the Word that was made flesh is not the wisdom and power of God.

I prove the major premise thus: Paul says: "Who was made wisdom for us" [I Cor. 1:30].

Response: He was even made sin for us [II Cor. 5:21]. For we can say: Christ is the incarnate and created wisdom of God, or however you wish to say it.

Argument 23

Christ says: "The word which you have heard is not mine" [John 14:24]. Therefore, the Father has a word internally in himself other than Christ himself.

Response: Christ refers everything he has to the Father, even his divinity, in order to call us to himself and to teach us that we should not seek the Father without or outside himself. What is more, he says elsewhere: "My teaching is not mine" [John 7:16]; it is not as if it is from him alone but as if it were received from the Father. And it is to be noted well and to be observed most emphatically that outside Christ there is no other God. On that account the Father wishes that the Son himself be heard, and there are most excellent passages to this effect in John and in Paul's Letter to the Ephesians.

Argument 24

Paul says that the power of God is also comprehended by the philosophers, Romans 1 [:20]. Therefore, the same thing is true in theology which is true in philosophy.

Response: The meaning of the law is, under various circumstances, known to the philosophers. But the promises of God belong to theology, and the gospel is not known to every creature because it is a mystery hidden from the world.

Argument 25

Whoever abolishes the method of syllogizing allows heretics the opportunity of interpreting matters arbitrarily. You are doing this. Therefore, you are providing the opportunity for heretics to exist.

Response: No, rather heretics, who have erred in this respect and who have rushed blindly into theology with this syllogistic form, permit themselves to reconcile all things by reasoning, and to infer everything by the syllogistic process in opposition to Scripture. For, having relied on this form and method, they have brought many difficulties and faulty inferences to Scripture even when the plain text occasionally shouts in disapprobation. Therefore, we speak thus: "Let the woman keep silence in the church" [I Cor. 14:34].[19] Advance anything you like from the Scriptures because of the saying, "Listen to him" [Matt. 17:5], or something which delights all those who listen to you; but always do it with him [Christ], since he remains immovable and does not contend against Scripture.

Argument 26

That which is not impious is able to confirm articles of faith. Reason is not impious. Therefore, reason is able to confirm articles of faith.

I prove the minor premise because no creature is impious; therefore, neither is reason impious. If reason is upright, therefore, philosophy, which uses human reason, is also upright.

Response: It is not impious that the Gentiles have come to know God, but there is a distinction to be made in regard to the word "upright." There are upright persons in theology and there are upright persons in philosophy. This [philosophical] uprightness is meant for a mother and a father. Thus, in the law of Moses there are upright persons. But we have a more excellent theology which speaks differently about uprightness.[20]

Argument 27

Philosophy is wisdom. Wisdom consists in understanding and intelligence. Understanding and intelligence inquire into the reasons for things. Through the reasons for things we arrive at true

[19] Reason is not to be mistress in the church.

[20] Civil righteousness is here differentiated from the righteousness or uprightness demanded by God.

knowledge. Therefore, philosophy inquires into this: "The Word was made flesh."

M[artin] L[uther]: Whoever inquires into the purposes of and reasons for things can understand this: "The Word was made flesh." Philosophy inquires into the reasons for things. Therefore, it also inquires into this: "The Word was made flesh."

Response: On the basis of particular things this does not in any way follow. We acknowledge that [philosophy inquires into the reasons] of many things, but not of all things, especially not in these matters; even if philosophy attributes power to the Word, it nevertheless does not subsequently ascribe to him the power to become flesh, as we said above.

Argument 28

Flesh and blood cannot inherit the kingdom of God [I Cor. 15:50]. Christ inherits the kingdom of God. Therefore, Christ is not flesh.

Response: With regard to the major premise: No flesh can inherit the kingdom, that is, flesh born of woman and having original sin. Christ did not possess such flesh. For "flesh" is taken here to mean lascivious faults themselves. Such flesh Christ does not have. For concerning this flesh he says: "He who hates his flesh will have life" [John 12:25]. But equivocation is the mother of error.

Argument 29

The power to bring forth something else is a reality in theology and philosophy. Therefore, faith is a reality in theology and philosophy.

Response: I acknowledge the first premise entirely in the area of the physical, even if philosophers deny that something is created out of nothing. Theology talks with sobriety: The Father is another person, not another thing, so the Son is another person, not another thing, but not another substance. He is to be spoken of in the masculine gender, not in the neuter gender, according to the Master of the *Sentences* in the first book, the fourth distinction.[21] However, it is explained here: Generation is one thing in divine affairs and another thing in philosophy, and among neuter things neither takes place.

Argument 30

There is to be no arguing about the Trinity. You are disputing about it. Therefore, you are committing wrong. The major premise is proved on the basis of the decretals.

Response: It is not to be debated by idle men, like those of the whole Roman Curia, who understand none of these things, and it would have been better to allow a prudent investigation of the Trinity in theology than thus to abolish the article of justification. By that command of his, the pope hindered more than helped, and buried all of Scripture, because he was concerned about Satan alone.[22] Surely the devil himself opposes us, and we, after we have learned how to investigate the matter of the Trinity, become more experienced in it, and inquire better and more suitably into the Scriptures by which our faith can be strengthened and we can persevere in the faith. We also despise their vain opinions, and say: "I have heard those things now for a long time and they are known to me and are clever. For thus the devil always stirs up his followers."

Argument 31

Christ has been created. Therefore, he is not God.

Response: In philosophy it is true. The Arians caused great trouble for the fathers by that passage from Ecclesiasticus 24 [:12] concerning wisdom: "The Lord created me from the beginning" [Vu'gate]. This text the Arians stubbornly emphasized. "He created the Word" is not in the Hebrew. Thus it is badly proclaimed in written prose. He was born of his mother, the Creator has been

---

[21] Peter Lombard, *Sentences* (*Sententiarum libri quattuor*), I, d. 4, 4 (*MPL* 192, 535).

[22] Literally: "he looked at Satan alone." That is, he was so concerned about evil that he forgot about the gospel.

created, is not good prose, nor ought it to be proclaimed in this way. I believe that any ordinary pastor could have done as well.

Argument 32

Substance and essence are the same. There are three substances. Therefore, there are three essences.

Response: Both the Latins with *persona* and the Greeks with *hypostasis* wanted to signify that there is not one person but three distinct persons that subsist and not one person in the way Sabellius[23] wanted it. But there are three distinct, separate persons, and you may call them different and not different.

B *The Disputation of Doctor Martin Luther: Whether the proposition is true in philosophy: "The Word was made flesh"*[24]

Arguments Opposed to the Thesis

Philosophy and theology differ from one another. Philosophy deals with matters that are understood by human reason. Theology deals with matters of belief, that is, matters which are apprehended by faith.

[*I*]

Against 2

Philosophy attributes infinite power to God. Therefore, it also attributes to him the power of the incarnation. I shall prove the premise on the basis of the definition: God is an eternal, infinite mind.

Response: I deny the inference. For even if it [philosophy] seems to think and say that God is omnipotent, nevertheless, it cannot understand and establish that God was made man because the infinite would be contained in the finite.

---

[23] Sabellius, who was teaching in Rome around 215, advocated modalistic Monarchianism, according to which God revealed himself successively in three different modes or ways as a person, first as Father, then as Son, and finally as Holy Spirit.

[24] Beneath this heading Theses 1-42 appear in the Wittenberg printing of 1539. Cf. *WA* 39^{II}, 3, n. 1 and 6, n. 1.

[*II*]

That which has been created is unable to become increate. The Word was made flesh from a virgin. Therefore, it is not impossible.

Response: This is in no way against us. Another question of the Scholastics is whether God can divest himself of the assumed flesh. The major premise has to do with created things and creatures, not with the Creator who was made [man].

[*III*]

Another Argument

The word "man" is predicated of God. Therefore, what is predicated of man is predicated of God.

Response: The Scholastics say: The term "man" is equivocal. (1) It is used of the created human race. (2) It signifies God who sustains a human creature. The failure to make this distinction is dangerous. They [the Scholastics] deny the minor premise.

[*IV*]

Every man is a creature. Christ is a man.

They say: According to the minor premise it signifies something other than according to the major premise. Here, therefore, we are arguing against the Parisians, for they say that the same statement is both true and false. They are driven to distinguish and to use the terms equivocally, by that fact implying that truth is different in theology from what it is in philosophy, because a word or a proposition must have the same meaning in philosophy and theology if it is to be true in both.

Gabriel[25] states that man is univocal and adheres to this steadfastly. Therefore, it is safer here to return to the word and abide by it. We are speaking of the God-man through the mutual participation of properties.

[*V*]

Against Proposition 16 and the Remaining Ones

Whatever is stated concerning a concept in the major premise,

[25] Gabriel Biel, exponent of Occam's theology. Cf. Heiko A. Oberman, *op. cit.*, pp. 120-145.

the same can be stated about it in the conclusion. Therefore, the conclusion in these syllogisms is true because the premises are true.

Response: The same thing is not true in theology and philosophy.

[V[a]]

Another Opposing Argument

One and the same cause cannot have, etc. The divine is one and the same cause. Therefore.

[*VI*]

Veit Winsheim[26] *Against 4*

The wisdom of God does not contradict itself. Philosophy is the wisdom of God. Therefore.

The minor premise is proved on the basis of Paul's statement: "The truth of God" [Romans 1:18, 25].

Response: I admit that the legal wisdom of God is not contrary to that wisdom of the gospel, but is not included in it. Theology, the incarnation, and justification are above and beyond reason and philosophy. Philosophers concede to God omnipotence outside himself in the things which he created.

[*VIII*]

Against 4

What is in harmony with the truth supports it. Philosophy is in harmony with the gospel. Therefore, the former supports the latter.

I prove the major premise: "Whoever is not against us is for us" [Mark 9:40].

Response: Whoever is for us, that is, has the same faith. All things are for Christ and work together for good in the elect; yet all things do not constitute the gospel.

---

[26] Veit Oertel from Windsheim. Evidently a master of theology at Wittenberg University. Cf. K. Hartfelder, *Melanchthoniana paedagogica* (1892), pp. 93 ff.

[IX]

Veit Amerbach[27]

Truth and falsehood are in themselves opposed to one another. Therefore, philosophy and theology are in opposition to one another in themselves because you said: One thing is true in theology, another in philosophy.

[*Response:*] Matters opposed to one another ought to be contradictory concerning the same thing, in the same category.

The God-man and God, not man, are not contradictory matters in the same category.

The Sorbonne is equivocal here about the designation "man."

[X]

Against 16

The Father generates in divine matters. The Father is essence. Therefore, essence generates.

I prove that this is a true inference from the Creed:[28] "God of God, Light of Light." Therefore, God generates God.

Response: We are making a false inference because the essence designates the entire Trinity. Moreover, if you say: The essence generates, it would be nothing other than: The Trinity generates.

[XI]

Against 14

Let the woman be silent in church.

An example of sacred Scripture opposes this command. Therefore, etc.

Response: It is an isolated example.

[XI[a]]

Against 8 Saxo[29]

Propriety is not to be disdained. Particularly, disdaining musical skills amounts to disdaining propriety. Therefore.

---

[27] Veit Amerbach was dean of the faculty of arts at Wittenberg University during the winter semester, 1538-1539.

[28] The Nicene Creed.

[29] Johannes Saxo from Holstädt in Holstein. Cf. *WA*, TR 5, No. 5391.

[XII]

Another Argument from Paul of Samosata[30]

The propriety of words is to be retained. The word itself does not designate a person, but thought. Therefore, etc.

Response: The Word is a new and different expression in theology and designates the divine person. It does not signify a word. "The Word was made flesh," that is, the promise of God was fulfilled. This interpretation of it is unreasonable.

[XII[a]]

Heinrich Schmedenstede of Lüneburg[31] *Against 9*

It is possible to have the same form in a philosophical and a theological syllogism. Therefore, logic is not to be rejected.

Response: But the conclusion is not valid in the same way in both. Whatever follows on the basis of truth is true in philosophy. However, whatever follows on the basis of truth in philosophy is not true in theology, such as: Image is not substance. Christ is the image of God. Therefore he is not substance. *Response:* The major premise, which is true according to reason in philosophy, is to be denied.

[XVI]

Dr. Jonas[32]

The distinction between unity and threeness is necessary in divine matters. But that distinction is a philosophical one. Therefore, a certain amount of philosophy is necessary in theology.

Response: The Trinity in theology is vastly different from the way it is accepted in mathematics.

[XVIII]

God is not at all visible. Christ is visible [as a man]. Therefore.

---

[30] Cf. above, p. 255, n. 17.

[31] Heinrich Schmedenstede from Lüneburg came to Wittenberg in 1524. He received his M.A. in 1532 and became a member of the faculty of arts the following year. Cf. *LW* 34, 302.

[32] The reference is to Justus Jonas, a member of the theological faculty at Wittenberg University from 1521-1541. Cf. Martin Lehmann, *Justus Jonas, Loyal Reformer* (Minneapolis: Augsburg Publishing House, 1963).

I prove the major premise: "No one has ever seen God" [John 1:18; I John 4:12].

[*Response:*] Christ is visible because he is true man.

[*XIX*]

Dr. Cruciger[33]

Christ is consubstantial with the Father and with us. The question is whether he is consubstantial in the same manner. The Greeks have said that he is *homoousion*[34] with the Father. The Latins have said that he is consubstantial, that is of the same substance. These matters seem to be contradictory—even as Christ is true God within the Trinity and is also true man.

[*XIX*[a]]

Against 4

Whatever is enjoined by God is true in theology. Philosophy is enjoined by God. Therefore, it is true in theology.

Response: The major premise is true in a theology which approves of this; otherwise, it is not so.

[*XXIII*]

Against 2

"The word which you heard is not mine but the Father's" [John 14:24]. Therefore, the Father has another inner word, and, consequently, the Word was not made flesh.

Response: Christ refers everything to himself which is in the Father; and indeed, he refers everything to the Father. Whoever wishes to listen to God, let him listen to Christ; this is a distinction of office, not of the person.

Another Argument

My teaching is not mine. Therefore.

Response: It is not his, as it were, from him, but his as though given him by the Father [John 7:16].

---

[33] Caspar Cruciger, a member of the theological faculty at Wittenberg University.

[34] The word means "the same essence."

[XXV]

Against 16 and the Rest

Any syllogism in which there is no defect of form or matter is valid. These syllogisms are of such a nature. Therefore, etc.

Against 4[35]

There are no contradictions unless they occur in the same subject.

[XXV[a]]

Philosophy and theology have a different subject. Therefore, they do not oppose each other.

Response: They are different and not contrary to each other.

[XXV[b]]

Master Battus[36]

Philosophy is a custodian leading to Christ [Gal. 3:24]. Therefore, it is not different [from theology].

[XXV[c]]

Against the Argument

Whoever assumes human nature is not a creature. The Word assumed human nature. Therefore, that which became flesh is not a creature.

The major premise is proved because a creature is made a creature by God.

[*Response:*] He who assumes human nature truly does not effect it by someone else's help. Therefore, the major premise is false. Whoever was made is a creature.

[XXVII]

Another Argument

Whoever inquires about the purpose and the causes of things inquires about the word of God. Philosophy inquires about purpose and causes. Therefore, it inquires about the word of God.

Response: It is a subtle argument.

---

[35] This is not a new argument but the response.

[36] An unidentifiable person.

[*XXVII*[a]]

I prove this:[37] Every syllogism, where neither the form nor the matter is invalid, is true. The syllogism, whatever it investigates, is not invalid in form and matter. Therefore.

Response: Things that are contradictory and diverse cannot be in the same subject.

[*XXVIII*]

Another Argument

Flesh cannot inherit the kingdom of God [I Cor. 15:50]. Christ inherits the kingdom of God. Therefore, Christ is not flesh.

Response: Flesh there signifies concupiscence in Paul. It is an equivocation. Every equivocation is the mother of errors.[38]

C *The Disputation of D. M. L. Concerning the Passage: "The Word was made flesh," the eleventh day of January in the year 1539*

D[octor] M[artin] L[uther]

Even if it is an order that each particular faculty deal with its own subject matter, nevertheless, for us theologians it is, in addition to this, according to the command of God that we deal with this subject matter in opposition to Satan and learn to search for sound doctrine, seeing that we are already a spectacle, as it were, in the world. Therefore, this disputation has been arranged against the Parisian theologians who want to measure all things theological with their philosophical reason; in order that we might know of their opinions and errors, these matters are now being discussed.

This is the proposition of this disputation, that the same thing is not true in theology and philosophy. For we know that it is one thing to understand, another thing to believe. Therefore, philosophy and theology are to be differentiated; it is the task of philosophy to understand by the use of reason; it is the task of theology truly to

---

[37] The following is a new argument, being a doublet of [XXV].

[38] The end of Report B, according to the extant manuscript.

believe what is above all reason. Faith is not bound by, or subject to, the rules or words of philosophy, but it is on that account free. And just as God has created many spheres in heaven, so, too, there are distinct domains among these faculties.

[*I*]

Against 2

Whoever concedes to God infinite power, that person also seems to attribute humanity to the Word. But philosophy does concede it. Therefore, all philosophers attribute infinite power to God, even as Plato believes that God is the Founder of the World. In this respect he is greater than Aristotle. They concede to the ruling God infinite power, that is, an infinite world.

[*Response:*] The major premise is simply to be denied. For even if philosophy would say that everything exists through God's infinite power, man can nevertheless not concede that he [God] can become man or anything else, because to enclose the power of God in the finite seems to diminish it. However, theology does concede it. Philosophy is concerned with these matters insofar as it speaks about things that were made, not about God [who was made flesh] because the fact that God was made [flesh] is intolerable to philosophy.

[*III*]

Participant Polner[39]

Even when the form is conceded, nevertheless, it may be that either the major or the minor premise is to be denied. But the form is to be conceded. Matter is that thing with which the form or syllogism deals. If there is an error in the matter and not in the form, it ought to be said: It fails in the major or the minor premise. But in this instance there is no failure in either the major or minor premise. Therefore, the matter is good.

Response: The subject matter taken by itself does not constitute either the major or the minor premise. It is the form that con-

---

39 Probably Hans Polner, Luther's nephew, who began to study in Wittenberg in 1529 and was still living in Luther's home at this time, serving as Luther's *famulus*, or assistant. Cf. *LW* 54, 428.

stitutes the major premise, the minor premise, and the conclusion. The subject matter is not confined within these boundaries.

[III[a]]

Another Argument

"Man" is predicated univocally, both in word and in meaning, of God. Therefore, it ought also to be predicated of God that he is a thinking animal.

M[artin] L[uther]

When I speak of God as man, I cannot deny that he is a thinking animal; here the Scholastic theologians have admitted that Christ was a rational animal and man. However, they distinguish senses of the word "man" and say that it is equivocal, so that, when it refers to anyone of the human race apart from the incarnation, it designates a person subsisting by himself. This is a philosophical meaning. It has another meaning when it is said about Christ. Here one does not interpolate that fictitious philosophical concept of a person. For here a new word is coined, designating the divine person sustaining our human one, as a white person signifies a man who maintains whiteness.

[IV]

Every man is a creature. The argument is not true, however, because there is an equivocation in it and there are four terms in the syllogism. In the major premise, "man" is made the middle term. Christ as man signifies the divine person incarnate, but in philosophy he signifies a fictitious person. So they destroy their own argument.

That the term "man" is taken univocally is not true in theology but in philosophy. But when the term is taken equivocally, you have a syllogism of four terms which does not subsist. But the Parisians themselves make this distinction and still they say that truth is the same in philosophy and theology. Why, therefore, do they make this distinction? If it were the same, it would have to be taken univocally, the same word, the same meaning. Therefore, not knowing what they say, they nevertheless distinguish theology from philosophy. Others have taken the word "man" univocally, like Gabriel [Biel] who objects [*incurrit*] to this syllogism: Every man is a creature. Occam did not want the term to be univocal but equivocal, so that humanity is one thing in Peter, another thing in Christ.

In philosophy man, according to his nature, does not signify a son of God or a divine person. This is the very thing which we say by the term "communication of properties." A syllogism is not allowed with regard to the mysteries of the faith and of theology. Philosophy constitutes an aberration in the realm of theology.

[*VI*]

Against 4 Master Winsheim[40]

The wisdom of God does not contradict itself. Philosophy is the wisdom of God, as Paul calls it. Therefore, philosophy does not contradict itself.

Response: We concede that it [philosophy] is not contrary to this legal wisdom but that it is not included in it.

We oppose the men at the Sorbonne who teach that that other theology concerning the Son, etc., is in agreement with philosophy.

There is, indeed, something innate in men that tells them that they should not kill, etc.; but that such things ought to justify them apart from grace is truly blasphemy.

[*VII*]

[*Response:*] That argument proceeds on the basis of contradiction. We do not say that the argument is contradictory. For philosophy is not in opposition to this one aspect of theology but opposes the other aspect.

In philosophy they argue about whether God is infinite or finite. Philosophy attributes to God what it does not comprehend. Philosophy deals with things that can be known, at least in part, but theology has to do with things that are to be believed. This is the difference.

---

[40] Cf. above, p. 264, n. 26.

[*VIII*]

Another Argument

Whatever is in harmony with the truth of the faith supports the truth of the faith, because Christ said: "For he that is not against us is for us" [Mark 9:40].

However, philosophy, if it is not against us, is therefore for us.

Response: Christ speaks there about the Spirit who is with us in the same faith. He does not oppose us. Furthermore, we admit that philosophy may be for us; but it does not follow from this that both are identical; heaven and the stars are devoted to the church, but they are not at once identical with it.

[*IX*]

Another [Argument] of the Dean[41]

Falsehood and truth are opposites. But what is true in philosophy is false in theology. Therefore, they are opposites.

Response: Contraries ought to concern the same matter or be in the same genus. God and man are two propositions, false in philosophy, true in theology. If both were in theology, then the objection would hold good.

We say: God is man, which is a simple proposition, not twofold as the Sorbonne has made it. We condemn the latter. Every man is a creature, this is a simple proposition; this is true in philosophy, but in theology it is false, which is proved in the minor premise, that is, Christ is man.

The Sorbonne compels us to make all words ambiguous. This is to be resisted. It is not to be allowed that in this proposition, that is, God is man, one may unite theology and philosophy, because a distinction is made between man and man. The man who uses words univocally speaks consistently, but not the equivocator, and by the fact that they equivocate they destroy their own argument.

[*X*]

Another Explanation of the Argument

The divine essence designates the entire Trinity. If we would

[41] The reference is to Veit Amerbach. Cf. above, p. 265, n. 27.

admit that the divine essence generates, it would be similar to saying that the Trinity generates.

[*Opposing Argument:*] On account of this inference we reject the syllogism in 16.

[*XII*]

Response: Paul of Samosata[42] was foremost in denying the divinity of Christ. When the word "man" is used in philosophy it signifies substance; in theology it also signifies the substance existing in Christ, but thus, that it is the substance which is at the same time God.

"Mother" in philosophy designates an impure woman; in theology the mother of Christ points to a pure woman and a virgin. And thus words that are employed by philosophy are invested with a new meaning.

When John says, "The Word was made flesh," he is designating a primary act, not a secondary act.

[*XIV*]

That which existed before creation was not born after creation. But Christ existed before creation. Therefore.

[*Response:*] This syllogism is valid in philosophy but not in theology.

[*XV*]

The person of Christ is God and man; that which pertains to his humanity suffered; but because he was one person, Christ is said to suffer, Christ ascends [to heaven], receives the kingdom, even though he was king before this, and all things were made subject to him, even though he possessed all things beforehand. All these things are said on account of the communication of properties.

[*XV*[a]]

Another Argument

"Let us see this word," Luke 2 [:15],[43] does not designate the person but the event. However, where the circumstances are such

[42] Cf. above, p. 255, n. 17.
[43] According to the Vulgate.

that it cannot be understood as an event, there "Word" is something else, namely, the divine substance. For God has generated in eternity, brought forth, and poured out the Word which, nevertheless, has remained in the same substance.

[XVI]

Dr. Jonas[44] *Against 4*

The distinction between unity and Trinity is necessary. In divine matters that distinction is necessary. Therefore, a certain amount of philosophy is necessary in theology.

Response: It is especially necessary to say that there is a Trinity in theology; but mathematics contends with theology, though it does not seem to oppose it: It is not possible for three to be one. This is a very true statement, but it is outside the realm of theology. Mathematics ought to go ahead in its own sphere and to argue about the unity and Trinity in its own way and not encroach on theology. That created Trinity and unity form a different Trinity from the one which is understood in arithmetic.

[XVIII]

Another Argument

God is not at all visible physically. But the apostles saw Christ. Therefore, he is not God.

Response: The property of both natures makes one Christ and each of the two propositions becomes true. Christ was visible and not visible; John says: "We have seen the Word" [John 1:14; I John 1:1, according to the Vulgate]. Mary is the mother of the Son of God; she is the mother of the Word of God.

[XIX]

It is a true statement that Christ is consubstantial with the Father according to his divinity and consubstantial with us according to his humanity. By generating, God pours forth his substance of divinity into the Son, and still the whole divinity remains in him in such a way that the Son is the perfect image of God.

---

[44] Cf. above, p. 266, n. 32.

[*XX*]

The art of logic is a seeker after truth in every field of learning, but in theology it may be a maidservant and bondwoman.

[*XXIII*]

Christ refers everything to the Father because he does not have his divinity from himself alone but from the Father; therefore, he says, "My teaching is not mine" [John 7:16], that is, it is not mine as if it were from me alone, but it has been received from the Father.

You do not listen to me as if the teaching were from me alone, but as the teaching I have received from the Father.

[*XXV*[a]]

Legal wisdom is sometimes known to reason, but in no wise the gospel or that which rests upon the promise.

Opposites are not in the same category. The subject of philosophy and theology is identical, that is, the human soul. Therefore, they are not opposed to one another.

Response: It is true, I admit, but they are different in character.

[*XXV*[b]]

Philosophy leads to Christ. Therefore, it is not different because as custodian it leads to Christ.

God does not generate something else, but someone else, that is, another person, even if similar to himself in all things, and consubstantial with himself. The Platonic philosophers have stolen much from the fathers and the Gospel of John, as Augustine says that he found almost everything in Plato which is in the first chapter of John.[45] Therefore, those things which the philosophers say about these ecclesiastical matters have been stolen, so that a Platonist teaches the Trinity of things as (1) the maker, (2) the prototype or exemplar, (3) and compassion; but they have mixed philosophical thoughts with one another and have falsified them.

[45] Augustine, *Confessions* (*Confessionum*), VII, 9 (*MPL* 32, 740-742).

[*XXIX*]

Whoever wants to debate ought to see to it at least that one of the two premises is reasonable [?] and affirmative, just as it is necessary that the contradiction of one of the two must be true, as for example the proposition that you are an ass [?].[46] Therefore, it is true.

Response: On the basis of purely particular things this does not in any way follow. It was necessary that all the answers be presented . . . .

The creature signifies that which is neither essence nor the divine person in philosophy. Therefore, it becomes a new word in theology, so that it signifies the subsisting person.

[*XXXII*]

Substance and essence are identical. Therefore, there are three substances. Therefore, there are three essences and not one.

Response: The Latins speak of *persona*, the Greeks of *hypostasis*. However, there are three subsisting persons but one divinity. The major premise is true. There are three different subsisting persons, but one divinity, yet they cannot be judged by human reason.

The value of this disputation lies in the fact that it does not allow us to argue on the basis of philosophical reasons in the mysterious articles of faith, but we must adhere strictly to the word and truth of the Bible. It is also clear from the disputation that the judgment of reason is not strong enough to oppose the word upheld by faith, but that reason should subordinate and submit itself to the obedience of Christ; second, that "man," "flesh," etc., become designations with a new meaning when they refer to Christ.[47]

---

[46] The Latin is not clear here. Cf. Thesis 3.

[47] At this point there follows an appendix, containing a very carefully worded series of arguments against a number of the theses. Since the responses to these arguments are lacking, Paul Drews convincingly conjectures that this section represents the work of an unknown scholar who was not given the opportunity of presenting his arguments during the course of the disputation. Cf. Drews, *op. cit.*, p. 486.

BRIEF CONFESSION CONCERNING THE HOLY SACRAMENT

1544

Translated by

Martin E. Lehmann

INTRODUCTION

Luther's closing sentence of the Marburg Articles aptly summarized the result of the Marburg Colloquy: "And although, at this time, we have not reached an agreement as to whether the true body and blood of Christ are bodily present in the bread and wine, nevertheless, each side should show Christian love to the other insofar as conscience will permit, and both sides should pray to Almighty God that through his Spirit he might confirm us in the right understanding."[1] In this way the controversy over the sacrament, though failing to end in agreement, was brought to an amicable cessation.

Literary polemics over the matter ceased for more than ten years. Significantly, too, the Wittenberg Concord of 1536 marked the formal agreement with respect to the eucharistic doctrine between Luther and the rest of the Wittenberg theologians, on the one hand, and Martin Bucer and Wolfgang Capito of Strassburg as representatives of the South German cities, on the other hand. Some two years later it even appeared as if an accord might be reached with the Swiss also. In a letter to Duke Albrecht of Prussia, under the date of May 6, 1538, Luther wrote: "We are getting along well with the Swiss with whom we have been in disagreement on account of the sacrament. . . . This pleases us . . . and disturbs the abomination at Rome; they [the papists] are very much frightened by this latest news . . . ."[2] Henry Bullinger, Zwingli's successor at Zurich, at that time also harbored the sanguine expectation of reaching complete accord with the Wittenbergers. In a letter to Luther he spoke about forming "a mutual friendship which is never to be broken."[3]

However, these high hopes were soon dashed to pieces. After 1538 the cordial relationship between the Swiss and the Lutherans

---

[1] See *The Marburg Articles*, above, pp. 88-89.
[2] *WA*, Br 8, 215.
[3] *WA*, Br 8, 207.

deteriorated progressively and in the early 1540's it became apparent that the doctrinal difference over the Lord's Supper could not be overcome.

The immediate impulse for writing the *Brief Confession Concerning the Holy Sacrament,* however, did not come from the Swiss but from Caspar Schwenckfeld. Schwenckfeld had at one time been an enthusiastic follower of Luther's evangelical teaching. Later he developed his own specific doctrines about the person of Christ and the relationship between the human and divine natures in him as well as a different understanding of the Lord's Supper. Luther labeled him as a heretic. The upshot was that Schwenckfeld became Luther's determined opponent.

In October of 1543 Schwenckfeld, writing at length to Luther, expressed his regret that the Wittenberg Reformer looked upon him as a heretic. He stated that he agreed with Luther in the essential points of the faith and that he was not in agreement with the Swiss followers of Zwingli with respect to the teaching on the Lord's Supper. At the same time Schwenckfeld had the temerity to point out to Luther his doctrinal errors and his deficient knowledge of Christ and the gospel.[4] When Luther received this letter, he became quite disturbed over it. Instead of dignifying Schwenckfeld with a reply by letter, Luther handed a note to the messenger who had brought Schwenckfeld's letter. In it he declared that he did not want to have anything more to do with Schwenckfeld because he was a Eutychian[5] and a sacramentarian. He called Schwenckfeld a "stupid fool, who is possessed by the devil, has no understanding and doesn't know what he's mumbling about."[6]

Schwenckfeld did not reply to the note but made it public among his friends and adherents, after appending to it his own commentary. "Therefore, I can say nothing more about Luther's evil, dissolute, unreasonable words than that I must have pity on

---

[4] *WA*, Br 10, 421-426.

[5] Eutyches, a monk of Constantinople, taught that in the incarnation the human and divine natures of Christ were so blended that there was but one nature left and that nature was fully divine. Christ, therefore, only seemed to be human. Eutyches was excommunicated for heresy at a synod in Constantinople in 448.

[6] *LW* 54, 469-471. Cf. *WA*, TR 299-301.

him."[7] Since Luther speaks of this rift between Schwenckfeld and himself in the opening paragraphs of the *Brief Confession*, it is clear that Schwenckfeld was in part responsible for inducing Luther to write another confession.

The second factor which caused Luther to plan and carry out this literary task was actually the primary motivating force in its composition. Lutheran pastors in Eperjes, Hungary, informed Luther by letter about a certain Matthias Biró Dévay, an evangelical minister, who was advocating a Zwinglian view of the Lord's Supper. Dévay had previously spent some time in Wittenberg and had gone from there to Switzerland where he became acquainted with the Zwinglian view of the Eucharist. After his return to Hungary he began to spread the report that the elevation of the elements in the Holy Communion had been dropped in Wittenberg because of a new understanding of the sacrament and that agreement between Lutherans and Zwinglians on this vital doctrine had been attained. In a reply to these pastors in a letter of April 21, 1544, Luther stated that it was hard for him to believe that Dévay had become a sacramentarian. He emphatically denied the report that agreement with the Swiss on the interpretation of the sacrament had been reached, stating that he and his colleagues were constantly opposing their teaching. The decision to do away with elevation of the elements in the Eucharist, he explained, had not been prompted by a new teaching about the sacrament. However, in view of this confused state of affairs about the sacrament, Luther felt compelled to clarify his own doctrinal position in the matter anew. He wrote to the pastors in Hungary: "After writing so many confessions, I must come out with one more. I will do this in the very near future, and it will be my last one."[8] This is the first reference Luther made to his plan of writing another confession of faith.

After that date Luther undertook with all the vigor he could command—about one and a half years before his death—the execution of that resolution. By August 8, 1544, he had completed writing

---

[7] *MA*³ 4, 425.
[8] *WA*, Br 10, 556.

three pages of his projected confession. Within six weeks it was in the hands of the printer and by September 30 it had appeared in print.[9] Caspar Cruciger, his colleague on the theological faculty, spoke of it as being moderate in tone.[10] All things considered, the book could be so designated. When he wrote it he was already an old man. Recurring illnesses had plagued him from 1537 on. Maligned by his foes, vexed by internal strife and misunderstanding, and burdened with excessive labors, he had become coarse and intemperate in his polemical outbursts against his opponents. Yet, in spite of his irascibility, the *Brief Confession* did not condemn or find fault with Melanchthon's and Bucer's compromising tactics in dealing with differences with respect to the Lord's Supper within the Protestant camp, although such a condemnation had been expected. In reality it was a statement of faith which reflected Luther's strong disagreement with the interpretation of the Eucharist as put forward by Zwingli, Karlstadt, Schwenckfeld, and others, as well as his positive emphasis on doctrinal integrity and evangelical freedom. In writing this last confession of faith Luther utilized his previous polemical writings against the radical Reformers in a supportive way.

His opponents, especially Bullinger of Zurich, impatiently awaited the publication of this confession. In December of 1544 Bullinger received a copy of it. He began almost immediately the task of framing a reply. His answer to Luther's *Brief Confession* appeared in print in March, 1545, under the title, *True Confession of the Servants of the Church at Zurich.* Luther, upon perusing it, was hesitant about answering it. After some reflection he decided not to reply to Bullinger's work. An indirect answer to the position taken by the Swiss was given by Luther in the fifteenth and twenty-seventh theses of his *Against the Thirty-two Articles of the Louvain Theologists,*[11] written in 1545. Still, the idea of engaging in a polemic as a rebuttal to Bullinger's work occurred to Luther again in September of 1545. However, his death on February 18, 1546, precluded any further possibility of carrying out such a plan.

---

[9] *C. R.* 5, 488.
[10] *WA* 54, 123.
[11] *LW* 34, 355-356.

The German text of Luther's *Brief Confession Concerning the Holy Sacrament* (*Kurtz bekentnis D. Mart. Luthers, vom heiligen Sacrament*) in *WA* 54, 141-167, translated below, was compared with the texts in *EA* 32, 396 ff., *St. L.* 20, 1764-1791, and *MA*³ 4, 294-315. In preparation for the *Brief Confession Concerning the Holy Sacrament* Luther devised an outline of which a fragment is extant. This fragment is included with the text of the *Brief Confession* in the Weimar Edition. A translation of this partial outline will be included in a lengthy note at the point where it parallels the thoughts developed in the final version of the *Brief Confession*. A comparison of this portion of the outline with the material in the writing itself reveals to what extent Luther was guided by it.

BRIEF CONFESSION CONCERNING THE HOLY SACRAMENT

Grace and peace in the Lord! My dear friend,[1] that Schwenckfeld is circulating my letter[2] to and fro and, together with his Eutychians and slanderers of the sacrament,[3] is maligning me behind my back, I must believe because you have just now sent me the copy of the same letter which you had received. It pleases me that he is circulating this letter for the sake of his honor and good name and for the sake of my dishonor and shame. For that reason, too, I did not wish to seal the letter but left it open; neither did I address it to him but to his messenger, for I did not want to honor his name. For such a damned slanderer is (God willing) not that important to me that I would address one letter of the alphabet to him or talk with him, or see or hear him. It makes no more difference to me if he or his accursed faction of fanatics, Zwinglians and the like, praise or scold me than if Jews, Turks, pope, and actually all devils would scold or praise me.

Since my death is now imminent, I want to take this testimony and this honor along with me before my dear Lord and Savior Jesus Christ's judgment seat, that I have earnestly condemned and rejected the fanatics and enemies of the sacrament—Karlstadt,

[1] It cannot be established who this friend was.

[2] The reference is to an open letter by Luther which he had sent to Schwenckfeld in reply to one written by the latter. See Introduction.

[3] "Slanderers of the sacrament" in all likelihood refers to the followers of Zwingli. "Eutychians" is used here to designate the followers of Schwenckfeld's understanding regarding Christ's true deity and humanity. Eutychianism is a teaching, deriving its name from Eutyches, a monk of Constantinople, who held that after the incarnation the two natures, divine and human, were so blended that only one nature remained and that this remaining nature was fully divine. The body of Christ, he asserted, is the body of God and therefore it is not consubstantial with our human body.

Zwingli, Oecolampadius, Stenckefeld,[4] and their disciples at Zurich and wherever they are—according to his command, Titus 3 [:10-11]: "As for a man who is factious, after admonishing him once or twice, have nothing more to do with him, knowing that such a person is perverted and sinful; he is self-condemned." They have been admonished often enough and also earnestly enough by me and others; the books are extant. In addition, we continue to preach against their blasphemous and deceitful heresy daily, as they know full well.

On this account it seemed very strange to me and it makes me uneasy that Schwenckfeld has become so frank and bold in approaching me with writings and books, because he knows or at least should know that he is my unreconciled enemy.

First of all, there is the matter of the holy sacrament, which in the province of Silesia he represented as mere bread and wine and thus misled many thousands of souls; he has not repented, but as Solomon says, "He rejoices in evil things,"[5] as if he had done well. And still he thinks that Luther should welcome his letters and books. He hopes in this way to foster the false idea that Luther is in complete agreement with Schwenckfeld and the fanatics and has recanted everything, for they are exchanging letters and books with one another like good friends, etc.

To be sure, I have often been told that the fanatics were boasting that I was in agreement with them, but I refused to believe it because none of them was willing to admit this publicly in writing. However, in this way I was supposed to be confirmed in my believing it before becoming aware of what was happening.

It is true that it is fifteen years since Zwingli and Oecolampadius and several of us assembled at Marburg and reached an agreement with respect to a number of articles of faith that were completely Christian, as the printed leaflet testifies.[6] However, with regard to the article on the sacrament we reached an impasse. Yet

---

[4] Luther here changed Schwenckfeld's name to Stenckefeld, literally meaning "Stinkfield." This derogatory term is frequently employed by Luther throughout the *Brief Confession*.

[5] Prov. 2:14, quoted in Latin from the Vulgate.

[6] The reference is to *The Marburg Articles*. Cf., above, pp. 85-89.

in other respects we were supposed to be good friends so that the sharp polemics against each other might cease and we might see whether in time God would grant harmonious understanding through our prayers in this matter also. Because Zwingli and his followers yielded in so many important articles of faith, I was quite hopeful that in time the one remaining article would also be agreed upon. So for several years there was among us a pause in writing against one another.

Meanwhile Zwingli was wretchedly slain on the battlefield by the opposing party, the papists,[7] and Oecolampadius, much too weak to bear such a misfortune, died of grief because of it.[8] This event also caused me heartfelt sorrow, so that for two nights I, too, could easily have died. For I was hopeful that they were changing for the better, and yet I had to be very much concerned about their souls because they were still steeped in error and would thus perish in their sins.

However, after Zwingli's death a book came out which he is supposed to have written shortly before his death. It was entitled *Exposition of the Christian Faith to the Christian King*, etc.,[9] and was supposed to be better than all his previous books. That it had to be Zwingli's was evident from his wild, confused language and from his previously held opinion [about the Lord's Supper].

I have become very frightened about that book, not on my account but on his account. For, because he was able to write this after our agreement at Marburg, it is certain that in every respect he dealt with us with an insincere heart and tongue at Marburg. Therefore I had to despair (as I still must) of the salvation of his soul, if he died with such a disposition, regardless of the fact that his disciples and successors made him out to be a saint and martyr. O Lord God, this man a saint and martyr!

In this book he not only remains an enemy of the holy sacra-

---

[7] The battle at Kappel, October 11, 1531.

[8] November 24, 1531.

[9] Written in the early summer of 1531 and addressed to Francis I of France, the *Exposition* was dispatched to the French Court by the hand of Rudolph Collin. Cf. G. W. Bromiley (ed.), *Zwingli and Bullinger, Library of Christian Classics* (Philadelphia: Westminster Press, 1953), XXIV, 239 ff.

ment but also becomes a full-blown heathen. This is the marvelous improvement for which I had hoped. You can see what I mean: In somewhat different words he addresses the previously mentioned king thus: "There[10] you will see in the same fellowship all holy, godly, wise, brave, honorable people, the redeemed and the Redeemer, Adam, Abel, Enoch, Noah, Abraham, Isaac, Jacob, Judah, Moses, Joshua, Gideon, Samuel, Phinehas, Elijah, Elisha, also Isaiah and the Virgin Mother of God of whom he prophesied, David, Hezekiah, Josiah, the Baptist, Peter, and Paul; Hercules, Theseus, Socrates, Aristides, Antigonus, Numa, Camillus, the Catos and Scipios and all your ancestors who have departed in the faith," etc.[11]

This is written in his book which (as has been said) is supposed to be his most excellent and best book, produced just before his death. Tell me, any one of you who wants to be a Christian, what need is there of baptism, the sacrament, Christ, the gospel, or the prophets and Holy Scripture if such godless heathen, Socrates, Aristides, yes, the cruel Numa, who was the first to instigate every kind of idolatry at Rome by the devil's revelation, as St. Augustine writes in the *City of God*,[12] and Scipio the Epicurean, are saved and sanctified along with the patriarchs, prophets, and apostles in heaven, even though they knew nothing about God, Scripture, the gospel, Christ, baptism, the sacrament, or the Chris-

---

[10] I.e., in heaven.

[11] Cf. *An Exposition of the Faith, op. cit.*, p. 275. In Greek and Roman mythology Hercules was said to have been the son of Zeus and was a man of great physical strength. Theseus was a legendary Greek hero and king of Athens. Socrates (469-399 B.C.), a renowned Athenian philosopher, is the chief character in the dialogues of Plato. Accused of impiety and innovation, he was condemned to death and was given a cup of hemlock to drink in prison. Aristides was a Greek statesman and general in the fifth century B.C. Antigonus Cyclops (382-301 B.C.) was one of the ablest Macedonian generals of Alexander the Great.

Numa Pompilius (715-672 B.C.) was the second king of Rome. Marcus Furius Camillus, a Roman soldier and statesman, was elected dictator five times. He died of the plague in 365 B.C. Marcus Porcius Cato the Elder (234-149 B.C.) was a Roman statesman. Cato the Younger (94-46 B.C.) was a Roman Stoic philosopher who committed suicide on learning of Caesar's decisive victory at Thapsus. Publius Cornelius Scipio Africanus the Elder (237-183 B.C.) was the Roman general who defeated Hannibal at Zama in 202 B.C. Scipio Africanus the Younger (185-129 B.C.) was a Roman general and consul who directed the burning of Carthage.

[12] Augustine, *The City of God* (*De civitate dei*), III, 9-11 (*MPL* 41, 84-87).

tian faith? What can such an author, preacher, and teacher believe about the Christian faith except that it is no better than any other faith and that everyone can be saved by his own faith, even an idolater and an Epicurean like Numa and Scipio?

Because Zwingli not only repudiated the Marburg Agreement in this book (in fact, did not take the agreement seriously), but did what was worse and became a heathen, and yet his comrades, the fanatics, praise and honor this book (which also contains many other abominations), therefore, I have abandoned all my hope for their improvement. In fact I have ignored them to the extent that I did not want to write against this book nor pray for them any more, because I had seen that all my previous writings and admonitions, in addition to my Christian love and fidelity demonstrated at Marburg, were so badly received and would thus necessarily be shamefully lost.

If now on the basis of the news of such an agreement or in some other way someone had heard or had been persuaded that I was siding with the fanatics and we were of one opinion, I sincerely entreat him for God's sake that he should in no way at all believe this. May God keep me, as he has done up till now, from knowingly protecting or endorsing with my name the most insignificant article of faith of the fanatics. For at Marburg, too, we did not agree with them in a single article of faith, but they joined us in assenting to all articles with the exception of the article on the sacrament (as the printed leaflet shows), in which (as has been said) there was no agreement but the hope that such agreement would eventually take place. However, you have now heard how this hope has fared.

I say that I would much rather let myself be torn apart a hundred times or let myself be burned before I would be of one mind or will with Stenckefeld, Zwingli, Karlstadt, Oecolampadius, and whoever else they might be, these loathsome fanatics, or before I would acknowledge their teaching.

For I can well remember, and it is also recorded in their books, how altogether scandalously they blasphemed us along with our dear Lord and Savior; they called him a baked God, a God made of bread, a God made of wine, a roasted God, etc. They called us cannibals, blood-drinkers, man-eaters, Capernaites, Thyesteans,[13] etc. Yet they knew that they were doing an injustice to the Lord and us intentionally and in an exceedingly blasphemous way and that they were inventing scandalous lies about us. This was a sure sign that there was no benevolent spirit dwelling in them. Still, we allowed all this to take place and to happen to us at Marburg in the hope that they would make a complete change for the better.

For they knew very well that we had never taught or believed this, although they would like to have spread this view among the populace to their glory and our shame to make it look as if we were such mad, senseless, raving people who held that Christ was locally [*localiter*] in the sacrament and was eaten up piecemeal as a wolf devours a sheep, and that we were drinking blood as a cow drinks water. They knew (I say) when they called us cannibals and blood-drinkers at the instigation of the devil that they were resorting to manifest, impudent lies. For even the papists have never taught such things, as they clearly knew, but yet they—these holy, spiritual people—wanted to hurt us with the name "papist."

For this is how it was taught under the papacy, how we still accept and teach it, and how it was accepted in the true, ancient Christian church of fifteen hundred years ago (for the pope did not institute or invent the sacrament, as the fanatics themselves also must admit, although they want to make it papistical): When you receive the bread from the altar, you are not tearing an arm from the body of the Lord or biting off his nose or a finger; rather, you are receiving the entire body of the Lord; the person who comes after you also receives the same entire body, as does the third and the thousandth after the thousandth one forever and ever. In the same way when you drink the wine from the chalice, you are not drinking a drop of blood from his finger or foot, but you are drinking his entire blood; so, too, does the one who follows you even to the thousand times thousandth one, as the words of Christ clearly say: "Take, eat; this is my body" [Matt. 26:26].

---

[13] Thyestes, an ancient Greek legendary character, who unwittingly ate the flesh of his own sons. Cf. above, p. 72, n. 79, and *LW* 37, 138, n. 237.

He does not say: "Peter, there, devour my finger; Andrew, devour my nose; John, devour my ears," etc.; rather, he says, "It is my body; take it and eat it," etc. Each person receives it whole.

No, God be praised, we are not such ignorant blockheads, neither can this be said of the church under the papacy, as the evil spirit, working through the fanatics to our great vexation and disgrace, would like to have made the people believe with such shameless lies, so that they might gloss over their heresy. Moreover, they knew that in this matter their tongue was a lying tongue, because undoubtedly they themselves had often sung or read the mass for *Corpus Christi* (as it was called), in which among many other things it clearly says: "One takes it, a thousand take it; this person receiving as much as that person; nor, having taken it, is it consumed."[14] Therefore, they certainly knew that we were not cannibals, drinkers of blood, Thyesteans, Capernaites, or localists, and that our God could not be a baked God, a wine God, etc. Still, we had to listen to their malicious, manifest blasphemy; and whoever does not want to cease doing so still blasphemes thus among them, for they read it in their books.

Yet we let it pass at Marburg (as has been said) in order that we might fully demonstrate Christian love.[15] For (God knows),

---

[14] Luther is quoting here from the hymn "Praise, O Zion, Thy Salvation" (*Lauda, Sion, Salvatorem*) by Thomas Aquinas. Cf. John Julian, *Dictionary of Hymnology* (New York: Dover Publications, 1957), I, 662-664.

[15] The following is Luther's partial outline which was referred to in the introduction to this treatise. Cf. above, p. 285. – [Zwingli] displayed great faith, holiness, love, and suffering. In short, he wanted to be a martyr, just as our fanatics like to resort to big talk about Christian love. They also scold the damned Luther, because he is so proud and hard-hearted, entirely without love, and because he rends the unity of the church, yes, dishonors and mocks the holy servants of Christ for the sake of such an insignificant article which is of no consequence at all and is unnecessary (as their masters Zwingli, Oecolampadius, and Stenckefeld rave). This means judging the splinter in the brother's eye in order to cover up their own beams; it means straining out gnats and swallowing camels. In fact, whatever they did to me, they claimed that I had done to them; whatever I had to suffer at their hands, they boasted that they had to suffer at my hands.

Very well, then! I can do nothing about it; I must let them boast and be holy. I shall gladly be a poor sinner insofar as my dear God and Lord Jesus Christ is accused by me of telling a lie and is censured for his words. As Psalm 51 [:4] says: "Against thee, thee only, have I sinned . . . so that thou art justified in thy sentence and blameless in thy judgment," when the fanatics and followers of Stenckefeld judge and censure you. Accordingly I pray to God, the Father of all grace and mercy, that he might sometime graciously deliver the good people, wherever they are, in Switzerland or Silesia, from the damned teaching of the fanatics Karlstadt, Zwingli, Oecolampadius, Stenckefeld, and their comrades, and instead give them upright teachers. Amen. For, as has been said, I do not want to have anything to do with these teachers because it is entirely useless. My books which I have written to oppose them are available, and the truth has been abundantly and powerfully enough proved by me for anyone who desires to have the right faith. So there need be no more quarreling or debating.

In the face of such faithful diligence on my part God has indeed revealed himself in opposition to them by means of a forceful exhortation so that they should have been able to recognize their error. For right from the beginning God permitted the spirit who blasphemes the sacrament to be separated into seven spirits opposed to one another. By this they should have observed that it could not be a good spirit who treated the same text [of Scripture] in such a manifold and dissimilar way.

The First Spirit

Karlstadt interpreted the text according to his erratic understanding thus: Jesus took bread, gave thanks and broke it, and gave it to his disciples and said: "Take, eat; this is my body which is given for you," etc. The "this" was not supposed to point to the bread which the Lord took and gave, but to his visible body sitting at the table, so that the meaning was: Take, eat. Here sits my body which will be given for you, etc. I have written sufficiently about this in another book, *Against the Heavenly Prophets* [cf. *LW* 40, 73 ff.].

The Second Spirit

This interpretation did not please Zwingli, and his spirit brought a different hodgepodge into the text, namely, the following: "Take, eat. This signifies my body," etc. Zwingli permits the word "this" to point to the bread and wants to maintain his point of view in opposition to Karlstadt's spirit. But the word "is" is supposed to mean "signifies" in this sense: The bread "signifies" my body which was given for you.

The Third Spirit

Oecolampadius interprets the text thus: "Take and eat. This is my body." He permits the two words "this" and "is" to remain, which Karlstadt and Zwingli had changed. But the word "body" is not supposed to mean "body" but "sign of the body" so that the meaning is: This is the sign of my body.

The Fourth, Fifth, and Sixth Spirits

It seemed to Schwenckfeld that he outshone everyone. For he appeared on the scene on his own without a call; moreover, he was uneducated but filled with a proud spirit. And, as was fitting for such a proud spirit, he brought a new, unheard-of rule into theology. It was this: The new rule of the holiest spirit [*Regula nova spiritus sacerrimi*].

One must overlook these words, "This is my body," and first of all think about the spiritual meaning. Afterward one must set the words in the right order. There you have the true master, the free, sublimest spirit. Now mark this well when a text presents you with difficulties.

how we were obliged to hear that we possessed no Christian love, that we despised the ministers of Christ, grieved and confused the church, etc. There were no sinners on earth except us alone, and there were no saints in heaven except the fanatics alone. Among them there was nothing but the fire of love, among us nothing but the ice of mercilessness; for we were cannibals, they were pure, clean, and unadulterated, the Spirit himself.

But how have such overflowing love and humility helped us? Not at all, except that because of them everything has become worse and our confident hope has wretchedly betrayed us. For love will be and must be deceived because it "believes and trusts all things," I Corinthians 13 [:6]. But faith cannot fail, for God does not lie, as man does, I Samuel 15 [:29].

How should and could I now place upon my poor conscience such coarse blasphemies by the unrepentant fanatics and blasphemers? This I would have to do if I became involved with them through books, writings, or words, as Stenckefeld now expects me to do.

St. John says in II John [vv. 10-11]: "If any one comes to you and does not bring this doctrine, do not receive him into the house or give him any greeting; for he who greets him shares his wicked work." Now you know who the man is who bids me neither to hear nor to see the fanatics, but to avoid and condemn them. It is the same thing that I also said above when quoting from St. Paul, Titus 3 [:10]: "As for a man who is factious, after admonishing him once or twice, have nothing more to do with him."

Even if the impossible were true, and they were right that mere bread and wine are in the Lord's Supper, should they for that reason rage and thunder thus against us with such hideous blasphemies, "baked God," "God of bread," etc.? Should they not spare the sacred words of Christ (which we have not invented), "This is my body," by which he clearly calls the bread, that is being offered, his body? Thus they might also blaspheme him as being a God of cloths or made of cloths, or a woven or a sewn-up God because he went about in a robe and garments that were sewn and woven. Likewise they might call him a watery God because he was baptized in the Jordan, a God wrapped in clouds because he ascended into heaven in the clouds.

I, too, would have been able to designate their God in a corresponding way and I could still do it, if I would not want to spare the name of God. I could also give them their true name and say that they are not only devourers of bread and drinkers of wine but devourers of souls and murderers of souls and that they possess a bedeviled, thoroughly bedeviled, hyper-bedeviled heart and lying tongue. Thereby I would have spoken the truth because it cannot be contradicted that they have shamelessly lied by means of such blasphemies of theirs against their own consciences. Yet they are not repentant; in fact, they boast about themselves in their malice.

Therefore, no one among the Christians should and can pray for the fanatics or receive them. They have incurred their penalty and are committing "sin which is mortal" [I John 5:16], as St. John says. I am talking about the leaders; may the dear Lord Christ deliver the poor people who are among them from such murderers of souls. They have (I say) been admonished sharply and often enough. They do not want to have anything to do with me; therefore, I do not want to have anything to do with them either. They have received nothing from me, they boast, for which I am thankful to God. Likewise, I have received much less from them, for which God be praised. Let that be as it may; the truth will come to light, if it has not already done so with a vengeance.

First of all, they were warned right at the outset by the Holy Spirit when they separated into seven spirits in their interpretations of the text, each one differing from the other at all times.

The first spirit, Karlstadt, interpreted the text, "This is my body," to mean: Here sits my body. Therefore the text should read thus: He took bread, gave thanks and broke it, and gave it to his disciples, saying, Here sits my body which will be given to you.

Oh, this was so certain that not only the Holy Spirit but the heavenly Father himself had revealed it to him. I have written enough about that in *Against the Heavenly Prophets*.[16]

---

[16] Cf. *LW* 40, 73 ff.

The second spirit, Zwingli, says that this was not rightly interpreted, notwithstanding the fact that the heavenly Father himself had revealed it. He interpreted the text by another holy spirit of his thus: "Take, eat. This signifies my body which is given for you." Here "is" had to mean "signifies."

The third spirit, Oecolampadius, brought forth the third holy spirit, who again interpreted the text differently, namely, thus: "Take, eat, this is the sign of my body."

To the fourth spirit, Stenckefeld, it seemed that his stench was musk[17] for the whole world. He brought forth from the fourth holy spirit this rule: One must disregard these words, "This is my body," for they hinder the spiritual understanding. If you want to become a theologian, you must carefully observe this rule, namely, where the clear word of God contradicts your understanding, look for some other word which pleases you, and say that it is the Holy Spirit. After that you may arrange and interpret the words as it seems good to you.

Here, for example, you must first of all comprehend the sublime, spiritual meaning, that bread is bread, wine is wine, something that neither the pope nor Luther, nor any baker or innkeeper ever understood. Accordingly, you interpret the text by placing the last part of it first, namely: "Take, eat, my body, which is given for you, is this" (namely, a spiritual food). There you have it. Now go and say that Stenckefeld does not have the Holy Spirit in a far greater measure than the three holy spirits of Karlstadt, Zwingli, and Oecolampadius!

The fifth holy spirit[18] and some of his vermin interpret it thus: "Take, eat, that which is given for you is my body."

The sixth holy spirit[19] interprets it thus: "Take, eat. This is my body for a remembrance." This is supposed to mean the same as this: Take, eat; this is the remembrance of my body (the nominative "body" is to be interpreted as a genitive, "of my body") which is given for you, etc.

---

[17] An ingredient used in perfume.
[18] Luther is referring to John Landtsperger, a former Carmelite monk in Augsburg, who opposed his doctrine on the Lord's Supper. Cf. *LW* 37, 41, n. 65.
[19] It is not certain who the person referred to here is.

The seventh holy spirit, John Campanus,[20] interprets it thus: "Take, eat; this is my body," namely, it is a body made of bread. This is supposed to mean: The bread, which I am giving to you, is a body or substance by itself, not my living, natural body, but a dead, lifeless body, even as stone or wood is a body. But because it is my creation, therefore it is also my body which I have created.

This is the most sublime holy spirit who opposes and is superior to all the others, except that he takes the honor away from the baker who, for all that, also does something with the bread, for God does not create the bread but the grain for the bread.

Above these spirits there roamed about still another holy spirit[21] (for the devil is holy and a great spirit), who speaks thus: There is no article of faith at stake here; consequently, one should not quarrel about it, and in this matter everyone can believe what he likes.

This holy spirit seems to me to be a young holy spirit whom the old holy spirit Stenckefeld has bred and hatched. For he adheres excellently to the rule of Stenckefeld and not only disregards the text but throws it overboard along with the faith and everything else, making it out to be nothing other than an empty nutshell.

All these holy spirits, no matter how completely they disagree about the text, nevertheless are in harmony about the sublime spiritual meaning that bread is bread, wine is wine. Whoever does not possess this sublime understanding, he had better become confused and believe that bread is not bread but wood or stone; this would then be a serious matter.

Thus the Lord's Supper among them is nothing other than a daily common meal at which they use bread and wine; during such

---

[20] A young man from Maeseyck who was matriculated as a student in Wittenberg in December, 1528. He sought to introduce a novel interpretation of the Lord's Supper at the Marburg Colloquy and also denied the classical doctrine of the Trinity. Cf. George H. Williams, *The Radical Reformation* (Philadelphia: Westminster Press, 1962), pp. 272-273.

[21] Luther also refers to this "spirit" in his treatise *That These Words of Christ, "This Is My Body," etc., Still Stand Firm, Against the Fanatics* (1527), *LW* 37, 42.

a meal one can talk about Christ, read about him, praise him, thank him, and also eat spiritually, as well as in the Supper of Christ. Christ is therefore an exceedingly great fool to institute a a special Supper when the world already is filled to capacity with suppers which take place daily. It would have been altogether sufficient if he had spoken thus: If and when you eat bread and drink wine, "do it in remembrance of me." This would be a complete Supper of Christ as the fanatics want to have it. It is the same as what St. Paul says about the whole of life: "Whatever you do, in word or deed, do everything in the name of the Lord Jesus, giving thanks to God the Father through him" [Col. 3:17]. What else is this other than observing a spiritual eating in all of our activities, that is, remembering the Lord and strengthening the faith. Thus, in time a fine party of drinking companions, as the Corinthians initiated it [I Cor. 11:20 ff.], might come about on the basis of the Lord's Supper.

They were warned a second time[22] by many, most especially by me, since I wrote against them so diligently, and convincingly refuted their basic arguments and explanations so that their consciences had to become aware of it. For they had two passages of Scripture on their side. The one was John 6 [:63], "The flesh is of no avail," which Oecolampadius[23] called his iron wall. The other passage was: Christ has ascended into heaven; for that reason his body and blood cannot be in the Lord's Supper. They adduced additional passages of Scripture which talked about the ascension of Christ. They informed us very insistently that Christ had ascended into heaven, just as if we had never heard of this event that happened about fifteen hundred years ago. However, that for this reason mere bread and wine were present in the Lord's Supper—this problem they did not want to broach, much less attempt to solve, as my books which are extant testify against them.

I demonstrated so convincingly to them that the first passage,

[22] The first warning, according to Luther, was the divisions among the sacramentarians themselves. Cf. above, p. 290. The treatises directed against them were the second warning.
[23] Not Oecolampadius but Zwingli himself. Cf. *LW* 37, 78, n. 133, also 78-79, 81-84, 95-96, 286-287.

"The flesh is of no avail," was not applicable,[24] that even Zwingli in his last book no longer makes mention of it. I also demonstrated conclusively that the other passage was not applicable.[25] I argued as follows: It is impossible that they should have been seriously misled to deny the body and blood of the Lord in the Lord's Supper on account of the passage, "He ascended into heaven," as they indeed always confidently asserted with arrogant words in many books. That they were surely lying in this matter, I proved on this basis: Christ instituted the Lord's Supper and gave his body and blood to his disciples, as the words, "Eat, this is my body," indicate, before he ascended into heaven; for in that instance he was sitting at table here below on earth and was observing the first Lord's Supper. For this reason their boast cannot be true, namely, that the passages about the ascension convinced them. For in opposition to this you can read that Christ observed the Lord's Supper before he ascended into heaven.

Now if his ascension does not stand in the way of the first Lord's Supper, how can it be a serious and honest concern when they say that the ascension convinced them and prevented them [from believing in the real presence]? For we have been celebrating no other Lord's Supper for the last fifteen hundred years than the one the Lord instituted and commanded from the beginning, as he says: "Do this in remembrance of me" [I Cor. 11:24]. Besides, they do not know and understand what ascending into heaven means, so how could it have convinced them?

They were unable to refute these arguments and they now sought ways and means to patch up and excuse their weak position and to be reconciled with us. At that point the colloquy at Marburg was arranged. During it they improved their position and admitted that it was not mere bread and wine in the Lord's Supper, as they had most vehemently contended until then, but that the body and blood were also in it, however, not bodily, but spiritually.[26] This contention could not be rightly maintained because spiritual eating and drinking are possible only for the holy and righteous. But St.

[24] Cf. *"This Is My Body," LW* 37, 78-101.
[25] Cf. *"This Is My Body," LW* 37, 55-78.
[26] Cf. above, *The Marburg Colloquy,* pp. 15-85.

Paul says that the unworthy receive the body and blood of Christ as well as the worthy, I Corinthians 11 [:27 ff.].

Zwingli had a long, absurd talk with me about local inclusion,[27] that the body of Christ could not be in the bread as it would be in space or in a vessel, just as if we taught that Christ's body was in the bread like straw in a sack,[28] or wine in a barrel. After that some of them excused themselves and said that they had understood that we and the papists taught that Christ's body was in the sacrament locally, like straw in a sack. Oh, that was a useless, insignificant, lame excuse!

For they knew very well that neither the papists nor we had taught that. Even if they had not understood it otherwise (which is entirely unlikely), they had to confess in this way that they, like mad persons, were attacking matters which they themselves had never heard of nor understood. For the papists' teaching was at that time far better known than now. Indeed, there was no other teaching abroad of which the fanatics could have known.

The papists teach, yes, not the papists but the holy Christian church and we with them (for the pope, as stated, did not institute the sacrament), that Christ's body is not present locally [*localiter*] (like straw in a sack) in the sacrament, but definitively [*definitive*]. That is, he is certainly there, not like straw in a sack, but yet bodily and truly there, as I have proved convincingly in my book.[29] I say that they knew this very well, or at least they should have known about it, since they wanted to rage so dreadfully against that of which they had no knowledge.

Thus we departed from Marburg with such hope (as we mentioned), because they agreed to all the Christian articles of the faith, and in this article of the holy sacrament they also abandoned their previous error (that it was merely bread). It seemed as if they would in time share our point of view altogether.

---

[27] *Locali inclusione*. Cf. above, pp. 30-32.

[28] Cf. *Confession Concerning Christ's Supper*, *LW* 37, 228, and Luther's earlier comment in *The Sacrament of the Body and Blood of Christ—Against the Fanatics* (1526), *LW* 36, 343.

[29] Cf. *Confession Concerning Christ's Supper* (1528), where Luther discusses more fully the difference between the presence of Christ *localiter* and *definitive*. *LW* 37, 214 ff.

However, on account of the devil's activity this did not happen, and I was badly betrayed. This I was bound to notice in the book which appeared after Zwingli's death,[30] for he became worse after the colloquy and certainly dealt deceptively with me at Marburg. Consequently, I am forced not to receive into fellowship any fanatic whether his name be Stenckefeld, Zwingli, Oecolampadius, Karlstadt, or whoever they may be, these fanatics, devourers of bread and drinkers of wine, that is, blasphemers and enemies of Christ; and in my heart I must neither know, nor see, nor hear of their letters, books, greetings, blessings, writings, names, or memory.

For because I am sure that they are wrong and blaspheme God, and because their own conscience must testify against them, I shall and can cheerfully say in the presence of my dear Lord Jesus Christ on the day of judgment: Lord Jesus, I have faithfully warned and admonished them of that which their own conscience convicts them; this they will have to confess before you, you know this, dear Lord.

For the third time[31] they were admonished by the dreadful judgment of God when Zwingli and with him about five thousand very excellent persons were so wretchedly slain, as the histories and their letters testify.[32] Nevertheless, they wanted immediately to interpret such a wrathful judgment as a gracious sign and wanted to boast of Zwingli as a saint who, like all saints, had to suffer much and was innocently slain. What good does it do, even if God sends them more plagues than he did Pharaoh, since they are disposed to make of it nothing but holy suffering? They are like the Jews who for fifteen hundred years interpret their suffering and misfortune in the same way and harden their hearts by means of the very things that are being used to admonish them so dreadfully. But because I am certain that Zwingli, as his last book testifies, died in a great

---

[30] Cf. above, p. 289.

[31] Luther is referring here to the third warning which the sacramentarians received, namely, their fate.

[32] This statement, made by Luther, was based on Carion's *Chronicle*, which proved to be inaccurate. Only two thousand troops from Zurich were involved in the battle at Kappel. Of these only several hundred were slain. Cf. *WA* 54, 132.

many sins and in blasphemy of God, therefore I cannot believe their interpretation.

Nevertheless, I ardently hope that God has applied to him the saying of St. Paul in I Corinthians 5 [:5]: "Deliver this man . . . for the destruction of the flesh, that his spirit may be saved in the day of the Lord Jesus." And I Corinthians 11 [:32]: "But when we are judged by the Lord, we are chastened so that we may not be condemned along with the world." Oh, how sincerely I wish that he would have fared according to these sayings, since his misfortune made me feel exceedingly sorry and still does.

If suffering is supposed to be holy and to make holy, innocence and a cause that is right in God's sight must be present beforehand, as St. Augustine says: "Not the punishment, but the reason for it produces a martyr."[33] Now they certainly know that Zwingli, apart from his blasphemy of the sacrament, had also incurred blame in a worldly way when he imposed a road blockade against the party hostile[34] to him and so acted wickedly. For this reason it seems more than likely that he was judged according to the passage: "All who take the sword will perish by the sword" [Matt. 26:52]. Indeed, this is the way we ought to think of and regard this matter. They may interpret, speak of, and excuse Zwingli's death in whatever way they desire; the historical narratives and their written testimony contradict them.

Also (I hear it said) that they are consoling themselves with the fact that they are writing many books and are performing a great work for the church and in the Scriptures. Of what use is it, as long as they falsify and twist God's word and sacrament and do not want to listen? Whoever does not listen to God, to him God in turn does not listen, but "his prayer is an abomination," Proverbs 28 [:9]. The Jews are also working hard on the Scriptures for about fifteen hundred years. Indeed, what heretics have not labored by

[33] This quote appears frequently in Augustine. Cf. Augustine, *Exposition of Psalm 34* (*Enarratio in Psalmum XXXIV*), 2, 1 and 2, 13 (*MPL* 36, 333 and 340); *Exposition of Psalm 68* (*Enarratio in Psalmum LXVIII*), 1, 9, (*MPL* 36, 848); also *Letter 89, To Festus*, 2 (*MPL* 33, 310); *Letter 108, To Macrobius*, 5, 14 (*MPL* 33, 413); *Letter 204, To Dulcitius*, 4 (*MPL* 33, 940).

[34] Because of this road blockade, the five Roman Catholic cantons were unable to import goods. This action led to a war with Zurich. Cf. *WA* 54, 132, n. 1.

means of teaching and writing even more than Christians? It is much harder for the devil's martyrs (as the saying goes) to earn hell than it is for the true saints to earn heaven.

Because so many of God's great warnings and admonitions have simply had no effect on them—I can boast with a good conscience and strong faith that my treatise which came out fifteen years ago[35] was also a divine admonition alongside the other two admonitions;[36] nor am I too insignificant that they should let themselves be admonished by me, even though they boast excessively; for I, too, am a servant of Christ, as much as, if not more than, they are; and I, too, have worked in his church, before they did (I do not want to boast too much)—therefore, I must leave them to their devices and avoid them as the "self-condemned" [*autokatakritos,* Titus 3:11] who knowingly and intentionally want to be condemned. I must not have any kind of fellowship with any of them, neither by letters, writings, and words, nor in works, as the Lord commands in Matthew 18 [:17], whether he is called Stenckefeld, Zwingli, or whatever he is called. I regard them all as being cut from the same piece of cloth,[37] as indeed they are. For they do not want to believe that the Lord's bread in the Supper is his true, natural body which the godless person or Judas receives orally just as well as St. Peter and all the saints. Whoever (I say) does not want to believe that, let him not trouble me with letters, writings, or words and let him not expect to have fellowship with me. This is final.

With this, my good friend,[38] you have my explanation why I have not wanted to listen or reply to that blasphemous tongue, Schwenckfeld. If you wish to do so, you can indicate this to those whom Stenckefeld has perhaps stirred up against me by defamation and by casting suspicion on me. I am pleased (as has been said) that such blasphemous tongues are reviling me and that they are so very angry with me. There is no one here who pays attention

---

[35] The reference is to *Confession Concerning Christ's Supper* of 1528, which, more precisely, was published sixteen years before. Cf. *LW* 37, 151 ff.

[36] The reference here is to the disagreement among the sacramentarians themselves and to their misfortunes. Cf. above, pp. 296, 302.

[37] Literally, Luther says that he considers "them all part of the same cake."

[38] See above, p. 287.

to their wrath. "If they have called the master of the house Beelzebul, how much more will they malign those of his household" [Matt. 10:25]. That is, if they dare to blaspheme and call our dear Lord Jesus Christ a liar in regard to his words, "Take, eat; this is my body," etc., and to turn and pervert his blessed, comforting sacrament into a peasants' drinking bout, what should not these most haughty spirits do to poor Luther?

In short, they have been found out and overcome by me time and again as the most manifest blasphemers and liars. First, this was the case when at the outset they taught that there was nothing except mere bread and wine in the Lord's Supper. They scolded us and reviled us in this respect as cannibals, drinkers of blood, Thyesteans, Capernaites, and called our Lord the baked God, the God made of bread, the God made of wine, etc., as extant books forever testify.

What Christian heart can or even wants to believe that the Holy Spirit, and not rather the loathsome devil, is continually at work in them because they interpret the clear words of the Lord, "Take, eat; this is my body," according to their own capriciousness and wantonness on the basis of their fancy that he is present spiritually and not bodily. For we know very well, even though the Lord Christ dwells in our hearts by faith (as St. Paul teaches in Ephesians 3 [:17]), which is called a spiritual indwelling, that he has nonetheless not assumed a spiritual body or blood nor given it to us, as he says, Luke 24 [:39]: "Handle me, and see; for a spirit has not flesh and bones as you see that I have." And yet he lives spiritually in our hearts.

Second, I have clearly proved that they have falsely interpreted the passages of Scripture which they had adduced, such as those that talk about the ascension and the unavailing flesh, and have employed them in an intentionally false sense. Consequently, they were caught telling many big lies, and even today they persist in such manifest blasphemies and lies without repentance, with a hardened heart, and in an obstinate way. Thus I would have to condemn myself into the abyss of hell together with them if I should make common cause with them or have fellowship with them or should be silent about it when I notice or hear that they presumed to be or boasted about being in fellowship with me. The devil and his mother[39] may do this or keep silent about it, but I will not.

I want to take my stand with the holy father Abraham and all Christians on the passage in Romans 4 [:21], "What God says, he can do,"[40] and again in Psalm 51 [:4], "So that thou art justified in thy sentence and blameless in thy judgment." I do not first want to seek counsel from my reason as to how it is conceivable or possible that I am able to receive his body and blood orally, and afterward, as a judge over God, explain his words according to my inclination. No, I do not want to rave thus. He has said it; I shall adhere to that. If he misleads me, then I am being misled for my salvation. He has never lied yet and he cannot lie. However, the fanatics are manifest liars, recognized as such by me and by themselves. They also have to lie continually because they rely on their ideas more than on the word of God.

Whoever does not want to trust in God's word and to take his stand on these or on similar passages, "What God says, he can do" [Rom. 4:21], and "God cannot lie"[41] [Hebrews 6:18], I faithfully counsel him to leave Holy Scripture and the articles of the Christian faith alone. For his interpretation constantly drags him deeper into error. It would be better for him to remain a condemned heathen than that he should become a condemned Christian.

O dear man! If someone does not want to believe the article of faith concerning the Lord's Supper, how will he ever believe the article of faith concerning the humanity and divinity of Christ in one person? If you have doubts about whether you are receiving the body of Christ orally when you eat the bread from the altar, likewise, that you are receiving the blood of Christ orally when you drink the wine in the Lord's Supper, then you must surely have serious doubts (especially when the end of your life draws near) about how the infinite and incomprehensible Godhead, who is and must essentially be everywhere, can be bodily enclosed and in-

---

[39] Luther often referred to reason as the devil's bride or mother or grandmother. Cf. *LW* 40, 174, n. 134, and *LW* 37, 210, n. 69.
[40] A paraphrase rather than a direct translation.
[41] A paraphrase.

cluded in the humanity and in the Virgin's body, as St. Paul says in Colossians 1 [2:9]: "In him the whole fulness of deity dwells bodily."

And how is it possible for you to believe that the Son alone became man, not the Father or the Holy Spirit, since the three persons are nothing but the one God in a most completely single essence and nature of the one Godhead? How can this be explained? How is it possible that the single, completely perfect Godhead of the Son should divide or separate itself so that at one and the same time it is united with the humanity, and the same single Godhead of the Father and the Holy Spirit is not united with the humanity? Yet it is at the same time one and the same Godhead; one person is in Christ with the humanity, and it is not the Father or the Holy Spirit. Oh, how they will really begin to rave, reel, and bluster when they arrive at this point! Then they will find occasion to explain it, even as I hear they are already vigorously starting to do with Eutychianism and Nestorianism.[42] For I thought and also said that they had to arrive at this point. The devil cannot be idle. Wherever he instigates one heresy, there he must instigate additional ones, and no error remains alone. If the ring is broken at one point, it is no longer a perfect ring; it no longer holds together and constantly comes apart

Even if they boast a great deal that they believe in this article about Christ's person and chatter much about it, you should not believe it; they are certainly lying in everything they say about it. With the tongue they indeed say it (as the demons in the gospel also call the Lord God's Son), but it is certain that "their heart is far from me," Matthew 15 [:8]. The Jews, too, swore by the living God; but they swore falsely, says the prophet [Zechariah 5:4]. The Turks also glory in the name of God, but when they are at the

[42] These were two heretical teachings about the person of Christ and his two natures. For Eutychianism, which Luther associated with Schwenckfeld, see above, p. 287, n. 3. Nestorianism reflected the teaching of Nestorius (died around 454), a presbyter and monk of Antioch, and later bishop of Constantinople, who differentiated sharply between Christ's two natures. He objected to calling Mary, the mother of Christ, "Bearer of God" (*theotokos*). Thus he separated the human nature of Christ from his divine nature, precluding the full and perfect union of the God-man, Jesus Christ. Luther interprets the Christology of the Zwinglians as Nestorian.

point of death they discover who their God is. For it is certain that whoever does not rightly believe in one article of faith, or does not want to believe (after he has been admonished and instructed), he surely believes no article with an earnest and true faith. And whoever is so bold that he dares to deny God or to accuse him of lying in one word, and he does this maliciously in opposition to that about which he was once or twice admonished and instructed, he also dares (and he certainly does it, too) to deny God in all of his words and to accuse him of lying.

For this reason we say that everything is to be believed completely and without exception, or nothing is to be believed. The Holy Spirit does not let himself be divided or cut up so that he should let one point be taught and believed as trustworthy and another as false—except in the case where there are weak believers who are willing to let themselves be instructed and are not stubbornly opposing his truth. Otherwise, if this attitude should obtain that it does not harm anyone if he desires to deny one article of the faith because he still regards all the others as true (although basically this is impossible), then no heretic would ever be condemned, indeed, there could not even be a heretic on earth. For it is charactristic of all heretics that they start by denying one article of the faith; after that, all the articles must suffer the same fate and they must all be denied, just as the ring, when it gets a crack or a chink, is totally worthless. And if a bell cracks at one place, it does not chime any more and is completely useless.

Let the examples of history teach you this: Arius[43] singled out this one article of the faith [and said] that Christ was not God but a creature. All the other articles of the faith, particularly that God the Father was one God, Creator of heaven and earth, that Christ died for our sins, that there were baptism, sacrament, keys, resurrection of the dead, and eternal life, he probably believed more reverently (to judge from his words) than true Christians believe. However, the Holy Scripture stands firm and testifies that he did

[43] Around A.D. 320 Arius, a presbyter in the church at Alexandria, denied that Christ as Son of God was co-equal and co-eternal with God, the Father.

not believe any article of the faith. For thus St. John says in I John 2 [:23]: "No one who denies the Son has the Father. He who confesses the Son has the Father also." Now if Arius does not have the Son and the Father, then he also has no God or Creator of heaven and earth. That is, it is of no use to him that with his mouth he calls God the Father and Creator of heaven and earth, and highly exalts him, even though no other God is Creator of heaven and earth than this one whom Arius mentions with his lying tongue. However, for Arius he is not a God, because he is denying and blaspheming his only Son, Christ, by saying that he is not God.

Thus baptism is no longer baptism for him, forgiveness of sins is no longer forgiveness of sins, the sacrament is no longer the sacrament; that is, it no longer does him any good even if previously he was indeed rightly baptized and had received true forgiveness and the true sacrament. Thus he has forfeited all articles of faith because he denies the true God of faith, Christ, and no article is of any use to him and he is also unable to believe any article with true seriousness, but must make use of all of them for his condemnation, as the second commandment states: "You shall not take the name of the Lord your God in vain" [Exod. 20:7]. Here it is brought to your attention that even the true, holy name of God does not help but rather hurts those who do not believe in it rightly and abuse it. For this reason, too, the ancient fathers debated whether the baptism of the Arians was indeed a true baptism.[44] Thus one misfortune always leads to another one.

The heretic Macedonius,[45] bishop of Constantinople, also believed all articles of the faith except the one that the Holy Spirit was true God. What good did it do him and his party? It amounted

[44] The controversy over heretical baptism (254-257) took place before Arius' time, although there was a continuing debate in various areas of the church about the validity of heretical baptism even after the controversy was over. The decision of the Church of Rome around 257 that baptism by a heretic, if done in proper form, was valid eventually triumphed in the Catholic Church.

[45] Macedonius, bishop of Constantinople, was deposed from his office in 360 because he held that the Holy Spirit is a creature subordinate to the Son, thus denying the orthodox doctrine of the Trinity.

to as much as believing in none of them. Even though he could articulate and speak of these articles quite correctly, he nevertheless has no God because he does not regard the Holy Spirit as God. That is why he also has no Creator of heaven and earth. Under these circumstances his baptism is no longer valid, there is no forgiveness of sins, no sacrament, no eternal life. Even if he lives in a disciplined way and leads a seemingly Christian life, he is still not a true Christian, but a big hypocrite. It would be much better for him if he were not a Christian, and did not thus abuse and falsely bear the Christian name, that is, bear and honor it so damnably.

Nestorius, too, who was also bishop of Constantinople, was a man who strictly adhered to all but one of the articles of faith, as did the other members of his party; but, with respect to one article he was a heretic, for he held that God's Son, Christ, was not born of Mary, the Virgin, and that Mary was not and could not be a mother of God. As a result, all other articles of faith lost their meaning for him except insofar as he was able to speak of them and to abuse them. Furthermore, from these three heretics there eventually emanated and came to light additional heresies (which had previously been hidden within them), until the abominable Muhammad emerged. For all history books testify that Muhammad was a product of the Arians, the Macedonians, and the Nestorians to whom he adhered right from the beginning.

How is it that the pope became so completely heretical and that he brought one heresy after the other into the world until there are now at Rome, especially at the papal court, nothing but Epicureans and mockers of the Christian faith? It is because they have fallen from faith in Christ and depend on works, that is, on their own righteousness. Of what use were all the other articles of faith to him? What good does it do him greatly to exalt with his mouth the true God, the Father, the Son, and the Holy Spirit, and to make a splendid pretense of living a Christian life? For he, nevertheless, is and remains the greatest enemy of Christ and is the true Antichrist. He has made himself the head of Christendom, yes, the anus as the place of excrement for the devil, through which so great an abomination of masses, monkery, and unchastity has been passed into the world, until finally the monks helped the dying

Christian on to heaven by means of their vermin-infested cowls.[46]

Consequently, it will not do the fanatics any good if, in connection with the sacrament, they do a great deal of babbling about the spiritual eating and drinking of the body and blood of Christ and about the love and unity of Christians. For these words are nothing but fig leaves with which Adam and Eve wanted to cover and adorn themselves so that God should not notice their shame and sin. Much less will their great labor of teaching and writing and their earnest, chaste conduct help them. All this is still a heathenish practice. It is also useless for them to believe in God the Father, Son, and Holy Spirit and in Christ the Savior. Everything, I say, is lost along with all articles of faith, no matter how correctly and blamelessly they speak of and represent the same with their false, blaspheming mouth, because they deny and call false this single article of faith when Christ says in the sacrament: "Take (the bread) and eat; this is my body which is given for you," etc. For what they chatter about spiritual eating and about love has solely this aim: They want to cover up and hide such harm and poison so that one should not take notice of or see the same but should regard them as remarkable and very good Christians. This is what we call placing an illusion before one's eyes and adorning the gloomy devil (as St. Paul teaches [II Cor. 11:14]) with the bright dress of the angels of light. Therefore, their great boasting and many works are in vain because they do not want to be Christians in this one article of faith.

The Lord talks about this in Luke 11 [:35-36]: "Therefore be careful lest the light in you be darkness. If then your whole body is full of light, having no part dark, it will be wholly light." Here you see that the Lord desires that everything should be light in us and that no particle of darkness should be in it. So, too, it is stated in Matthew 6 [:23]: "If then the light in you is darkness, how great is the darkness." And Paul says in Galatians 5 [:3]: "I testify again to every man who receives circumcision (which was a small part of the body) that he has fallen away from Christ and from grace and

[46] The practice of burying people in monks' cowls, supposedly to assure them of salvation, is mentioned several times by Luther. Cf. *LW* 34, 21, and *LW* 47, 52, n. 66.

that he is bound to keep the whole law." From this passage the saying of James 2 [:10-11] is derived: "For whoever keeps the whole law but fails in one point has become guilty of all of it. For he who said, 'Do not commit adultery,' said also, 'Do not kill,'" etc. It is one God who has commanded everything. Whoever provokes God to anger in one thing will in turn experience the anger of all creatures and of the commandments of God, and even of his own good works which he thought he had done in obedience to the other commandments, for they were not done in true obedience to God or in faith in Christ.

Perhaps you would like to say: "My dear Luther, it is to be hoped that this is not so, or at least there is no use being anxious about the fact that God should be so very vehement and relentlessly strict that he would want to condemn people on account of one article of the faith if they faithfully adhere to and believe all other articles." This is the way not only the heretic comforts himself but also other sinners comfort themselves. Sirach [7:9] writes that they want God to take into consideration the rest of their good works and to be gracious to them, as King Saul, too, wanted to cover up his disobedience with his religious devotion and sacrifice, I Samuel 15 [:15]. So they proceed securely and with self-assurance, as if they lacked nothing; the many great works and the labor which they do will outweigh a single failure. Over against this [attitude] it must be said that God could scarcely hope or expect that his poor, miserable, blind creation should be so senseless and proud in opposition to its Creator and Lord that it would deny, regard as false, and blaspheme his divine word; rather, he should be able to hope that his humble, submissive, obedient creation would not deny and blaspheme a single word but sincerely receive all words [in general] and every word in particular, and give thanks with great joy that the creation is worthy to hear one single word from its dear God. Yes, it is fitting for God to look at it in this way.

Now, however, the heretics treat God's word as though it were man's word, or a fool's word, which they can despise, mock, and blaspheme. They think they can do everything better according to their own good judgment. Nor do they want to let themselves be corrected. So there is no help for them. In this situation their many great and good deeds and labors will not outweigh the one bad point. There are neither many nor few, neither small nor great, good works before God, but only vain, evil, condemned works, for unbelief or blasphemy destroys and condemns even the good (as they call them) works; yes, such good works are worse than plain sins are, because they are performed and take place in the midst of blasphemy and stubborn denial of God's name and word. Indeed, it would be much better and would be desirable if instead they would commit sin and do evil works; then they would at least recognize and come to know what they are doing. They are now faring according to the saying of Solomon, Ecclesiastes 5 [:1]: "Guard your steps when you go to the house of God; to draw near to listen is better than to offer the sacrifice of fools; for they do not know that they are doing evil." A sacrifice is actually a good work; nevertheless, it is called evil when fools, who do not want to listen (that is, the godless or heretics), perform it. But one of these days the passage from Psalm 50 [:16] will judge and strike them much more sharply: "To the wicked, God says, 'What right have you to recite my statutes . . . . ?'" Let this be enough. Whoever does not want to listen, let him be.

In conclusion I must also append this: I hear it said that some persons have been induced to think that we are in agreement with the fanatics because we have permitted the practice of elevation[47] to be dropped in our churches in order that we might acknowledge that Christ's body and blood are not in the sacrament, and that they are not orally received. However, the matter stands thus: Twenty or twenty-two years ago when I began to condemn the mass[48] and wrote sharply against the papists that it was not a sacrifice or our work but a gift and present or a testament from God, which we could not sacrifice to God but which we should and had to receive from God, even as baptism was not a sacrifice but a gracious gift of God, etc., at that time I was indeed inclined to

---

[47] The elevation of the bread and the wine during the recitation of the words of institution in the Lord's Supper.

[48] Luther was thinking of the two treatises *The Misuse of the Mass* (1521), *LW* 36, 129-230; *WA* 8, 482-563; and *The Babylonian Captivity of the Church* (1520), *LW* 36, 51-54; *WA* 6, 497-573.

abolish the elevation on account of the papists who regarded the mass as a sacrifice and a work by us sacrificed to God, as they still do and have done up until now for over six hundred years.[49]

However, because our teaching was at that time new and exceedingly offensive to the entire world, I had to proceed with forbearance and accommodate myself a great deal for the sake of the weak, which I afterward no longer did. Accordingly, I let the elevation remain because it could in fact have a valid meaning, as I had written in the treatise, *The Babylonian Captivity of the Church,*[50] namely, that it was an ancient custom, taken over from Moses' writings and continued among the first Christians uninterruptedly. For what Moses writes about *thnupha* and *thruma,* particularly in Deuteronomy 16[51] [Lev. 8:27; 10:14], every layman can now read in the German Bible; it was not a sacrifice to propitiate God on account of sin, as it was when the papists celebrated their sacrificial masses and sold them in a most shameful way; rather, it was nothing other than a sacrifice of thanks or thanksgiving in response to the blessings they had received from the land, etc. This, too, would be a fine interpretation, if the priest would with the elevation of the sacrament do nothing other than illustrate the words, "This is my body," as if he wished to express by means of his action: Look, dear Christians, this is the body which is given for you. Thus the elevation would not be a symbol of the sacrifice to God (as the papists foolishly imagine) but an admonition directed toward men, to provoke them to faith, particularly since he immediately elevates the bread right after speaking the words: "This is my body which is given for you." Nor does he mention one word about a sacrifice along with it. This you will find in the treatise *The Babylonian Captivity of the Church.*

While I am thinking thus and abiding in my faith, Jack Ab-

[49] It is not clear why Luther made mention of this period of time; but it is a fact that during the ninth and tenth centuries the idea of a sacrifice in the mass gained increasing importance.

[50] *LW* 36, 51-54.

[51] For a description and explanation of the terms *thnupha* (wave offering) and *thruma* (heave offering) (Lev. 8:27-29; 10:14), see the article on "Wave Offering" by W. Bruggemann in *The Interpreter's Dictionary of the Bible,* 4 vols., ed. by George Arthur Buttrick (Nashville: Abingdon Press, 1962), IV, 817. Cf. *LW* 40, 138 f. and 138, n. 91.

surdity, Dr. Karlstadt, comes blustering and jolting against me with his heavenly prophets and directs a book[52] against us. In it he chides us Wittenbergers for being murderers of Christ, crucifiers of Christ, new papists, etc., and becomes very rude and repulsive. Yet he had no other reason than that we were elevating the sacrament. This kind of elevating he interprets as offering a sacrifice. Furthermore, he interprets offering a sacrifice as being the same as having crucified, slain, and slaughtered Christ and as having dealt far worse with him than the Jews had ever done. Now he knew exceedingly well that we Wittenbergers did not regard the sacrament as a sacrifice; for by this time we had contended for almost three years with the papists that it could not be nor could it be called a sacrifice, but was a gracious gift and testament of God (as was said above). We were not obliged to him for the teaching that the sacrament was not a sacrifice, for we had not learned it from him in the past. Rather, he was obligated to us, for he had learned it from us; otherwise it would perhaps never have occurred to him at all.

Now when I saw such a mad spirit raving against us without cause and saw that he wanted to make it a sin for us—and such an abominable sin—even though it was no sin nor could it be, I decided that in opposition to, in defiance of, and to the chagrin of this same devil I would retain the elevation which I was nevertheless inclined to drop in opposition to the papists.[53] For I did not want to permit, and still will not permit, the devil to teach me how to arrange or determine something in our church. I especially did not want to permit it because if I retained the elevation and did not abolish it as the mad spirit insisted, he wanted to give me a very bad conscience, as if I had slain, crucified, and desecrated Christ. On account of such a bad conscience I would be forced to abolish the elevation. No, no, I had no reason for such a guilty conscience; this I knew full well, and it could not be made applicable to me. He was well aware of it, too.

---

[52] *Against the Old and the New Papistical Mass.* Also, in his *Dialogus* Karlstadt calls the Wittenbergers "new papists." Cf. *WA* 54, 164, n. 1.

[53] Carl F. Wisløff, *The Gift of Communion* (Minneapolis: Augsburg Publishing House, 1964), pp. 156-165.

Before I would admit to or take upon myself such a guilty conscience, on account of which I would have to drop the elevation because it would make me feel like a murderer, crucifier, and hangman of Christ, I would still today not only retain the elevation but, where one would not be enough, assist in introducing three, seven, or ten elevations. Therefore, I wanted to have it regarded as a free choice (even as it is a free matter and must be that), in which no sin could take place, whether one upheld it or dropped it. For this reason the elevation was retained among us. For whatever is free, that is, neither commanded nor prohibited, by which one can neither sin nor obtain merit, this should be in our control as something subject to our reason so that we might employ it or not employ it, uphold it or drop it, according to our pleasure and need, without sinning and endangering our conscience. In short, we want to be free lords and not slaves, who can proceed in this matter how, what, where, and when they wish. We do not want to be compelled to abolish the elevation because it is such a grave, great, and horrible sin, as Karlstadt's spirit wanted it to be; we also do not wish to be forced to retain it because abolishing it would mean the loss of the soul's salvation, as the pope's devil wants to have it; but it should mean: If you do not want to elevate, then let it lie; if you do not want to let it lie, then elevate it. What does God care about that? What does my conscience care about that? It is as little concerned about that as the altar is concerned about whether you want to elevate something above it or place something on it; both procedures are a matter of indifference to it.

Accordingly, the enemies of the sacrament have no reason for boasting, as if we let the elevation be dropped in order to please and oblige them. No one should get the idea that thereby we want to incline toward their blasphemous error, much less give in to it. Rather, steadfastly and firmly we want to regard them as God's and our condemned enemies. We do not want to deny, desecrate, and pervert Christ's word along with them, as if we had to learn from them how to eat bread and drink wine. We can indeed do this apart from Christ's Supper, and the whole world does it daily far too much, apart from God.

However, the sole reason why we are discontinuing the elevation is because nearly all of the churches have given it up for a long time already. Consequently, we wanted to agree with them and not practice something distinctive in a matter that in itself was open and could be retained or discontinued without endangering the conscience. I particularly [wanted to agree] because from the beginning I had been inclined to drop the elevation and certainly would have done so at that time if Karlstadt had not made such an abominable sin of it, as has been mentioned. For where it can be done without sinning and endangering the conscience or without giving offense, it is indeed fine for the churches to agree in external matters, which are in any case voluntary, even as they agree with one another in the Spirit, in the faith, in the word, and in the sacrament; for such agreement makes a fine impression and pleases everyone.

Agreement is also good because such dissimilarity, since it is unnecessary, looks very much like a schism or disunion and discord. For from the time the church first began, ceremonies have caused much offense in the churches; so, for example, the dispute about the Easter festival caused such a commotion that few churches were in agreement with one another about the matter. The bishop of Rome, Victor, placed all the churches in Greece and in the East under the ban because they did not observe Easter on the same day with the Roman Church. However, he was rebuked by the bishop of Lyons, Irenaeus, and had to desist and let every church celebrate the Easter festival in its own way and on its own day, for agreement could not be reached without danger and without causing offense, and there was nothing to be apprehensive about if Rome observed Easter on one day and the Greeks on another day.[54]

[54] Luther is referring to the quarrel between Asia Minor and Rome over the proper date for the observance of Easter. It was the practice of the churches in Asia Minor to observe Easter through the night of the fourteenth of the month Nisan (the seventh month of the Jewish year). This was probably the ancient Christian custom, and the festival, like the Jewish Passover, was celebrated regardless of the day of the week on which it might fall. At Rome and in some parts of the East it was customary for the church to hold the Easter feast always on a Sunday. The problem of settling the dispute over the right date became so acute that around the year 190 synods were held in Rome, Palestine, and elsewhere to discuss the matter. At these gatherings it was decided to follow the Roman practice. When the churches in Asia

There are many other matters about which the Greeks did not agree with the Romans; they do not agree even today. What does the bishopric of Milan, a bishopric which is located in Italian territory and is under the pope's jurisdiction, do even nowadays? In this bishopric not only the elevation or a part of the mass is dissimilar to the mass in other churches, but the entire mass is dissimilar, particularly in that the bishopric does not possess the small canon[55] and in every respect retains its special character in the mass. So when I journeyed through that area in the year 1510,[56] I could not celebrate the mass anywhere. The priests said to us: "We are priests of the Ambrosian rite;[57] you cannot celebrate mass here."[58] But why should I go into detail? There is no church on earth where there are so many differences and customs in worship and in churches as in the Roman Church. Not only experience shows this but also the books on canon law, of which there would indeed be fewer if more uniformity had remained in the Roman Church. But it proved beneficial to the pope that much or everything was taking place in a dissimilar way, if only they would be alike in regarding him as the head of all Christendom.

As a result, the saying was current among them: When in

Minor refused to conform to this decision, Victor, bishop of Rome (189-198), excommunicated the dissenting churches. Irenaeus, bishop of Lyons in southern France, who was a native of Asia Minor and was reared in its theological tradition, raised his voice in protest against this high-handed assertion of authority by the bishop of Rome. However, the protest proved to be in vain, because eventually the Roman custom of observing Easter on a Sunday prevailed within Christendom.

[55] The canon of the mass is the essential and unchangeable part of the mass in which the consecration of the bread and the wine is effected. Luther is here referring to the "small canon," or "lesser canon," as opposed to the "greater canon." In printed missals prior to the Council of Trent (1545-1563), the term "lesser canon" was used to denote the offertory prayers within the canon of the mass which immediately preceded the consecration of the elements. Cf. *LW* 36, n. 104.

[56] Luther here confirms the fact that 1510 was the date of his official trip to Rome with a fellow monk of his order.

[57] The Ambrosian rite, which is still used in the old archiepiscopal province of Milan, is one of the few non-Roman rites which have survived in the Roman Catholic Church. Its name is derived from St. Ambrose, bishop of Milan (*ca.* 345-407), but there is no convincing evidence that this rite was developed by him. It is a rite that differs considerably from the Roman one.

[58] Cf. *WA*, TR 4, 475; *WA*, TR 5, 621.

Rome, do as the Romans do.[59] Therefore, I would like to say here: If you come to a place where they still observe the elevation, you should not be offended nor should you condemn them, but accept it because it is taking place without sinning and without endangering the conscience. Perhaps they are as yet not able to change it. Nevertheless, it is of course more desirable and makes a better impression if one agrees about this matter in all churches. Because the elevation has not been commanded and is unnecessary—for it is something that has arisen apart from the divine command on the basis of human devotion—it is consequently fairer that one should agree with the churches that do not practice the elevation than, on the contrary, to agree with those that do practice it. For St. Paul faithfully teaches us everywhere that we should be diligent to teach and to live in unity and harmony with one another and to be on our guard against discord or differences wherever we are able to do so: Romans 12 [:16], "Live in harmony with one another"; and I Corinthians 1 [:10], "I appeal to you, brethren, by the name of our Lord Jesus Christ, that all of you agree that there be no dissensions among you."

However, where this is not possible, then let the fourteenth chapter of Romans direct us: "Do not confuse the consciences. One believes he may eat everything, while the weak man eats only vegetables" [vv. 1-2].[60] "One man esteems one day as better than another, while another man esteems all days alike. Let every one be fully convinced in his own mind" [v. 5]. "For the kingdom of God does not mean food and drink but righteousness and peace and joy in the Holy Spirit" [v. 17]. "Let us then pursue what makes for peace and for mutual upbuilding" [v. 19]. To that end may our dear Lord Jesus Christ together with God the Father and the Holy Spirit, who are praised throughout eternity, help us all. Amen.

---

[59] *Si fueris Romae, Romano vivito more.* This Latin sentence appears in the text along with a translation into German.

[60] Luther's translation of v. 1 differs considerably from the translation of both the Authorized and the Revised Standard Versions.

INDEXES

INDEX OF NAMES AND SUBJECTS

INDEX TO SCRIPTURE PASSAGES

Type used in this book
Body, 10 on 13 Caledonia
Display, Bulmer and Caledonia